TEDDY BEAR ARTISTS

Romance of Making & Collecting Bears

by
Carol-Lynn Rössel Waugh

Carol-Lynn Rössel Waugh

1985

Hobby House Press, Inc.
900 Frederick Street
Cumberland, Maryland 21502
(301) 759-3770

"Having a Teddy Bear in a way is like being in love and never getting over it....You can remain in love with him forever. You never have to fall out of love with your teddy bear. You never have to come down to earth. You never have to learn to accept the bad with the good with a bear. A bear can be all good. I guess that is what makes them so special...They are a magical fantasy creature."

CATHERINE BORDI, Teddy Bear Artist, 1983.

Additional copies of this book may be purchased at $12.95
plus $1.75 postage/handling from

Hobby House Press, Inc.
900 Frederick Street, Cumberland, Maryland 21502

© 1984 by Carol-Lynn Rössel Waugh   2nd Printing — May 1985

ISBN: 0-87588-226-9

TABLE OF CONTENTS

Introduction 1
Real Musgrave 5
The Reverend Chester Freeman, Jr. 8
Doris King 12
Bob and June Beckett 16
Sarah McClellan 20
Sylvia Lyons 24
Helen Hull 27
Janna Joseph 29
Carole Bowling 32
Miriam Hughes 34
Joyce Stafford 37
J. D. Clark 40
Barbara Isenberg 42
Karen Walter 45
Whim C. Bear (Dean Hansen and Sandra
    Haroutunian Hansen) 48
Tommy and Patsy Lewis 51
Sue Kruse 54
Pat Marrison 58
Lori Gardiner 60
Terol Reed 63
Marianne Anderson 65
Lois Beck 67
Rebecca Iverson 70
Penny Noble 73
Sandy Williams 76
Mereart Bears (Suzy Stewart and
    Joanna Meredith) 78
Margory Hoya Novak 80
Maria Kwong 83

Herta Forster 86
Elaine Fujita-Gamble 88
Ballard Baines (Karin Mandell and
    Howard Calvin) 90
Judy Lewis 93
Bonnie Harron 113
Mary Olsen 116
Kimberlee Port 120
Maxine Look 125
Lois Carlisle 128
Garrett and Janet Sakamoto 130
Sara Phillips 132
Faith Wick 136
Theresa May 138
Catherine Bordi 142
Roberta Viscusi 145
Jacqueline Robinson Tapley 150
Deanna Duvall 153
Kelly Reuter 157
Pat and Mimi Woolley 160
Cheryl Lindsay and Joanne Purpus 162
Earl Krentzin 168
April Whitcomb 170
Bob Raikes 173
Cappi Warnick 175
Frank and Susy Bird 179
Terry and Doris Michaud 182
Barbara Sixby 185
Beverly Port 189
Carol-Lynn Rössel Waugh 195
Directory of Artists 202

Dedication

To Beverly Port:
with love and a dozen bear hugs.
Winthrop, Maine.
May, 1984.

Acknowledgments

Without the help of every single artist in this book, *Teddy Bear Artists* never would have happened. I want to thank them all for answering my endless questionnaire and providing me with photographs and bears to photograph, especially Elaine Gamble, who sent me piles of stuff. The Winthrop, Maine, postal service deserves special thanks for bringing us all together. They delivered boxes of bears in the worst Maine winter weather.

Thanks to my publisher, Gary R. Ruddell, for believing in me, to my editor, Donna H. Felger, for steering me along, to Bill Eugley for teaching me to use the word processor in an amazing hour and a half (I would have been stuck without it), to Ted Menten for his friendship, and to my family for bearing with some pretty weird times, with love and forbearance. Most of all, thanks to Beverly Port, whose marathon phone calls and support kept me going. I love you all.

All photographs by Carol-Lynn Rössel Waugh unless otherwise credited.

INTRODUCTION

Since his birth in 1902, the teddy bear has been a popular artistic motif. Universal in appeal, he reaches out and touches the child within, dissolving age, class and cultural barriers.

Artwork featuring teddy has a magical quality. It gently seduces the viewer. He stops, smiles, transported for a moment. Teddy acts as a time machine, drawing him into his past, into a world simpler, more content, where a furry hug made everything right. The therapeutic touch of the teddy bear, remembered with fondness, remains as the traveler returns to the "real world." Content he moves on.

Few subjects in art have this effect on an audience, and it is natural that artists, gifted with perception, seized upon the teddy early, and have returned to him for over four-fifths of a century.

These artists, for the most part, were not "teddy bear artists," as I would define them. In my reckoning, a teddy bear artist must devote a substantial chunk of his original output, in whatever medium, to the teddy bear. This sort of artist is of recent vintage, say, since about 1980.

This does not mean there were not teddy bear artists before that date. It is just that nobody thought of them that way. Right from the start, there were teddy bear artists. In fact, if two artists, in two different media, had not "done their thing" in 1902, teddy bears might not exist.

I am speaking, first, of Clifford Berryman and his 1902 political cartoon, "Drawing the Line in Mississippi," which pictured Teddy Roosevelt's refusal to shoot a tethered bear while on a political jaunt-cum-hunting trip in Mississippi. The widely-distributed cartoon struck a popular chord. People began to speak of "Teddy's bear."

Mr. Berryman's drawing inspired the Morris Michtoms of Brooklyn, New York, to design the first American plush bear, and to name it "Teddy's bear." These first handmade original bears soon found their way to commercial production and the rest was history. The teddy bear was born.

Was Mr. Berryman the first teddy bear artist, then? It is hard to say. His career was certainly enhanced by his association with the popular cartoon, and he drew lots of pictures with bears and President Roosevelt in them, but they were not his main interest, methinks.

How about Mrs. Michtom? I am sure when she was stitching up the bears in her Brooklyn novelty store, she would never have thought of herself as a bear artist. She was inventing a way to draw customers into the shop. A plush bear in the window was timely, calculated to snag a crowd. It did; demand for her homemade original bears was more than she could handle. Soon they were mass-produced, by the first company founded by and for the teddy bear —Mr. Michtom's new Ideal Toy Company.

But, the first Michtom bears can be considered a form of original art. If any of them are still bearing up, they have first dibs on the premiere bear artist award.

Since teddy made his debut in 1902, he has been a source of aesthetic insbearation, making guest appearances in all manner of fine and commerical art. Children's books, and their illustrations, have featured him from his inception;

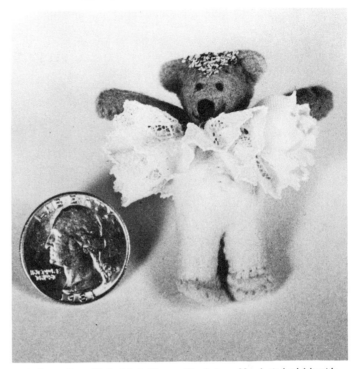

Ballerina Bear Pin by Maria Kwong. Stock item. Hand-stitched felt with nylon lace tutu and gold glitter cap; pink body to look like tights; natural (browns, gold, rust) heads and arms; white rosette on left side (which does not quite show up in photograph). 1n (2.5cm) bar pin sewed and glued on back. Size: 2in (5.1cm) tall. *Photograph courtesy of Maria Kwong.*

teddy's position in the juvenile literary world is solid. Zena Sutherland of the University of Chicago's Center of Children's Books states: "Excluding dogs and cats, there are probably more children's stories about bears and mice than anything else." Just about all of them are illustrated.

Still, artists seldom specialized in teddies. Those who did considered themselves artists — fine or commercial — artists who just liked teddy bears.

The term "teddy bear artist" is of recent vintage and it came from the doll world, as did the first people who called themselves by that name. And, I am afraid, I was mixed up in its coinage.

A bit of history is in order.

In the early 1970s, there were four of us — all doll artists, all working independently, who decided, for one reason or another, to design original teddy bears as art objects. Three were on the West Coast, which is, today, teddy bear heaven, largely because of their influence. I still work in central Maine, where my influence is undetectable.

Maria Kwong, a Californian, was a pioneer. She worked, and still works, in felt. Moving from fabric dolls, she developed terrific, inspired, technicolor bears. The other three of us worked in clay, designing original porcelain dolls. For one reason or another, we branched into bears.

Lois Beck and Beverly Port, in the Pacific Northwest, combined porcelain faces with plush bodies, marrying doll making and bear making techniques, to produce marvelous art bears, which they would bring to doll conventions, and sell out, even though bears were (and often still are) looked down upon by the heirarchy of the "official" doll world.

Theodore B. Bear by Beverly Port. © 1974. 5in (12.7cm) tall. Fully-jointed of old fabric; button eyes; black embroidered nose and mouth; long arms; wearing vest with buttons on front. *Theodore B. Bear* is the first teddy bear author to write a monthly column about teddy bears. He lectures and appears at shows and rallies. His well-known motto and trademark is: "Be a Benevolent Bear to Someone Today!" *Photograph by Beverly Port.*

I have always wondered about the sanity of this discrimination. Bears, after all, are humanoid. Theodore Roosevelt considered them the closest animal to man in intelligence, and what better recommendation could one want? Bear-faced dolls can be more human than people-faced dolls because they can caricature man in a way a people-doll never can.

I made bears, too, out of porcelain. Actually, they were a bit strange. They were bear-dolls, all-jointed, like dolls, with molded-on clothing. This was 1975, and, at the time, my bears were considered "mighty peculiar" by the general populace. Up here in Maine, one can get mighty lonely when one has a peculiar avocation. The local citizenry, those who took time to think at all about me, which was not all that overwhelming a number, considered me weird enough when I would drag around the porcelain dolls I designed. The most common comment about my work ran something like, "Why do you make a doll out of clay? It breaks."

You can imagine the popular appeal my bears had. People here are big on practical things. I can't think of many things more impractical than a porcelain bear. You can't even hug it. It takes a rarified taste to warm up to a cold, hard bear. And, in 1975, not many Mainers had an educated palate. So, I began searching for my peers, out of self-preservation. And I rediscovered Beverly Port.

The year before she had shown a doll named Percy at the International Doll Makers' convention in Reno. From his hand dangled an original teddy bear named *Theodore B. Bear*. I remember thinking at the time it was good that somebody had shown a teddy.

Bev and I never met until years later, but she was making her influence felt on the West Coast by teaching bear making techniques and disseminating information on bears. At shows, her bears were snapped up, albeit surreptitiously, by closet-case bear lovers, not ready yet to admit their mania. Word was spreading. Bears were art objects if they were made by artists. Art is, after all, whatever an artist says it is.

As her following on the West Coast increased, pockets of bear makers sprang up, and the craft-art-whatever-it-was, was passed along. She's still at it, like Johnny Appleseed: writing, lecturing, designing and making. It is largely because of Bev Port's generosity that enthusiasm for artist bears has reached its current level and has a tradition of excellence.

Lois Beck, at the same time, in the same area, was designing and making her originals, in both porcelain and fabric. She designed paper doll bears and other bear items. Collectors took notice and spread the word.

Still, at doll conventions, resistance to the showing of bears remained obdurate. They were frowned on at sales tables and excluded from competition.

I remember one year one of the little bears I had entered into competition was draped with a fat sign reading "NOT A DOLL." Phooey! It's funny how these not-dolls sold to doll collectors who smiled at them, patted them on the head and stuffed them into the depths of their tote bags with a "who, me?" expression.

The time was not quite ripe.

Of course, simultaneously, artists in other media were using the teddy bear for subject matter. Working alone for their own reasons, they were making personal artistic statements oblivious of the world outside. Content with their production, they were not even waiting for the world to catch up with them.

It finally did.

A book made the difference. Actually, it took two books, since the four of us (and many others) had been, separately, touched by Peter Bull's *Teddy Bear Book* (1968). More than any book on the subject, the *Teddy Bear Book* has turned more people onto bears, or brought out courage in the secret bearaholic, than can be calculated.

The second book to influence the field was *The Teddy Bear Catalog,* by Alan and Peggy Bialosky, published in 1980. It did not list a whole lot of teddy bear artists, mainly because, at the time, there were not a wad of us, but Bev, Lois and I were there. The Bialosky book alerted the world at large that teddy bears were valuable and worth paying attention to. And it did it with dollar signs attached to pictures.

Probably the time was ripe, anyway, but *The Teddy Bear Catalog* tapped into that readiness and spurred it on to unprecedented heights. Bears became big and valued. And, as antique bears' prices skyrocketed, collectors' tastes rarified. They craved rare bears — not necessarily old, but good and collectible. Bear artists were born overnight to fill that need. And most of them were on the West Coast, the territory primed by Bev Port.

California has a tradition, left over from the 1960s and 1970s, of craft excellence, especially in fiber arts, and of artistic experimentation. Bear making tapped into this ready seedbed. With an ever-growing market available, consisting of ravenous bear collectors and new stores specializing in bears, bear makers sprang up like mushrooms, some calling themselves "Original Bear Artists."

Some were good, some not. Some were neither artistic nor original. Few were tied to, or aware of, the traditions of doll making, or the ethics involved, and some problems began to surface, born of ignorance.

Novice bear makers, in search of secrets, began to buy bears or patterns and take them apart, or put them together, and then copy them, changing them a bit. Because they made the bears with their own two hands, they considered themselves somehow artists. They were craftsmen, imitative ones at that. Art revolves around invention, inspiration and originality.

The key word here is *originality,* as it separates artist from artisans, quality from quackery. As it is vital to the understanding of the works in this book, I thought I would take a few minutes to explain this term to the prospective or practicing bear artist.

ORIGINAL comes, obviously, from the word ORIGIN — or beginning. So, when you do an original anything, the essence has to come from you. You, as an artist, have to come up with every scratch of that piece of art.

The seed has to come out of your brain and you have to nurture it to fruition with your own two hands and ingenuity. Or, in other words, an original bear has to be wholly the artist's design. The artist can't use commercial kits or molds or purchased patterns or bodies. And she can't take a casting from a purchased or borrowed mold and change it slightly and call it an "adaptation."

Apparently many bear makers don't realize it, but to claim such works as original is dishonest, dishonest both to the buyer, and to the original designer, whether he is contemporary or deceased.

Sure, there are concepts that artists grab onto, for various reasons, that give them ideas or inspirations and they use them as springboards for their original efforts. This is perfectly valid. Sometimes there are ideas flying through the air, and, simultaneously, for one reason or another, a lot of people come up with something similar. As long as they aren't deliberately copying the work of someone else, even if the works are similar in conception, each of these products is a valid original statement.

The things we have to distinguish between are the general ideas in the air which a lot of people can get inspiration from and what is then done with them. It's what they do with their ideas that counts.

Goethe once said: "The most original authors are not so because they advance what's new but because they put what they have to say as if it had never been said before."

This is what distinguishes the artist from the artisan and what lives in the work of the people in this book.

The collection of data on them was a three years' project. The book could have been twice as thick. It started with a thirst for knowledge about my peers. In 1981, I wrote a two-part article for *Doll Reader*™ magazine called "The American Bear Artist." Up to that time, the idea of bear artistry, or the term, had had scant dissemination. But the response from readers was phenomenal and gratifying. The time was ripe for the original bear artist to gain acceptance, both from the doll world and the public at large. As the movement grew, I collected names and addresses and, sometimes, bears. I began to feel less alone.

As months passed, unforseen elements began to creep into the burgeoning bear movement: some good, some not. Speaking as an all-round arctophile, I guess the one I liked the least was the collectors who began to buy the artist bears — and the old ones, for that matter — for status value, rather than for love.

I understand that artist bears are art objects, since I am involved in their creation. But sometimes I wonder at the motives of some collectors, who look at the bear's price tag instead of his heart, or *eyes,* when they make a purchase.

I guess the problem is that of love objects vs. art objects. Can a teddy bear made by an artist be both?

Bear by Lois Beck, 15in (38.1cm) tall. Fully-jointed; made of 1/2in (1.3cm) long gold European mohair; shoe button eyes; growler; red bow; tag. Same style was made into a mechanical bear with a tail that made head say "yes" and "no." *Photograph by Lois Beck.*

I certainly hope so. But can one love a bear that costs $500 with the same freedom, in the same way, as one that costs $.75? I guess it depends on one's makeup and motives, but I do not think the love would be for the same reasons.

One can admire a $500 bear, but love — I mean, hugging-type love? Love that doesn't care if it sort of wears out the loved one — for after all, teddies are meant to be hugged, not looked at from afar, because that is the only way they get Real? I do not know.

Personally, I think it's wrong to select a bear for rarity alone, for its price tag. The proper criteria, in my opinion, for choice, are humbler: simple things, but vital and it doesn't matter whether it is an art bear or one that's been pre-loved. They remain the same, or should.

They are: the bear's huggability, and the way he looks at you. One or both must suit the two of you. A look of love is universal. Every "perfect bear" bears it. But the hug on a clay bear is mighty tricky.

A bear knows if he is picked for the wrong reasons. To be right, he must speak to his owner — preferably before he goes home, or he may never speak, and then you are both in for a dreadful time. Bears are sensitive about adoption motives. Those that call out for adoption are the ones to invite home.

Most bear lovers have heard this call. I did, most clearly, in November 1983, when I met my bear, *Oop.* Even though he is not an art bear (although he thinks he is arty), I thought I would describe the experience for those who have yet to undergo it.

I was in New York for a writers' conference and my mother and I were visiting a flea market in Tottenville, Staten Island, where I grew up. On top of a pile of junk lay a brown knitted bear. Since I am always on the prowl for bears, I gave him a quick once-over and decided to pass. He looked like a lumpy sausage, with legs somebody had forgotten to stop

knitting, and was sort of a cross between bear and gingerbread boy.

I plodded about four steps down the path when I heard a little voice cry out: "Save me! Bring me home with you!" I peered back at the bear and queried, carefully, "Did you say something?" I could have sworn he noded earnestly.

Finding myself in front of the junk pile once more, I asked the saleswoman how much she wanted for the sausage-bear and she said, "Seventy-five cents." It is a good thing he was within my budget, which nears $1.50 a day, because, by that time, I had determined to rescue him.

It was love at second sight. I probed the bear's eyes, which were embroidered in an expression of perpetual wonder, and knew he was For Me. Lovingly cramming him into my bag, I made for the shop next to the flea market, which sold old dolls and toys and was/is run by a nice lady named Ellie Oop. I wanted to show off my prize. She appreciates bears — most of the time.

With my usual panache, I unstuffed the bear from the bag and wagged it in the air, exclaiming, "Look at what I found, Ellie!" Eyes round with disgust and amazement, she shook her head, and grinned wanly. "Where did you get THAT?," she asked. "I just got RID of it." She had given my prize bear to the flea market.

Dumbfounded by her lack of perception of the innate lovability of my newfound companion, I decided to forgive her. "Ellie," I said, "We know you didn't mean that. He's so sincere. I'll name the bear after you to show we've no hard feelings. I'll name him *Oop.*"

That is how *Oop* got his name. He has since acquired a select, extensive wardrobe, a Gucci bag stuffed with jogging clothes, a creamsicle minus one bite and a red and white checkered apron (because he is a gourmet cook). This $.75 bear has become my traveling companion. He's loyal and squashproof.

Bears of all kinds, artist products or not, should be picked for similar reasons. Artist bears may be art objects, but they are also love objects. When an artist really understands a teddy bear, this is reflected in his output — whether it be a painting, print, sculpture or plush bear. Usually this understanding is visible in the bear's eyes. Look into them carefully when you consider adopting an artist's work. You can usually tell if a bear is made with love.

I have tried, in this tome, to give a representative sampling of the work of bear artists, in many media, who were active as of this writing (Spring 1984). Choices were difficult: the book could have doubled. All display two vital qualities: originality and technical excellence. Not every artist herein has universal appeal, naturally. I certainly don't. That's why this book is a smorgasbord.

The artists have been introduced to you on a personal level, to let them speak to you in their own words as much as possible about their art: what they do and why they do it. Perhaps, by their example, a whole new generation of bear artists will be born.

This was my sneaky goal all along. You see, up here in Maine, I was tired of being alone.

Carol-Lynn Rössel Waugh and *Oop,* March 1984.

REAL MUSGRAVE

Real Musgrave and *Theobearus*, his mascot and drawing instructor, at work on the 1982 Texas Rennaissance Festival poster. *Photograph courtesy of Real Musgrave.*

"Escape from the Nursery." Etching. 1982.

Until I came across the work of Real Musgrave, I imagined I was the only one who saw bear wizards.

I had been working on a fantasy book about one, living for several months in an alternate dimension. That February, I was strolling through the art exhibit at the Boston science fiction convention, *Boskone,* and a bear wizard peeped at me from a frame. Heart pounding, I stopped and smiled. Here hung a kindred soul.

He was nothing like my bear wizard, who was large, bumbling and bespectacled. The perky little bear wizard who smiled out from the brown-matted etching was soul mate to mine, but more teddy than bear. His inquisitive, satisfied expression was the perfect foil to the terrified gulp of the dragonlet clutching the runner of the craft the bear was piloting — a flying pegasus rocker balloon.

Sometime later, Real Musgrave sent me his photograph for this book. Standing beside him was *Theobearus,* a bemused-looking bear wizard with star-spangled robe and pointed cap. He is not *Bearo,* my wizard, but he is probably kin.

Wizard teddies are relative newcomers to Mr. Musgrave's repertoire. He specializes in fantasy art but he takes his time before he admits this to just anybody. "When I am asked what I do for a living, there usually comes a rather lengthy pause while I assess the general psyche and humour of my conversation-mate. One simply cannot declare 'I draw dragons for a living' to everyone," he writes.

Gentle dragons, both big and pocket-sized, as well as other creatures; unicorns, gargoyles, benevolent wizards who fly air ships join the wizard teddies in Mr. Musgrave's personal world. They are brought to life through meticulous, detailed drawings and paintings, and limited edition etchings that combine fantasy and reality, until the viewer is unsure of their boundaries.

Real has lived in this world almost all his life; he started drawing it at five years of age. He "liked drawing realistic things that no one could really see.

"I liked being able to take things that were in my mind, but then putting them in a fairly realistic setting so that even now my wizards and dragons are often in a Victorian setting," he told a reporter.

Musgrave pictures are often embellished with runes, conveying secret messages. These words, when translated from *Futhorc,* his private language, add to the enjoyment of the work. For example, the word "wizard" is almost always written on a wizard's garments. His hat may read, "Ideas, ideas."

The artist explains why, "Even the most wondrous of creatures can sometimes use a little extra enchantment which is why I often decorate borders and trim in my drawings with messages or words written in runes. The words are nearly always in English, with occasional lapses into Latin, and they are written in an early Germanic futhorc (very powerful). Everyone loves secret messages, but they are even more fun if you can translate."

His art training began early, with tutors and special classes. But it was almost waylaid by his father's insistence that Real attend engineering school. Lucking into a new BFA program at Texas Technological Institute, he followed his muse.

After a stint as art director for a department store and a trip to Europe, he and his wife, Muff, settled down in Dallas, Texas, and opened a studio where he was free to live in his alternate world.

As he works, often long into the night, dragons and creatures peer out, supervising his work. A dragon-shaped teapot and tea cosy and other magical objects give atmosphere to the place. And, as usual, *Theobearus* is there for insbearation.

"There is nothing more fun than to sit down at my drawing table and to work with those characters," the artist said. "It's like I can call all the characters back to my drawing table and become completely involved with them and they live in a world with certain problems, but nothing insurmountable. The biggest problem is where to find the next jelly bean."

Mr. Musgrave is fond of jelly beans.

Musgrave pictures are usually drawings or prints. Sometimes he combines media. This is the way he describes his output: "Drawings are sometimes done in color, sometimes in black and white (occasionally versions are done in each) but each drawing is unique. Each one is intended to be sold

"Famous Artist," etching by Real Musgrave.

FUTHORC INCLUDING RUNES FOR DIPTHONGS:

ᚠ ᚢ ᚦ ᚩ ᚱ ᚲ ᚷ ᚹ ᚻ ᚾ ᛁ ᛃ

F ◊ U ◊ TH ◊ O,A ◊ R ◊ C,K ◊ G ◊ V,W ◊ H ◊ N ◊ I ◊ J,Y,GE, A

ᛋ ᛈ ᛇ ᛉ ᛏ ᛒ ᛖ ᛗ ᛚ ᛝ ᛞ ᛟ

I,EO ◊ P ◊ AI,K,X ◊ S ◊ T ◊ B ◊ E ◊ M ◊ L ◊ NG ◊ D ◊ O,OE

ALPHABET IN PHONETIC FUTHORC:

ᚣ ◊ ᛒ ◊ ᚲ,ᛋ ◊ ᛞ ◊ ᛗ ◊ ᚠ ◊ ᚷ ◊ ᚻ ◊ ᛁ ◊ ᚩ ◊ ᛝ ◊ ᚲ ◊ ᚱ ◊ ᛗ

A ◊ B ◊ C ◊ D ◊ E ◊ F ◊ G ◊ H ◊ I ◊ J ◊ K ◊ L ◊ M

ᛏ ◊ ᛟ ◊ ᛈ ◊ ᚾ ◊ ᚲ ◊ ᚱ ◊ ᛋ ◊ ᛏ ◊ ᚾ ◊ ᚹ ◊ ᛈ ◊ ᚲ,ᛋ ◊ ᛃ ◊ ᛋ

N ◊ O ◊ P ◊ Q ◊ R ◊ S ◊ T ◊ U ◊ V ◊ W ◊ X ◊ Y ◊ Z

"Futhorc," Real Musgrave's secret language, with a key to translation.

as an original piece of art, although it may be produced as an illustration (which is not an original piece of art). In my drawings, a concept may go through a number of subtle or radical changes which will result in a series of finished pieces, each having its own merit. Often I begin with very small "complete" drawings which are used to solidify an idea which will be used in a larger and more complex design later.

"Prints are an entirely different matter. Prints are produced in limited editions of multiple originals from a plate.

That means that although each signed and numbered print is an original piece of art, it is not unique. It is very much like each of the other members of its edition (normally 25-150 identical prints)."

Real's bears are a relatively new addition to his roll call. Originally they were patterned after his first teddy, *Growler*. Increasingly *Theobearus* has taken on the modeling role.

The teddies fall into two categories of copyrighted characters: *Wizard Teddies* and *Guardian Teddies*.

"*Wizard Teddies* are the apprentices to kindly old wizards and normally wear red pointed hats (with ear flaps, white stars and magic green stones) and red bow ties (very fashionable when conjuring). They are good at parlor tricks and are excellent drawing instructors. They are friendly, intensely curious and tend to be reliable and imperturbable. If they are not in the laboratory or studio, you can most often find them in the music room listening to chamber music by Teleman. (Incidentally, they enjoy music but for the most part have mastered no musical instruments and only their very best friends can endure their occasional singing or bugle playing.)

"*Guardian Teddies* are small winged bears very much like guardian angels, only better. They never moralize and will defend their people to the last bit of stuffing. They tend to be very patient and are good listeners. They are talented hummers and singers of soft lullabies."

Pocket dragons are often companions to *Wizard Teddies*. Real says, "These magical mischievous creatures speak in Middle English, are slightly vain, love junk food and have an overwhelming compulsion to be 'helpful.' The next time you fumble through your pockets hoping for some loose change, only to find a bit of lint fluffed into the shape of a pillow and a half-nibbled red jelly bean, you'll know what a wonderous little visitor you've had."

These little visitors have delighted fantasy fans since 1974, when Real began marketing a series of fantasy fine art prints. His work was collected in book form, *Real Fantasies*, in 1976. By 1978, he moved his studios to 3611 Marsh Lane Place in Dallas and Muff became his business manager. Under her tireless guidance, his career took off. Soon pocket dragons and wizards began attending science fiction and fantasy conventions all over the country.

In 1979, he joined the Texas Renaissance Festival as exhibitor and later became its official artist, producing posters and advertising. In between, he holds forth at his medieval cottage-like booth on the permanent festival site, which recreates a European Renaissance Fair each fall for six weekends.

With widespread exposure, Mr. Musgrave's art has attracted a substantial following. His characters even appear in a line of full-color signature greeting cards.

By the time I discovered his teddy bear wizards in 1983, they were already well-known to fantasy fans. But they were a revelation to me. After all, I had been living in my own alternate world.

I took the etching of the pegasus-riding wizard from the wall of the Boston art exhibit, paid for it, and exited with a secret smile. I was not alone. Others believed in bear wizards.

"My Guardian Teddy" by Real Musgrave. Full-color drawing. *Teri and Ed Dodd Collection. Photograph courtesy Real Musgrave.*

"Trojan Teddy," 3¼in by 4in (83.cm by 10.2cm) drawing. 1983. *Photograph courtesy of Real Musgrave.*

"Bear Wizard," 3¼in by 4in (8.3cm by 10.2cm) drawing. 1983. *Photograph courtesy of Real Musgrave.*

The Reverend
CHESTER DANIEL FREEMAN
JR.

Teddy bears are a means of sharing love and faith for the Reverend Chester Daniel Freeman, Jr. "Bears have become a symbol of my work. As one who is committed to ecumenical and interfaith dialogue, I believe that we seek a beloved community and the teddy bear as a symbol of love which we struggle for in our daily lives."

Reverend Freeman has firsthand experience of the power of teddy bear love, as chaplain at Amherst College, and, more recently, as hospital chaplain. He finds almost universal acceptance of the teddy bear as a conveyor of love and comfort.

"I know of many college students who still have their teddy bears with them in their dormitory rooms. This comes about as a result of preaching sermons on teddy bears, using them as symbols of good listeners and lovers," he wrote, as he completed his stay as college chaplain. More recently he added, "As I make rounds in the hospital each day, I see many patients with their teddy bears and other friends. For some elderly people this is the only thing they have to hold onto in their lives."

Reverend Freeman's insight into teddy bear power stems from personal experience with his childhood bear. It led directly to his career as a bear artist.

"My memory does not recall the exact year in which I received my teddy bear but it must have been around five or six years of age. Consequently, I have been fond of bears for a long time. As a matter of fact, I was given only one teddy and he was named *Timmy*. I do not know what the significance of the name was but it must have been very special to me at the time.

"A few years ago I went home to visit my parents and I found *Timmy* sitting in my closet. When I picked him up, one arm and one ear were torn. These were the two places where he had been pulled around with me. His nose was worn and one eye was missing — a little fellow in much need of repair.

"A friend of mine saw him and decided that she would repair his arm and ear. Another friend repaired his nose and I replaced his eyes. It was interesting to see all my friends taking such an active interest in my teddy bear from childhood. One could say it was a bear affair.

"As I reflect on my relationship with *Timmy,* I think it was a very special one. Being an only child, I did not have a brother or sister to play with so much of my time was spent alone. During those times when friends were not around, *Timmy* became my playmate. He became my trustworthy friend. We would play together and sleep together.

"I also remember when I was being punished for doing something wrong — *Timmy* was always there to comfort me. At those times, we cried together and hugged each other until the pain was over. One of my interests as a child was photography. I can remember taking a photo of *Timmy* on my bed. Recently I found that photo in the family album and it brought back such wonderful feelings of growing up. Today *Timmy* sits on an exposed post in my house. He is

learning to share space with the new bears which are gradually filling the house. But he is coping well."

Chester has been making original bears since 1981, and he credits his friend — now his business partner — sculptor and artist, John McGuire, with getting him started and keeping him going.

"When I created a pattern, or prototype, he would make suggestions as to what he thought might improve the look and personality of the bear. With his keen eye for design and frank criticisms, I was able to achieve what I feel is a perfect bear."

Mr. McGuire and Reverend Freeman have combined talents in an enterprise called "Baskets and Bears." Mr. McGuire is the interpreter of basketry at Old Sturbridge Village in Massachussetts. As such, he recreates traditional New England baskets, as well as contemporary ones. Reverend Freeman talked John McGuire into miniaturizing some of his designs for the bears. Today, Freeman bears are known for their backpacks and picnic baskets.

Each Freeman bear is hand-sewn. Chester puts great emphasis on hand work. "When I work, I do it carefully...so much time is spent in the hand-sewing. I think that this actually takes most of the time. Once the sewing is complete,

The Reverend Chester Freeman, Jr., and *The Intellectual Bear. Photograph courtesy of Chester Freeman.*

Timmy, friend of Chester Freeman. *Photograph courtesy of Chester Freeman.*

Chester Freeman sewing on the body of a bear. 1983. Original creations in the background. *Photograph by Neil Hammer.*

the work goes rather quickly. Usually I can make a bear a day from start to finish. It takes several hours (about seven) from cutting the fabric to placing the finished bow."

Sewing is a skill that has passed through generations of Freemans. "Both of my grandmothers made quilts for me. My father has designed and upholstered furniture as a hobby. He also sews." Chester finds hand-sewing relaxing. It enables him to have complete control over the creation of each bear. And each one is done with affection.

"Perhaps the word which best sums up my bear designing is patience. I spend a great deal of time placing the eyes, ears and nose on the bear. The mouth is done with great care and feeling depending on the other features. The most fun comes when creating facial expression and defining features. Probably the thing that I enjoy least is making joints and putting them into the bear. That is no fun, it is my opinion that when one sews a bear by hand as I do, the look of that bear is created and influenced by many factors. For example, the mood that I am in, the music or the silence which fills a country home in the woods. For me, character is influenced by those factors and more."

Freeman bears come in three graduated sizes: 9½in (24.2cm), 12½in (31.8cm) and 16½in (41.9cm). They look like the Three Bears family when placed side-by-side. The largest bear wears handmade spectacles made from copper, giving him an intelligent air and folks have noted some resemblance between this bear and its designer. "Some people have said that the bear looks like me because I wear glasses. I don't think so. But perhaps every artist has a little of himself/herself in the work they make. Many people have said that because of my working in academic ministry, my bear would naturally take on an academic look. Perhaps that is so!" he remarked.

Chester feels that the three sizes of his bears almost determine to whom they will go. "The smallest bear is great for little babies and toddlers. It is easy for them to handle. The medium bear is appropriate for the seven or eight year old. The largest bear is favored by the teenagers and adults because of the glasses and air of sophistication which surrounds him or her."

As he began designing prototypes, Chester discovered that different fabrics drastically changed the bears' personalities. "For example, I made a set of bears in camel hair.

Off for a Ride, 9½in (24.2cm). Short honey pile plush. Label on back. Original for this bear. 1983. *Photograph by Neil Hammer, courtesy of Chester Freeman.*

shops, catalogs and at the shows the partners attend.

Early bears are not marked because they were given away. But Reverend Freeman feels they stand on their own and are recognizable as his. "When you compare different teddy bear artists, I think it is easy to see the difference and you will easily recognize a Freeman bear from another...in the future." Now they are marked with a cotton label, but are neither numbered nor dated.

Chester says he plans to continue making bears "as long as I can or until I get carpel tunnel syndrome. It has been a very rewarding hobby for me."

Many of the rewards have been intangible. Sometimes these are the finest. Chester wrote me, "Recently I received a letter from a lady in Florida who received one of my bears near Christmas. Her father died and she took the bear down

LEFT: *Off To Camp,* 12½in (31.89cm). Short honey pile plush. Label on back. Backpack custom made by John McGuire. 1983. *Photograph by Neil Hammer.*

BELOW: 9½in (24.2cm) bear. Short honey pile plush; brown felt pads. Label on back. 1983. *Photograph by Neil Hammer.*

They are quite stunning but I don't know if the general public would like them. So I have decided not to use them for some time."

Reverend Freeman's absolute favorite bears are the second prototypes he created. "They are made from an old fur which I found in a large fabric shop in Boston. When I made them, they seemed to take on a character immediately and I knew that I would keep them forever. The largest one, 16½in (41.9cm) is *Grandpa.* Over the years he has acquired a wardrobe from flea markets and antique shows. The glasses on his face are small human spectacles. A plaid shirt adorns his chest with hues of red, green, white and black. His pants are white silk which has aged to a cream color. He wears a pair of button-up leather shoes which are in mint condition. Located in his shirt is a small stud with a photograph of Teddy Roosevelt on it. His expression is that of an aged bear who has enjoyed his years and is now settling in for a long rest. *Grandma* is adorned with a handmade straw hat with small dried flowers on its brim. The flowers in her hat match the colors of her blue and white dress. She wears a pair of lace-up shoes made in Germany. A set of pinch nose glasses allow her to see better. She holds a miniature Nantucket lightship basket made especially for her by Mr. McGuire."

Most Freeman bears are bare, however. Chester prefers it that way. Occasionally, he will add a hat. Once he produced, in this way, a whole series of character "portrait bears" of fellow participants in a Black Artist Festival sponsored by Amherst College.

Because of the demands of his chaplaincy, Freeman bears are made in Chester's spare time, but they are quickly growing into a full-time business. They are now found in

Teddy Bear Muff. 1984. Photograph courtesy of Chester Freeman.

Sitting in the Park, 9½in (24.2cm). Short honey pile plush. Signed on back. 1983. *Photograph by Neil Hammer, courtesy of Chester Freeman.*

South with her to the funeral. She said that it was a great help to her during that time of grief and loneliness. She even named him *Theophilus Chester* which was very touching."

Freeman bears have a mission — to spread love and comfort. "I think that bears are to be held, to be touched, to be caressed. That is their function. They give support. Knowing that my bears have brought a smile or giggle to someone's face is great reward to me." Chester explains.

He becomes philosophical. "By its nature of being silent — of listening, the teddy bear has a mystical quality. When talking to our bears, it is the 'silence' which allows us to reflect and to make decisions about our lives. Normally we don't take time to reflect critically, but with our teddy bears we listen as they listen.

"Teddy bears have another quality which is that of healing: a healing which comes from touching, hugging, holding.

"When you give a bear to a child, the immediate response is to hold — to touch the bear. I think that we are aware of the power of touch but we do not utilize that gift as much as we should. The teddy bear breaks down some of those barriers and allows us to be free to respond.

"The third quality which I find in the teddy is his/her availability. The bear is always there on the bed or sitting on the shelf waiting patiently for us to pick him/her up."

The bear maker, responding to these qualities in the bears that he has designed, finds that his reasons for creating them have evolved. "I began to make bears as an artistic challenge. Today I make teddy bears as a symbol of love which we struggle for in our daily lives, a love that is patient and kind, always ready to excuse, to trust, to hope, to endure whatever comes. The teddy bear is the embodiment of all those things and that is why they survive broken arms and torn ears. We believe in them because they listen to our joys, our sorrows, our disappointments and still love us regardless."

Chester is grateful, for many reasons, that he retains his childhood ted. It is not only because the bear started him in business. "For those of us who are fortunate enough to have their childhood bears, they serve as a fond reminder of our growth from childhood to adulthood. Consequently they are the mediator of love from parent to child. Because the bear was given as a gift in the spirit of love, it carries that love in its stuffing and becomes the embodiment of love for a lifetime. We never forget our teddy bears!"

It is obvious that Chester Freeman's bear, *Timmy,* has kept the faith.

Thread Bear. The first of the "Pre-Loved" teddy bears, he is 9½in (24.2cm) tall and dressed in worn and faded overalls and a white sweater. He is a copy of a very old teddy. There were 25 in this (now closed) edition. He is pre-loved, with some spots on his elbows and nose and on his clothing to simulate the kind of wear a teddy gets from a lot of loving. 1983. *Photograph courtesy of Doris King.*

Hucklebeary. Second of the "Pre-Loved" bears, he was an edition of 75. He is dressed in overalls and a beat-up straw hat. 14in (35.6cm) tall, he made a big brother for *Thread Bear.* With his paws stuck in his pockets, he is a picture of innocence. In his back pocket, though, he carries a slingshot. The right paw is reaching for ammunition. 1983. *Photograph courtesy of Doris King.*

Ursa Major, 14in (48.3cm) tall. He comes in a variety of acrylic fake fur; stuffed with excelsior; plastic eyes; movable joints. 1983. *Photograph courtesy of Doris King.*

Ro-Bear, 13in (33cm) tall. Stuffed with excelsior; shoe button eyes; movable joints. Wears a paint-spattered muslin smock gathered at the neck with a red bow and a matching red beret. He is a French painter. 1983. *Photograph courtesy of Doris King.*

Angelique, 13in (33cm) tall. Stuffed with excelsior; shoe button eyes; movable joints. Limited edition of 25. Made exclusively for "Pilgrim." With her classical tutu and her satin slippers, *Angelique* felt she was well on her way to being "Prima Ballerina." After hours of practicing the five basic positions, we find her at her exercise bar in the "sixth position" — fatigue. She is the second King "cultured teddy." 1983. *Photograph courtesy of Doris King.*

Skip-Bear, 13in (33cm) tall. Short-napped plush; shoe button eyes; movable joints; stuffed with excelsior. This fearless mariner wears a yellow sou'wester of sailcloth with a matching hat. Open stock bear. 1983. *Photograph courtesy of Doris King.*

Beach Bear, 13in (33cm) tall. Stuffed with excelsior; made of short-napped plush; shoe button eyes; movable joints. Wears an old-fashioned swim suit done in red and white striped knit. Open stock bear. 1983. *Photograph courtesy of Doris King.*

JUNE AND BOB BECKETT

Bob and June Beckett, 1983. *Photograph courtesy of Bob and June Beckett.*

June Beckett and some of her bears. *Photograph courtesy of June Beckett.*

Every once in a while June Beckett goes on a teddy bear binge and her studio swarms with heaps of bears. She does it for a change of pace. "Their reason for being made is for me to get away from carving at times. Gotta take a break and I do it with teddy bears...."

June and her husband, Bob, are well-known doll artists, and members of ODACA, the Original Doll Artist Council of America. Their hand-carved wooden dolls, personal interpretations of American children, have a long list of enthusiasts. These are the main products of their Tennessee studio. But now and then June makes bears, and they are snatched up eagerly by collectors.

It has been this way for over a decade.

June has loved bears since her Uncle Clarence gave her his childhood bear, " a real teddy from the pre-1910 era," in 1930. At first she made bears from patterns by other people. "Mrs. Hutchings' book (Margaret Hutchings' *Teddy Bears and How to Make Them)* was my teddy bear school," she says. She started with felt. "Somebody sent me a little bitty pattern in the mail for felt 3in (7.6cm) bears — probably originated in *Teddy Bears and How to Make Them"* and she made hundreds of little bears in sizes from 1¾in (4.5cm) to 5in (12.7cm), all hand-sewn. Later, fake fur became her medium and the bears grew as big as 24in (61cm) tall.

She must have done something right, for "everybody liked 'em, everybody bought 'em," so she continued, finally designing her own *Oldster © Bear* pattern in 1982.

Oldster is usually 17in to 19in tall (43.2cm to 48.3cm) tall because this size is "easiest to handle in sewing and stuffing." She makes him out of atypical stuff. "I use any fabric I feel like, enjoy the lovely old woolens in old coats the best."

Since there is not a bundle of usable fabric on any given coat, it is hard to make more than a couple of bears from it. These coaty bears have a special "limited eidtion" quality, therefore. A nice touch June gives to *Oldster* bears is the coat's label she sews to one of the pair she'll make. The buyer has a special sort of distinctive documentation this way.

The *Oldster* has a smaller sibling, 5in (12.7cm) tall, made in felt. "These are made to satisfy my memories of the (bear) Uncle Clarence gave me — the one someone stole from me when I was just a little, bitty kid." June says.

Her bears are usually jointed, "though occasionally some other one gets through to me." She uses a special trick to make the joints come out even.

"When cutting out fabric bears, have a package of notebook reinforcers handy (the self-stick type). Each place where you mark for a joint, surround the mark with a reinforcer. Later, when you are working with the joints, your fingers can feel the circles on the inside of the arms, legs and body; also if the fabric is a bit ravelly (as is some of the tweed and plaid coat fabric I use), the sticky reinforcer will help keep the ravelling down. Try it — it works! Just leave the circles in there; your joints work better and the fabric is strengthened."

Some of her bears are dressed, but at times, clothes are superfluous. "We have bears with neat, tidy overalls and

One of the first *Oldster Bears* made by June Beckett, 17in (43.2cm) tall. Fully-jointed, 100% cashmere (made from old coat); hand-knitted wool scarf. © 1982. *Photograph courtesy of June Beckett.*

Bear by June Beckett. Doll by Bob Beckett. 1981.

some girl bears wear pinafores, but a bear made out of hounds-tooth brown check (from an old sports-coat — gorgeous!) has no need of clothes, believe me. We--el, maybe a hand-knitted scarf!"

Bears seem to have definite ideas about what they will wear, June found out. "I remember the bear that I wanted to be a girl bear. When I finished it, I dressed 'her' in the baby dress (I'd) laid out — forget it. Unhappy bear — until I located a pair of overalls for HIM. Don't know if 'twas the fabric...the way HE was stuffed...or what!

The whole Beckett clan seems involved in bear making. June's daughter-in-law now supplies her with 2in (5.1cm) and 3in (7.6cm) bears to sell at shows. "Daughter Cyndi has made many tiny bears and sold 'em all. Son John made a dear little velour one about eight years ago just to prove he could do it," June reports. For Christmans, 1983, her "very best Christmas present" was the 3in (7.6cm) felt bear her six-year-old grandson, Johnny, made for her.

Bob Beckett, June's husband and partner, is a full-fledged bear artist in his own medium. He has designed hand-carved wooden bears. Some have fabric bodies. Some have jointed limbs. Some are clothed and some are bare and they all have a wonderful distinctive roundish bear shape that makes one smile.

For special people, Bob carves bear-bola ties, but he does not do many as they take just about as much time to do as does a wooden doll.

And dolls after all, are the Becketts' business. "I'm a wood sculptor and really love the wooden doll making that

we do for a living," June says. "If I'm not away from home, I'm involved either with that, or sneaking time in for bear making. If I wanted, I believe I could just make bears — but then who'd make my dolls?"

June is very particular that her bears are well marked. "It only takes a few minutes with an indelible pen to mark a bear in detail. I take great personal pride in my work and the marking is something I've decided is part of that feeling. At the Baltimore regional one year a lady came tearing back to me with the bear she had just purchased. 'My friends insist this bear is from Germany — you didn't sign or mark it.' Valuable lesson learned!"

June's bears are marked the following ways:
1) A label in the back seam says: Made by June Beckett.
2) Right paw: JB © 82 (Copyright shown only on *Oldster Bears*).
3) Left paw: Name of individual bear and year made. If bears are from a special coat fabric, they are numbered and this is shown on the left paw.

Beckett bears are only available at shows and from the Becketts' studio.

Fortunately for June, her leisure-time bears have been extremely popular. She has made over 2000 of her 3in (7.6cm) bears alone. "I'm not complaining," she says. "When I get on a 'teddy bear binge,' somebody'd better buy some or we'll be shoved out into the cold to make room for them. The studio is supposed to be for doll making and display. I'm only allowed one shelf...so why should I complain that bears are a 'hot item?' "

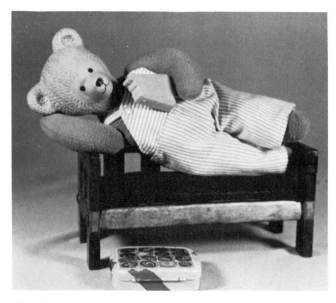

Baggy Bear, 8in (20.3cm). Carved wooden head designed by Bob Beckett. Balance of body fuzzy knit fabric. Baggy blue striped overalls.

Bridget Bear and *Belly Bear*. Carved wooden brown bears; jointed at arms. Designed by Bob Beckett.

Bridget Bear, 8in (20.3cm) carved wooden bear designed by Bob Beckett. Joined at arms; carved-on yellow-painted apron. Wife of *Belly Bear*.

Belly Bear, 8in (20.3cm). Carved brown wooden bear; jointed at arms. Designed by Bob Beckett.

Bromleigh, 18in (45.7cm) tall. Green Donegal tweed bear; fully-jointed. Off-white scarf; old shoe button eyes; corduroy paws. Original by June Beckett.

8in (20.3cm) unnamed bear. Prototype of the carved bears designed by Bob Beckett enjoying popcorn. Dark brown carved wooden head; fuzzy tan body fabric, hood; brown overalls. One-of-a-kind.

Felt jointed bears by June Beckett. They range in size from 2in (5.1cm) to 3½in (8.9cm).

SARAH McCLELLAN

FAR LEFT: Sarah McClellan and some of her creations. She has a firm grip on the open-mouthed grizzly bear. 1983. *Photograph courtesy of Sarah McClellan.*

LEFT: Early McClellan bears. *Melvin Oh, My* stands lower right. *Photograph courtesy of Sarah McClellan.*

"I am best known for the 'traditional' long-snouted, jointed teddy bear, who also just happens to be wearing clothes (usually)."

Sarah McClellan is describing her bears. They may be some of the most elaborately costumed bears around. And they are the only Wild West bears I have seen.

Sarah is the former editor of *The Grizzly Gazette,* an arctophile publication hailing from Scottsdale, Arizona. Sarah tries to capture a bit of the local culture in her bears.

A Texas native, McClellan moved around a lot as a child; her father was with the space program. Now married, she finds herself once more out West, drawing from her location inspiration for her bears.

The Grizzly Gazette Bears began around 1980. Sarah, who had let her sewing skills disintegrate since grammer school, decided to make a bear for her anticipated baby. "I wanted very much to make something very special for my child, something he/she could keep forever and I thought that the teddy bear was the most appropriate choice." In grammar school Sarah had wide exposure to art, winning art competitions. In college she took art as electives and studied sculpture.

Working from a commercial pattern, the Arizonan made bear after bear and started improvising. Long-lost sewing skills returned, ("I used to sew clothes for my dolls as a child but after about age 11, completely quit sewing and I barely passed Home Economics in Junior High.") and soon she was designing her own teds.

"Since then it has been one bear after another (and lots of dolls, too). I now have a couple of sewing machines and a fully-stocked workroom and have learned to sew by the seat of my pants," Sarah reports.

An early bear was called *Melvin Oh My,* which she calls a "pancake bear." "There are only three pieces — a front, back and snout. I will always be partial of *Melvin* because of his simplicity, but the bears that I seem to always surround myself with are the girl and boy cubs. If I had to pick one all time favorite, it would probably be the 'school age girl cub,'" she says.

Her real love is *Bongo.* He was a sort of adopted bear. However, he was not her first.

"I have liked bears since early childhood although I was much more partial to my dolls. My first bears seemed very crabby, not at all the kind you would want to cuddle up with in the dark. Then I began to find them in all sorts of places, on playgrounds, in parks, and once my dog even brought home a wonderful bear (covered with fertilizer).

"My favorite bear was an old Steiff (1907) that belonged to my cousin. She was six and I was seven when I first set eyes on it and I didn't know how I could possibly go on living without it. She was quite indifferent to him and my incessant wailing finally convinced her that the bear was really meant for me. We have been together ever since and "The Bear" (or *Bongo,* as he is more commonly known) went on to win the 1983 Teddy Bear Calendar Contest and to model for Christmas cards," she says.

McClellan bears are plush and largeish, ranging in size from 2in (5.1cm) to 3ft (91.4cm). "And someday lifesize!," Sarah adds.

She describes how she designs a bear.

"A lot of what I call inspiration comes to me from looking in books of the old west and in books on bears. I will see a certain outfit or cowboy and think about a bear in a similar outfit or with a similar look about him and then try to personify that. I get ideas about the actual shape of a bear from looking at the real thing and then, finally, when I have an idea of what I want, I will look through pictures of teddy bears for the qualities I would like to see expressed in my teddies.

"Next I sketch out the idea and take newspaper and begin drawing and cutting the patterns. I have some scroungy old fur I use for prototypes and when I have the bear 'down,' cut the pattern out in hardboard and from then on just trace the bears onto the back of the fur."

Sometimes inspiration comes from sources other than books. Once, it came first hand, and resulted in one of Sarah's most unusual bears.

Sarah tells it this way. "A few years back two friends and I toured Glacier National Park and the Canadian Rockies for three weeks, camping with just a tent for shelter (it snowed the first night — June!). After spending a few nights in the deep woods, the 'Beware of Bears' signs were beginning to get to us, especially since they are so full of graphic warnings of what can happen to you. I began to be afraid to venture too far from camp in the evenings and this newly found fear (terror) of bears became sort of a joke between us. At this time the book, *The Night of the Grizzly*, had just been released and was on every book stand in the parks. I told myself I wasn't to read it, but curiosity got the best of me. (It is the tragic story of two young women who had both been mauled to death on the same night by grizzly bears on opposite sides of the park. One of them had been pulled right out of her tent.) A very sad book and my fears were increased.

"Then, one morning, about 4:00 a.m., just as the sun was beginning to rise in Banff, Canada, a bear wandered into our camp. I woke up with my heart in my throat, pounding like a drum in my ears and was absolutely paralyzed with fear. As I lay there in my bag motionless, I could hear his grunting and snorting as he sniffed around the perimeter of the tent, just inches from my head. With just the thin sheet of canvas between me and his jaws, I was sure I was soon to experience a painful ending to my life.

Sarah and the toothy *Grizzly*. 1983. *Photograph courtesy of Sarah McClellan.*

"The only thing I could think of to try and save myself was to somehow use the hard shell of my suitcase as a shield. With one trembling arm I reached out, opened it, emptied it and tried to cover my body with it.

"My one friend had been sleeping in the car (fear of beasts in the woods) and had been awakened by the bear peering in at her. She watched in dumb horror as the bear lurked around for an opening to our tent. My other friend slept peacefully through the ordeal, even though the pounding of my heart sounded like thunder to me, and awoke after the bear finally lumbered off, to find me still white with fear peering from under my suitcase. (While I was laying there the thought had occurred to me that this might make a good Sampsonite commercial).

"Anyway, I have been afraid of bears ever since and created the bear with the big jaws as a representation of what my mind was picturing on the other side of the tent that early morning. The only difference is my bear is quite small — a foot and a half (45.7cm) — and I am sure the real one was at least 14ft (4.3m)!"

The bear with the big jaws (and clay teeth) is undressed. But most other McClellan bears are elaborately garbed. For Sarah, this is one of the best parts of bear making.

"A great many of the bears I make wear clothes. This is half the fun and it helps define their roles (though not their personalities) in life. For example: a hired-paw or a gambler. The clothing also helps differentiate between the series I have.

"All my bears are marketed under the trademark, "Sal's Pals," and the old west bears are in a series called the 'Grizzly Gazette Bears, Teddy Bears from the Wild West.' These bears are dressed and come in a variety of costumes and characters."

The character bears include a *Gentleman Gambler* bear (more often referred to as *Ace*, because of the royal flush up

The Gentleman Gambler bear, 22in (55.9cm), more often referred to as *Ace*. Fully-jointed; white pin-striped suit; "diamond" tie clasp in rose-colored tie; "gold" watch chain; white Panama hat with black ribbon band; shirt dickey tucked with lace; silvery gray fur. Keeps a "royal flush" tucked up his sleeve. *Photograph courtesy of Sarah McClellan.*

RIGHT: *Cowbear*, 18in (45.7cm) or 22in (55.9cm). Cotton print work shirt with western yoke; leather vest; leather belt with "silver" buckle holding up well-worn jeans; large bandana around neck; broad-brimmed cowboy hat. *Photograph courtesy of Sarah McClellan.*

LEFT: *Bongo*, Sarah McClellan's longtime friend, ready for the beach. *Photograph courtesy of Sarah McClellan.*

Quicksilver, the Gunfighter and *Dance Hall Gal Bear*, 22in (55.9cm). Fully-jointed. *Quicksilver* wears black jacket with long tails; lacy shirt dickey; black vest with silver buttons; "silver" gun in holster on right hip; "silver" belt buckle; "silver" trim on black cowboy hat. *Dance Hall Gal* wears silky dress trimmed with black lace; ribbon spaghetti straps; bloomers trimmed with ribbon and lace; black garter around leg; boa around neck; large ostrich feather adorning head. *Photograph courtesy of Sarah McClellan.*

his sleeve, *Quicksilver, the Gunfighter*, who totes a "silver" gun on his right hip; Cowboy Bears; *Grizzly Lily*, "The Grand Lady of the West," replete with Victorian fashions and lacy parasol; *The Dance Hall Gal Bear*, who flaunts a feather boa; a *Southern Belle Bear*, in a fancy white lace dress; a whole family of bears; a *Circus Bear* with baggy suit and a jester's collar with bells, *Bluebear'd, the Pirate*, with peg leg and parrot; and, my favorite, *Pawcahontas with Papoose*, who is dressed in a fringed rawhide dress and "turquoise" beads.

Most of Sarah's bears sport her label, which reads "SAL'S PALS." It is sewn at the top of their backs. The special series bears are signed and numbered. They are made with the collector in mind, "mostly because of the detail and the price. However, I would like to believe they are all made durable enough to withstand some regular use by small people."

Sarah's bears have become so popular she has had to find people to help her sew. She feels that her designs will still maintain their high quality, however. "Since I maintain very close contact with those doing the work, I feel my bears are as good (if not better — there are some excellent seamstresses out there) but still they are no longer manifested by me. Sort of like an artist dictating a picture, it is still his although he uses someone else's hands to realize it."

The analogy is apt. Bear making has become Sarah McClellan's art form.

"I am a frustrated painter. I have drawn and painted for as long as I can remember, but do not feel I am as successful expressing my ideas in that medium as I do working in the three-dimensional. I look forward to going into clay sculpture whenever time permits. Bear making in its highest form is self-expression."

Sarah's work is making its way into galleries. "My bears and dolls spent some time in the Heit Gallery in Phoenix, Arizona, and were actually part of a special showing of Picasso and Dali last spring (1982). It was a marvelous feeling to have my dolls and bears sitting just a few feet from those great artists' works."

What is the best part of bear making for her? "I think the most satisfying element of bear making is being able to form a physical counterpart to a thought; creating a tangible out of an intangible. Somewhere in their evolution from a piece of cloth to a finished bear they become an entity with a distinct personality, one that they seem to keep as long as they are in my possession. I guess that makes them 'people' to me."

They are people to her customers, too. "I always find it interesting to see the reactions of people to my bears. Often a person will come into my house who has had no previous interest in teddy bears and strike up a conversation with one, and if they stay long enough, actual friendships develop. I am always fascinated by the 'magic' bears seem to create."

Some feel the Grizzly Gazette's Bears' magic is in their elaborate wardrobes. Sarah knows it runs deeper. It is more than clothes that make the bear.

ABOVE: *The Grizzly Lily*, 22in (55.9cm). Fully-jointed ornate dress trimmed with ruffles and cream-colored lace; matching bonnet with ribbons and lace; coordinating underclothes; lacy parasol hanging by a satin ribbon from wrist. *Photograph courtesy of Sarah McClellan.*

BELOW: Small teddies by Sarah McClellan, approximately 7in (17.8cm) tall. *Photograph courtesy of Sarah McClellan.*

SYLVIA LYONS

Sylvia Lyons and friends. *Photograph courtesy of Sylvia Lyons.*

Eric-Jon Rössel Waugh (5 years old) and *Vanilla Pudding* by Sylvia Lyons, May, 1984. Bear is approximately 28in (71.1cm) high; fully-jointed; white plush; wide-open pink felt lined collie-like snout, plastic eyes; embroidered nose; growler; personality.

Eric-Jon and *Vanilla Pudding* get acquainted, May 1984.

As I sit punching words into the computer, one of Sylvia Lyons' bears is energetically nibbling at my son's nose. I can hear Eric-Jon's squeals of delight as they wrestle on the chair, then settle down in the bay window to build a castle.

The UPS man brought him this morning for a visit (the bear, not the boy), and he literally leapt out of the carton —which was half his size — when I opened it. E-J dragged him away and I have not yet been able to get him back.

"What's his name,?" Eric asks. "*Vanilla Pudding,*" I reply. "That's a disgusting name," he says. "HE isn't disgusting, though. I'll feed him a chocolate egg."

Sylvia's bear is a success. Reeking with verve and humor, he begs to be picked up, squashed by small arms (or big ones, for that matter) and carried off. As far as I can see, all of Sylvia's bears are of this ilk.

Sylvia's work has always been that way. Her "Porcelain People," with which she established herself in the doll world, are whimsical miniature porcelain dolls which developed from traditional doll house-style people into complex all-porcelain multi-jointed figures. About 1976, she started making porcelain bears. These were anthropomorphic bear-dolls, jointed like her people, insouciant and outrageous.

She has just (1983) branched out into plush bears. They are not small, either, and they are as outlandish as ever.

Their shapes are uncommon, certainly not traditional. Most are jointed, floppy and scrunchable. They are equipped with humorous, unexpected expressions. *Vanilla Pudding* has an enormous collie-like open snout with bright pink innards.

Sylvia's bears are the most easygoing bruins I have encountered. And they mirror her attitude.

"I make bears because they feel good to make and to hold when finished. They make ME feel good," she says. "I will make whatever calls to me — size or medium."

She has another reason for making bears.

"I have liked bears FOREVER. My favorite bear was about 12in (30.5cm) tall, probably an old Steiff. He became so loved that "Mummy-dear" tossed him out (when I was about seven) into the garbage can. I can remember like yesterday his wonderfully worn out ear which I used to twitch as I sucked my thumb. I know she figured that if bear was tossed out I would stop sucking my thumb. It didn't work. I sucked my thumb anyhow. But, alas, bear was lost forever. I never have forgiven Mum!

"I like my plush bears because of this. I feel I was successful in reconstructing my thrown-out bear."

The bears' personalities seem to reflect the way Sylvia thinks. She describes her bears' coloring: "My bears come in the following taste experiences: caramel, chocolate, nutmeg, licorice and more to come."

Lyons bears have suede paws, plush bodies "in all candy and spice colors," and are stuffed with fiberfill. They are extremely responsive to hugs. Joints, when used, are made from washers, cotter pins and leather. The bear artist does not much like making joints or bending cotter pins — this seems to be a common complaint. She prefers embroidering the nose and mouth. "The character lies therein," she explains. "Each bear is VERY carefully constructed."

But sometimes disasters still occur. This is the reason she prefers to make bears of multi-flavored plush.

"I made the same bear pattern in mohair. I bought a great deal of mohair in several colors. The same bear was absolutely unbelievably ugly. If there were a prize for ugly at any show, this bear would have won the prize hands down. I MUST design a new bear to use up all that gorgeous mohair."

Sometimes Lyons bears are dressed — not often. "I look at each bear and decide who should be dressed in what. Bears are seldom dressed unless going to some special affair. Bears are well dressed in their birthday suits, anyhow."

I asked Sylvia if her bears had a didactic purpose. She replied: "Good grief, what is didactic? My dictionary says 'Fitted or intended to teach' — I think not. My bears give their love unquestioningly, without strings one way or another."

Jenny-Lynn, 15, has just returned from Winthrop High. "Wow, Mom," she exclaims, grabbing up *Vanilla Pudding*, raising his arms in a Richard Nixon gesture and waggling his head. "This is MY kind of bear. Can we keep him? He's a nice bear for all sorts of perverted positions. You gotta take my picture with him!"

None of the squadron of visitor bears has elicited such unsolicited enthusiasm from my ursinely astute offspring. Sylvia Lyons' bears are a resounding success.

Post script:

As the result of transcontinental negotiations, *Vanilla Pudding*, rechristened *Van-My-Man* by Jenny-Lynn Waugh, has taken up residence at 5 Morrill Street, Winthrop, Maine. He was the only "visitor bear" we just could not send back.

Caramel by Sylvia Lyons, approximately 18in (45.7cm) tall, most of it in the legs. Fully-jointed; beige plush; brown felt paw pads; long wide blue satin ribbon, black eyes; embroidered nose and mouth; growler.

Caramel and *Vanilla Pudding* by Sylvia Lyons discuss the technical aspects of writing, May 1984.

Caramel and *Vanilla Pudding* by Sylvia Lyons. Fully-jointed plush bears with growlers. 1984.

Jenny-Lynn and *Van-My-Man*. He has just heard that he will remain in Maine.

Vanilla Pudding meets Jenny-Lynn Waugh, age 15, May 1984. Love at first sight!

LEFT TO RIGHT: *Caramel, Red Bearon (Ted Menten Collection)* and *Licorice* by Sylvia Lyons. *Photograph courtesy of Sylvia Lyons.*

HELEN HULL

LEFT: Two Helen Hull bears made of low-fire clay; jointed at limbs with wire. Approximately 1in (2.5cm) tall.

RIGHT: Helen Hull bears made of low-fire clay; jointed at limbs with wire. 1in (2.5cm) tall. 1983.

Helen Hull, of Framingham, Massachussetts, sculpts secret pocket companions. She sews them, too, but the 1in (2.5cm) ceramic-like jointed bears are her favorites.

"They're good listeners," she says. "They can 'hear' you spelling words, help you with verbs in Latin or French or Spanish, and, if you need them, they can be tucked in a match box to help you remember the answers on a quiz or your S.A.T.s. Some of my bears have done that. They're good luck; very good luck."

Luck — perhaps it should be termed serendipity — started Helen off. She loves miniatures and bears, but she had never really connected the two before meeting a teddy bear artist.

"I was attending a National Association of Miniature Enthusiasts convention (NAME) in Washington, D.C.," she explains. "One of the workshops was 'Sculpting a Miniature Jointed Bear.' It was being taught by Sylvia Lyons from California. I had made bears before but not jointed, so I signed up.

"Sylvia liked my bear and because the workshop was so popular she asked me to help her teach a second session the following day. (People who could not get into the workshop were getting grouchy and ugly!) I was pretty happy about that — working with Sylvia, and I was encouraged to make a few more bears and test the market.

"I passed! Actually, the teddies passed."

Mrs. Hull is an arctophile. "I've ALWAYS liked bears," she says, "but I didn't begin to LOVE bears until I bought a Steiff teddy for my daughter, Stephanie, when she was two years old — Christmas 1969. My favorite bear is hers. For many years and through some near-disasters, Stephanie and her bear were inseparable. Oddly enough, her bear does not have a name! He's showing 'bear pattern' baldness and he doesn't get around as much as he used to but he is still very much loved."

Helen began making sculpted bears from a low-fire ceramic-like compound in 1980. They are usually about 1in (2.5cm) tall, (doll house scale) are individually sculpted and are jointed at the limbs with wire.

"I combine two sculpting compounds which can be low-fired in a home oven. I've worked it out so that the bears are neither shiny nor too transluscent. They are usually caramel-colored but sometimes I make them brown like the antique Steiff.

"There is no actual design. It has to LOOK like a bear but other than that, it just happens. I use toothpicks, a tapestry needle and my fingers.

"They are painted with a 00 paintbrush which has lost a few hairs and I clipped some so I don't know what size it is now. I'll die when I have to get another one."

Helen also makes fabric bears. She describes their genesis.

"Our teddy bear collection wasn't growing as fast as our camel and frog collections. I found a nice furry remnant in a fabric store. Thinking it would make a nice bear, I bought it. It sewed like a dream, made a cute bear, except under our lights, which are not fluorescent, the sweet little bear is sort of camouflage green.

"Meredith, our camel collector, loves it anyway. Subsequent efforts have been more successful. I've learned to tell (in any light) which browns have too much gray or red or green in them. Bears can come in all shades of brown EXCEPT 'greeny brown'!"

But she prefers the clay ones. Maybe this is because of the reactions of her customers.

"My favorite bear is the sculpted one because no two are alike. Each one has a distinct personality. I enjoy watching people choose one.

"Some are fat, some thin, some have big feet, some have long arms, some have turned heads, some are looking up, some have big ears. Some people can't make up their minds at all and they pick one with their favorite color bow. And SOMETIMES two people fight because they want the EXACT SAME BEAR. When that happens, I wish I could make two alike but I can't and that's that!"

Mrs. Hull marks her bears with a tiny "HH" inside their left leg on the body.

Since, by nature, her bears are one-of-a-kind, the Massachussetts bear maker does not experiment much. She has her design formulated; it comes out differently each time. But once, she did.

"I decided to make three bears, one for each daughter and one for a friend. I wanted them to be different so I made them with open mouths. They were adorable! Apparently the open mouth bothered one of my daughters. She was just 11 at the time. To her dad's horror, she fashioned a tiny cigarette for her bear. He was NOT amused. The bear still has his cigarette but I never made any more open-mouthed

RIGHT & BELOW: Helen Hull bears made of low-fire clay; jointed at limbs with wire. 1in (2.5cm) tall. 1983.

"*Hershey* is my favorite. *Hershey* was fired too long and most people would consider him unattractive. It was nobody's fault. The timer was malfunctioning. I never tried to sell *Hershey* because he takes a while to get to know and love. It's difficult to explain"

Her chief problem seems to be food.

"It's no fun when hungry husbands and kids start to pace back and forth through your work area. I would like to figure out a way to make t.v. dinners look like gourmet meals. Nobody complains on the airplane!," she says. "My family loves the bears — really. They have always encouraged me. There isn't anything they could actually do to help me with the bears (I'm too fussy). They simply aren't as willing as I am to skip a meal when I'm in the middle of a bear project, and, needless to say, they NEVER forget whether or not they've eaten."

It is times like this when Helen considers the good points of associating with bears. "I've met a lot of people," she says, "and on the average I like bears better! Bears are consistent and dependable. And they do not eat much."

She has definite opinions on bears.

"I don't like to see a lot of inferior bears, with no character, quality or workmanship. I think a bear needs to be/become a truly cherished possession. I'm fussy about bears, very fussy. They don't have to be beautiful, or new or even whole, but they have to have a certain 'something.' I found a very nice bear in a drugstore.

"A teddy bear has to be one that I love or that someone else has loved practically to pieces. I like the basic, average bear and I love to see a toddler dragging a teddy that's obviously had a lot of hugs and kisses and shared a popsicle or two. There's something a little sad about an old bear that's still in its original box. I keep wondering why and every reason I can think of is a sad one."

Helen believes that teddies are for kids, especially children-kids. But, because of their small size, delicacy and relative high price, Hull bears do not reach most small people. Those that do are cherished.

"After receiving one of my tiny bears, Kristie from Michigan made it blankets and a bed in a matchbox. Later, she saw a tiny brass bed, antique, which she wanted desperately. Her parents thought she could do without it. They thought she had forgotten it until she announced one day that she had saved enough money from gifts and was buying a gift for her bear — the brass bed. She was probably five or six years old then."

Such devotion is not uncommon in children or adults. Just ask anyone whose special friend is a secret pocket companion — or ask Helen Hull.

bears lest I encourage a bad habit. Stephanie calls her bear with the cigarette "Smokey" — no relation to Smokey, the Bear for obvious reasons!"

Mrs. Hull does not dress them, either, though, she does have ideas. "The bears are naked except for a bow," she says.

Working on such a small scale, sculpting one-of-a-kind bears is exacting. So is sewing tiny bears. Helen lists some of the negative sides of bear making.

"Cutting out fur fabric is not my favorite part. It gets all over and clogs the sewing machine. That means getting out the vacuum. Every bear maker knows that you can't do both — make bears and clean house. Bear makers need spouses who are patient.

"The ceramic bears cause your hands to dry and crack. Then, if your hands are not in good condition, you leave marks in the bears which show up even more after they are fired. There is no way to remove such a mark or a speck of dust or a hair once it's fired in.

"The absolute hardest part of the whole process is parting with a finished bear. I like all of them. I pack them almost as soon as I finish them; otherwise I'd keep more than I sell.

"Wiring a bear is also a bit nerve wracking. One twist too many and you can break an arm or leg or bump into an ear, ruining about three hours of work. I have a bear with a plaster cast and a tiny crutch...the result of an accident. The crutch is 3/4in (2.0cm) high!"

Sometimes accidents have more positive results. Helen's favorite bruin came about this way.

Janna Joseph. *Photograph courtesy of Janna Joseph.*

Janna Joseph looks at original bears through a doll maker's eyes, and what she sees is thought-provoking.

"Dolls often seem to reflect the appearance of the doll artist," she wrote, "easy to do as the face the artist sees most often is her own and it is reflected in the created doll faces.

"Bears can also resemble their maker — not so much in facial appearance (although there can be a likeness) — but in the type of bear selected and the feeling the bear conveys."

Janna's bears do not look like her; she is tall, slender and fair-haired. Her eyes are lively and intelligent. As with many bear artists, she entered the world of teddies by way of dolls, actually, through the influence of another doll artist.

"I have only made bears for the past few years," she wrote in 1983. "I was selling dolls in California and bought one of Sylvia Lyons' *Winnie* bears, which I thought about the cutest thing I'd seen and then decided to try to make some of my own."

Janna's bears, like Sylvia's, are miniatures, made of jointed porcelain parts. But they are as different as are their dolls, and — Janna is correct — each reflects its maker.

"I think my bears tend to reflect some qualities that I have tried to cultivate in myself," she writes, "a sense of independence and resourcefulness. They stand on their sturdy little back legs and determinedly look for the silver lining. I think that the dolls I've made are set in the same mold. I've generally selected personalities that portrayed these qualities in the movie roles they played. None of my bears or dolls are whimsical, wistful or innocent-appearing. Not to say that any characteristic is more desirable than another, but that the artist's bears reflect their personalities. I especially like my *Sam* bear, who is really me."

She proceeded to "read" my *Santa* bear, like tea leaves, and to relate the qualities she saw in him. I wonder if it would have worked if we had never met. I suspect it just might have. An artist can only impart to a work qualities and sympathies which he has within himself. To attempt otherwise usually courts failure and stillbirth. Although, I expect, sometimes, if

one is talented enough, it might work. But the finished product probably would not ring true.

Janna's bears are small in scale, as is all her work. "I have always most appreciated something lovely that I can hold in my hand," she says. They are meant to be play bears, even though made of porcelain.

"My Mitzi plays with them as I design them. If she doesn't like them to play with, I may drop them. I use her interest as a test of their appeal. I also use myself and figure that I am pretty much a barometer of what will appeal to the people who usually buy my work. If I really like it, they will, too."

Janna's designs come at once, or not at all. "I do not spend a great deal of time designing the bears or the dolls.

I work very quickly. I have observed that if I can't get the face I am trying to create in the first or second try, I am not going to get it and will best drop it and do something else. If I keep working it over, trying to improve it, I will ruin it 'fer sure.' "

She makes her bears like porcelain dolls, which is, of course, what they are. "I am people-oriented — my bears are people in bear costumes," she says. "I usually make a model and a mold, pour it, clean it up in ceramic so that it is as smooth as possible, fire it, remark the mold separation line as accurately as possible (can't do this in the water clay I use to model), make a second mold and unless I get air bubbles in a bad spot, this is my pattern mold. Later on I may see where I

Sam, 2in (5.1cm) tall, a studious young brown bear. *Sam* hopes some day to win the affection of the flirtatious *Theodora*. *Sam* sometimes wears specs and a sweater vest. Porcelain, jointed at limbs. *Photograph courtesy of Janna Joseph.*

can improve the pattern mold and do so, but I rarely change a face after I've first made it."

Recently, Janna has switched her emphasis from porcelain production to designing and mold-making, so that others can make her creations. Unlike many doll makers, she enjoys making molds and figures that others who may lack in design skills may derive pleasure from reproducing her ideas.

She is probably right. Janna's critters are full of whimsy and good humor. They range from a multi-jointed *Fred Abear,* the dancer (plans are underway for his partner, *Ginger),* through a cast of characters: *Rhett Beartler* and *Scarlett O'Beara, Mitzi* and *Moe,* the terrible twins, *Bearishnikov* and *Beverly Bearanova, Dr. Brownie* and *Nurse Bonnie* (who is madly in love with the doctor), and a whole family of bruins. Although some are bare, ("Many collectors have told me they prefer their bears nude," she reports) most of Janna's bears are dressed, either with fabric or with molded-on garments.

Some of her teds, like *Scarlett* and *Rhett,* were made in limited editions and sold quickly. "I don't know as they appealed to the bear crowd as much as they did to the GWTW collector group who will buy anything related to that movie," she says. Janna did a whole series of Gone With the Wind miniature porcelain dolls, and the word got around among fans of the movie. She remarks on this phenomenon.

Fred Abear, 2in (5.1cm) tall. Porcelain bisque; jointed at arms, legs, elbows and knees; molded-on tuxedo and bow tie. 1982. *Photograph courtesy of Janna Joseph.*

Scarlett O'Beara and *Rhett Beartler. Scarlett,* 1¾in (4.5cm) tall, is a yellow-brown bear; long green and white print gown; wide-brimmed, straw hat. *Rhett,* 2¼in (5.75cm) tall, is a handsome brown bear; molded-on collar, cravat and shoes; painted moustache; felt hat; gray felt vest. Both bears are porcelain bisque, jointed at limbs. *Photograph courtesy of Janna Joseph.*

Mitzi and Moe, 1¾in (4.5cm) tall. Porcelain bisque; jointed at limbs; molded sailor suits; molded-on bow on *Mitzi;* molded-on hat on *Moe;* white fabric skirt on *Mitzi.*

"It is interesting to me that we (doll artists and bear artists) acquire a following much like a hairstylist — a clientele that buys just about whatever we make. Now that I've started selling molds, I notice I am picking up a different following altogether and will be watching to see if they are a 'like' group — that is, like each other."

Like many doll and bear artists, Janna most appreciates the work of others in her field. "The bears I collect are primarily the artist bears. I like them as bears and as a link with the artist who made them," she says, again stressing the connection between the artist and his production.

"Many years ago," she continues, "when I was doing cloth dolls, I made a *Mona Lisa* and, contrary to my usual pattern, I did read up on Da Vinci and noted he wrote that the picture remained in his studio about four years after he had finished it, during which period he was constantly touching it. I feel that many artists impart something of their inner selves to their work (bears, dolls, paintings, etc.). Through the touch of their hands and by touching the work, it is possible to pick up a faint residual vibration."

Perhaps this is what makes the work of bear artists and doll artists so special. Maybe they contain just a little bit of the soul of their creators, in a way no manufactured bear can.

Janna Joseph's bears do not look much like her, but, maybe she is right. When I look in their eyes, I can see that same good humor, that same intelligence I have seen in hers. They are a reflection of the artist.

The Great Bearishnikov and *Beautiful Beverly Bearnova,* brown porcelain bears, 2in (5.1cm) and 2¼in (5.75cm) tall. Molded-on leotards and crowns; jointed at limbs; painted gold ballet slippers. They wear the blue and orchid outfits they wore for their starring roles in the Bear Ballet Theater's production of "Bear Lake." *Photograph courtesy of Janna Joseph.*

The Bear Family's Christmas. Six all-porcelain, jointed miniature bears by Janna Joseph celebrate Christmas, 1981. *Photograph courtesy of Janna Joseph.*

CAROLE BOWLING

Carole Bowling and *Tuffy*. *Photograph courtesy of Carole Bowling.*

Carole Bowling's bears are floppy, contemplative and quizzical. They seem to take the world with a grain of salt.

"All my bears look either astonished or worried about the state of the world," Carole says. "They are me."

The bears are an offshoot of her doll work. Carole is a doll artist, member of the National Institute of American Doll Artists (NIADA), and received her art training at Parsons School of Design.

She designs and makes uncommonly realistic portrait dolls of children. The dolls are so fine they stand on their own as sculpture, and at times they evoke strong responses from viewers.

"The dolls elicit an almost reverential response, which I am uncomfortable with," the artist remarked. This is one reason she has turned to bear making. It is a release, a chance to play and yet still be a designer. I love the simplicity of statement I can make, and the happiness it gives to those who buy them," she says.

The real impetus for bear making came from her good friend, Beulah Franklin, the person who had interested her in dolls. "She began to collect bears, just as my dolls became more serious art, and the bears satisfied the child in me which was not being expressed in the dolls. *Beulah Bear* is named after her."

Carole's dolls are portraits, painstakingly sculpted in clay from photographs blown up to the exact size of the doll's head she is working on. Her bears derive from photographs, also, ones obtained from National Geographic. From these she did bear drawings and then "found the logical seamlines

for constructing bears from the drawings. Then it was trial and error to get the proportions correct. I work intuitively," she says.

The bears that resulted are crossbreeds, realism and abstraction. Because they are floppy and almost unstructured, they can assume languid, inquisitive, comfortable positions that are almost lifelike. They almost beg to be cuddled. Their eyes are perky, intelligent and innocent.

"I think they look more innocent because the need for innocence in the world is far greater," Carole explains. "But the bears' designs are a result of sophisticated design and advertising."

They range in size from 8in (20.3cm) to 25in (63.5cm). The collection includes: *Beulah Bear, GRRUF McDuff, Tillie* and her cub and *Tuffy.* The largest, *GRRUF McDuff,* sports a leather nose and leather foot pads. He seems irresistible to kids.

"My large bears always receive the ultimate response from small children," Carole says. "They immediately roll on them. If they don't, I either have a repressed bear or a repressed child!"

She is insistent on quality. The fur she uses is from Germany and very expensive. Her philosophy of bear making is: "Quality, craftsmanship, the best materials, thoughtful design, humor. I don't skimp!...Bears will come and go, but quality will always sell. I don't worry. Those that want and buy junk eventually throw it out and it is erased from the culture. The quality design remains and is absorbed into the society, and eventually filters down to be accessible to all!"

Bowling bear production is limited. "I have to share the time with dolls." she explained. Another reason for the limit on her editions is artistic impatience common in many creative persons. Once an idea is realized, she wants to go on to other challenges. "I hate tediousness of too much repetition, in either dolls or bears."

For this reason, not many Bowling bears are around and the question of future editions is uncertain. When asked what she will do in the future, Carole replied: "I'm not sure; I may have made the only statement I want to do with my bear family."

Carole's human family has mixed reactions about her bear work. "Tom, my husband, thinks I'm daft half the time," she says. "But Matthew, age 9, has to have one of each and loves it."

Her bears are marked © date

    Carole Bowling   or   + bear number
    CAROLEKINER.

Some early bears have only her name on them. They are sold primarily by word-of-mouth and she describes her audience as "anyone who appreciates quality of design and craftsmanship."

Above all, she says, "I love the happiness (the bears) give to those who buy them."

They help their owners take the world with a bear-sized grain of salt.

ABOVE: A family portrait of Bowling Bears, circa 1983. Left to right: *Ozzie, GRRUF McDuff, Tillie* and *Cub, Tuffy. Photograph courtesy Carole Bowling.*

LEFT: *GRRUF McDuff,* 25in (63.5cm) tall. Non-jointed bear made of German plush; leather nose and foot pads. This bear is also available as *Beulah Bear* in a lighter color. 1982. *Photograph courtesy of Carole Bowling.*

MIRIAM HUGHES

Miriam Hughes and bears, June 1983. *Louise* is at right.

The *"Family Portrait"* that started it all. Watercolor by Miriam Hughes. *Photograph courtesy Miriam Hughes.*

Miriam Hughes is a former medical illustrator who found out that drawing teddy bears was more fun than drawing medical specimens. She once worked for a firm that frowned on its employees bringing their bears to work. She dressed for success, took her art painfully seriously and was not particularly happy. Now she runs a mail order teddy bear portrait service and life is more low-key.

She got into her work informally, almost secretively, because, at the time, she was not sure how teddy bear art would be received by the "formal" art world. All she knew was that drawing bears made her happy.

She describes the way it all began.

"I have been drawing bears for years as a way to relax, but after one public showing of a portrait I did of *Ted*" (her bear — more about him later) "and *Raggedy,* in a watercolor class, where my instructor had a fit, I did not share that aspect of my work with people for a few years.

"About four years ago my husband framed a 'family portrait' I did for him (of bears) and when friends saw that, they all wanted either that one or one of their 'family.' So I started drawing peoples' bears for them and giving them away as presents. I never considered those drawings to be serious art and never seemed to suffer the same anxiety that I would suffer when doing my 'real' art or medical art. I did notice that the more teddy bear art that I did, however, the more relaxed I was about my other art. I also realized that I had fun — simple, giggle as you draw fun when doing my teddy bear drawings."

Ted, mentioned above, is a bear Miriam bought in Marshall Field & Co. when she was 20. She had been looking for a Mother's Day present, and bought him for herself. "My mother liked him so much I went back and adopted another *Ted* for her. We were not into creative names." He was a wise purchase. For *Ted* has changed Miriam's life.

It happened this way.

"For several years *Ted, Raggedy Ann* and I lived a peaceful life and then Joe came along. He was very quiet and when he used to come over to visit, I would have *Ted* ask him questions about life or how his research was going. Joe felt very awkward talking with a bear at first, but then all of a sudden he would come over and sit and talk to *Ted* only and I would be left out. *Ted* was looking for a father, but I was beginning to get jealous, so I adopted a friend for *Ted.* And then Joe adopted another bear for his place and before we knew it we were married with at least 40 creatures."

Ted was not Miriam's first bear. "My first bear was a blue corduroy bear with a sailor suit. My mother said she bought him from Marshall Field & Co. and she thought the bear was from England. I was about six months at the time, but I had him until I was about 14. His name was *Bear* (how original I was at six months). He was skinny with long legs and arms that ended with white fuzzy paws. His face was also white fur and he spent most of his life undergoing surgery on his limbs — they pulled off easily."

Bear, lost in a move, was replaced by *Ted.* And nothing has been the same.

Now Miriam finds her days full of bears. She works in

watercolor, primarily, using pale washes over pencil draw-ings. Some work is in pen-and-ink, and she has had prints made of some of these drawings. All the watercolors, though, are one-of-a-kind. Sometimes she plays with off-beat techniques like using eye shadow for shading. This has its drawbacks, though. "The shades are very subtle, but since I started using it myself on my eyes, I have become cost conscious," she says. "My style has not changed that much since I began, but like all artists, I am constantly experi-menting and trying to learn new things. My bears, however, really like the way I draw them and get exceedingly obstinate if I try to change too much. Every once in awhile I have to kick everyone out of the studio just so I can work my own way."

She finds some bears to be picky and temperamental. Others just will not sit still and be good models, especially visiting bears.

"The most difficult thing about illustrating bears," she says, "is anticipating their moods and complying to them. I find that I must have a stash of goodies to bribe some of them to sit still, or worse, to get them to be quiet and let me draw my way. I find that one must be very diplomatic and patient and also willing to take a lot of tea breaks (my weight is a constant problem because of this). But not all bears are so difficult and absolutely all of them love the finished piece (bears have huge egos) so I feel sufficiently rewarded."

Most of her bear portraits are in 5in (12.7cm) by 7in (17.8cm) format, and are matted, to a final size of 8in by 10in (20.3cm by 25.4cm). She is ecumenical in her approach to models. All bears are welcome. "I draw all types of bears. Bears, I have found, are very sensitive and can be easily hurt, so I try not to have favorites. Except with Louise, who thinks she is the best and my favorite, so I humor her a bit too much. I do particularly enjoy drawing bears who show obvious signs of love. New, fresh bears are actually more difficult to draw — like new babies. Their character has not developed yet. PLEASE do not tell Louise, but I love jointed bears and she does not have joints. Actually, I love all bears — even some of the more tacky commerical ones, (I figured someone has to love them). All bears have the power and potential to be good friends and make someone happy, so I try not to prejudge them."

Louise is one of the more important Hughes bears. She and Miriam have been collaborating on a book, which Miriam is illustrating. Miriam feels she has been greatly influenced by her collaborator.

"In spite of the fact that Ted has been with me for almost 12 years," she wrote in 1983, "and in spite of the drawing that I have always been doing, and my other bears (et al), I wonder if I would have pursued the direction I am if I had never met and adopted Louise.

"I literally ran into her one day. I was running my usual (at the time) eight mile circuit, but it was not going well. I was dehydrated and crabby. Someone had cut me off in an intersection where I clearly had the right of way. I was furious and pounded and kicked this fellow's car as he barely slid by my body; to no avail. He kept on going with a sneer on his grimy face.

"Well, I had two miles to go and I knew I was not going to

Louise jogging. Print of a drawing by Miriam, 8in by 10in (20.3cm by 25.4cm). 1983. *Photograph courtesy Miriam Hughes.*

Louise and a friend. Print of a drawing by Miriam, 8in by 10in (20.3cm by 25.4cm). 1983. *Photograph courtesy Miriam Hughes.*

"Tea Party." Print of a drawing by Miriam, 8in by 10in (20.3cm by 25.4cm). *Louise* and her friends are pictured. 1983. *Photograph courtesy Miriam Hughes.*

make it. So I called Joe and asked him to come and get me. While waiting, I wandered into a small and very cluttered craft store. Everything was so crammed in that you really could not see anything. But then this caramel-colored face in a dark chocolate body caught my eye.

"There *Louise* sat with a consort of dainty dolls and she looked as disgruntled as I felt. I picked her up and said 'Hello.' She just frowned at me. I thought that Joe would probably not like living with two grouches and put her down.

"I heard a little 'hurumph,' but walked out of the store. By the time Joe arrived, however, I knew I could not desert that crabby little bear.

"Life seemed to change after we adopted *Louise*. She is/was very much like myself, which sometimes is not a very flattering thing to see, so we have both grown — or else accepted ourselves more. More than any of my other bears, *Louise* has been a great inspiration. She tends to dictate orders a bit. *Louise* used to come to work with me quite often (before the portrait service) and she would say, 'All this is fine and dandy, but don't you think we would have more fun working together?' So here I am, her editor and she my business manager.

"*Louise* helps to keep visiting bears in line. It is sometimes difficult to get any work done while bears are posing for portraits. Unlike *Louise,* they are not well-versed in etiquette.

"One of the reasons I work from photographs with my mail order business," Miriam says, "is because if a bear comes to visit and get his portrait done, it could take months. My bears have welcome parties, happy you are here parties

and good-bye parties. I am supposed to work in between all these parties. Also we grow very attached to visiting bears and have a hard time parting. So it is best not to take a chance with us."

Miriam's bear portrait service is growing. She finds clients through word-of-mouth and advertisements in teddy bear publications. *Louise* modeled for the ad. Sometimes she trades portraits for services. She and Louise are flexible.

What is Miriam's audience? "I try to appeal to any bear lover who wants to immortalize their bear. It is an unfortunate fact that it is actually us humans who could use immortalizing, but we have more money than bears, so humans are my intended audience. And all the responses I have received so far indicate that I am dealing with alleged adults like myself."

Bear illustrating has revolutionized Miriam's outlook on art and on life. "My philosophy about life and my art is that you should enjoy it. Be grateful for having a talent that others can enjoy. Bears are to me like vitamins. Hugs are important. Accepting things easily is important and I like to draw bears in hopes that others will learn to relax and enjoy life. I am not sure what the connection is between my drawings and people relaxing, but the people who have bears seem to have a humorous point of view about life. They don't take themselves too seriously — or do they? There is too much to get out of life to waste it and bears always seem to remind me of that. So it only makes sense that if you can't bring your bear to the office, you can bring its portrait and keep your perspective." Miriam no longer worries if painting teddy bears is serious art. If she has doubts, she will just ask *Louise.*

JOYCE STAFFORD

Joyce Stafford with *Old Ted* and *Sniffy*. 1983. *Photograph courtesy of Joyce Stafford.*

Sniffy and *Old Ted*. *Sniffy* is 23in (58.4cm) tall. He arrived Christmas 1982. Light tan plush; fully-jointed. *Old Ted* is 24in (61cm). Made from old coat; white wool plush; fully-jointed. *Photograph courtesy of Joyce Stafford.*

I met *Ted* in Washington, D.C. He had just returned from the National Zoo where he had met the zookeeper, who had made him Honorary Zookeeper. He had the button to prove it. (The following year, he did the same in St. Louis, Missouri, I understand.) *Ted* seems to like zookeepers, as long as they do not lock him up.

He often, as that day in Washington, wears a handmade vest on which he displays the many buttons and medals he has garnered on his travels.

Ted is not so young anymore. In 1984, he was 54 years old. He spent the first 49 of them as a coat.

Joyce Stafford liberated him in 1979. He immediately became fast friends with her husband, John. John usually includes *Ted* in his travels. He could not bear to leave him home.

Joyce is a doll artist. Member of NIADA, the National Institute of American Doll Artists, she specializes in exquisite original porcelain dolls. Occasionally, she designs a bear. When she does, it is a real flight of fantasy.

Joyce's bears are of two sorts; the "art bears," for the collector and the "personal bears" for the family. *Ted* is a personal bear. He certainly has personality and he seems to have personal magnetism, especially with the ladies.

"*Old Ted* has been to all U.F.D.C. (United Federation of Doll Clubs) conventions and has been photographed with most U.F.D.C. presidents. He has a girlfriend who lives in Calumet City (*Sweet Bearina*). She gave him a button that says, 'I love Ted.' People send him gifts and buttons in the mail. You can see how special he is." Zookeepers like him, too.

Joyce made him from "an old child's coat, circa 1930." His fur is white wool plush; his eyes are brown. An original design, 24in (61cm) tall, he is fully-jointed, the first bear Joyce made for John.

John Stafford has a collection of antique bears, about 200 or so. Every year since *Ted* came around, his wife has made a new bear for Christmas. Usually John gets it; sometimes it goes to son, Gus. They seem to be rapidly assimilated into the family.

Sniffy arrived on Christmas, 1982. 23in (58.4cm) tall, fully-jointed, with brown eyes, he is made of light tan plush. An upturned proboscis gives him a slightly snooty, removed air; actually, he is just preoccupied with making scents of his environment. *Sniffy* likes reading about other bears who enjoy his predilections. One day, after reading a story in *National Geographic* about mirgrating polar bears who stopped off at a pig farm in their path, he spent the day sniffing for pigs. John captured him on film "in the act."

Theodora arrived on Christmas, 1981. 13in (33cm) high. She was made from a light yellow "real fur" lamb coat. Her paw and foot pads are leather. She belongs to John, too. Or maybe she belongs to *Old Ted*.

Then, there is *Elvis*. He preceded *Old Ted,* but does not live with the immediate clan. Made in 1979, *Elvis* came to life on the day Elvis Presley died. Jo's sister Nancy lives with him.

The NIADA artist holds a Bachelor of Arts degree in art and a Master's degree in education. A former teacher, she concentrates on original dolls made of porcelain bisque. When she makes bears for sale, and she does not make many, she does not even try to sell them; they are "bears that tell a story," as she terms them.

Jo's "art bears" have an entirely different reason for being from the family bears. Their appearance and audience reflects this.

Her four "art bears," to date, include *Super Bear* and *The Three Bears* (and *Jenny*) — no Goldilocks, thank you. That is another story. *Papa* stands 15½in (39.4cm) high, *Mama* 14½in (36.9cm) and *Baby* 11in (27.9cm). With fully-jointed brown plush bodies and porcelain faces, all are variations on the same theme, more "bear" than "ted." *Super Bear* bears the same face as *Papa Bear.* He stands 16in (40.6cm) tall, is constructed similarly to *The Three Bears,* but is a bear with "something extra," electric eyes. They are ear-controlled: push an ear forward, the eyes go on — back, they go off. He wears a *Super Bear* cape which helps him fly — maybe.

Joyce does not much care for clothes on bears. "I don't like to see them all gussied up," she says. "We prefer the plain old bears! They had personality without clothes. But *Old Ted* has a fantastic wardrobe."

Some of this wardrobe Joyce captures on paper, like the eagle-crowned hat he wore to cheer the Philadelphia Eagles on to victory. She designs writing paper and paper dolls, using *Ted,* his adventures and wardrobes as models. Often, the Stafford Christmas card, as well, will feature *Ted.* Christmas in the Stafford house seems to revolve around the bears.

The rest of the year they are hardly forgotten. *Ted* accompanies John on many of his travels; the highpoints of each trip are immortalized on film. His button-jacket (or is it a vest?) has become crowded with souvenirs.

The high point of the year for the bear may be the annual U.F.D.C. Convention. When I saw him at the convention in Washington, D.C., fresh from visiting the National Zoo, he was looking forward to the banquet. Never one to travel second-class (except, perhaps on airplanes), he was contemplating the menu and thinking of the ladies he would share the evening with. If they were really nice, maybe he would show them his zookeeper's badge.

He was certain to be comfortable. John had bought him a banquet ticket.

Old Ted seated at desk. He wears his "button vest." *Photograph courtesy of Joyce Stafford.*

Theodora, 13in (33cm). Made for Christmas 1981 out of lamb coat; real fur; leather feet pads and paws. Only one — John's. *Photograph courtesy of Joyce Stafford.*

Super Bear, 16in (40.6cm). One-of-a-kind. Electric eyes. Push ear forward, eyes go on — back, they go off. Porcelain masque face; balance of body brown plush; jointed. *Photograph courtesy of Joyce Stafford.*

ABOVE: *Elvis,* 28in (71.1cm). One-of-a-kind. First bear made by Joyce Stafford. Dark brown plush. *Photograph courtesy of Joyce Stafford.*

The Three Bears, © 1981. Porcelain faces; brown plush bodies. *Papa:* 15½in (39.4cm), *Mama:* 14½in (36.9cm). *Baby:* 11in (27.9cm). Edition of five. *Photograph courtesy of Joyce Stafford.*

Old Ted wearing Philadelphia Eagle hat he wore to root the team on to the Super Bowl. *Photograph courtesy of Joyce Stafford.*

JIM D. CLARK

J. D. Clark, with *Bung Bear* and new bear head. *Photograph by Marla Shelton Murphy, courtesy of Jim D. Clark.*

J. D. Clark is probably not a typical bear lover; his hand-carved bears certainly are not. His first love is the cowboy life. Art comes second — Western art.

But ranching and art do not always pay the bills. So he has tried his hand at construction, janitorial work and caretaking, fitting art around a busy schedule.

The Napa Valley in California where he lives is famous for its wineries. Perhaps someday it will be famous for its wine-derived bears. J. D. Clark's bears are hand-carved from "bungs," the redwood plugs used in wine barrels. They are shaped like big corks and seal the casks for aging.

Eventually, the bungs become saturated with wine stains and are sometimes riddled with worm holes, and are discarded. However, they have a special beauty for the wood carver, who delights in just these imperfections because they make each piece one-of-a-kind.

Jim's brother works at Modair Winery in the Napa Valley, and collects the discards, which slowly turn into hand-carved bears.

The bears began around 1979, when J.D.'s wife, Grace, asked him to carve her a special teddy bear. Grace is really "the teddy bear lover of the two of us." She says, "My favorite bear is a blue velour one I made from a pattern soon after we were married. He is a special friend and has been repaired many times as nieces and nephews have played with him. Most of my bears are factory bears and I have a good Steiff.

"They mostly sit on an antique high chair. The kids all know where they are and are allowed to play with most of them, but some sit up high (out of reach). My bears wear J. D.'s baby shoes."

When she asked her husband to carve a teddy, it was a departure from his production, which was small carved figures. These sold to the local shops and to friends, and were popular, partly because they were made of the area's winery bungs. Although an odd request, the teddy was so

attractive that, during a "low financial spot," the couple decided to find a good shop for him.

And they did — the Toy Cellar. When the owner, Marla Murphy, bought teddy outright and encouraged the artist in his work, a special relationship developed between the two, which has given birth to a whole sleuth of bears.

Bung Bears, as they are called, are usually 6in to 9in (15.2cm to 22.9cm) high, the height determined by the size of the bung and the intentions of the carver. Each is hand-hewn, and the positions and actions of the bears vary. Occasionally, Mr. Clark will sketch his ideas and follow them, but usually he creates as he goes, feeling his way as he works with the individual variations of the redwood piece.

Although some are carved in one piece, most often *Bung Bear* is made from six bungs. Head, body and legs are carved separately. He looks like a jointed bear, but, at this writing, is not. J. D. is thinking about it, though.

He marks each one on the bottom with a number and signature as follows:

The Bung Bears © By Clark Napa Calif.

There is a masculine energy, a vitality to these bears that is reflected in their positions and expressions. Some seem worried, eager, contemplative. One bear, who holds a fish, grins and the viewer can almost see him think about how dinner will taste.

The bears are realistic because the artist admires real bears. Grace Clark explains. "J. D. feels bears are special creatures created by God for our enjoyment and they enrich our lives. Teddies are special friends created by people for much the same reason. They are a plus."

So far, the bears have been bare, sometimes sporting red bows, but J. D. is considering making personality bears. He tries to give each teddy its own "look." And he plans limited edition bears in numbered series.

They take about eight hours each to carve and J. D. fits this time around a demanding six-day work schedule. He feels strongly about his work, the care and craftsmanship that go into each bear.

Grace Clark says, "There is no way J. D.'s hand-carved bears can be mass-produced. You can use some power equipment, but only in the rough stage and then with an artistic eye. There are no plans or patterns. Each is an original.

"It has been a major source of discouragement to J. D. the way people don't understand the quality of his work. Marla Murphy has been a great source of encouragement. Most in our families don't really understand, because counted 'by the hour,' he makes very little. Only another artist can really understand."

Marla Murphy, a photographer, does. She calls his bears "fantastic," and refers to him as "a wonderful young man —super shy, so it's hard to get him to pose."

The Clarks are upbeat about the future for teddies and for their art. "Teddies represent love, security, good memories and friendship. Today more than ever people need these qualities. Different bears represent different things to people. Some want a stuffed one to hug, a jointed one to play.

"And ours are still different. They reflect the love given and bring a smile. We hope to make a livng someday in art, and bears will always be a part of that work, and also our home life."

The differentness of *Bung Bears* is the key to their charm. They somehow seem to marry J. D. Clark's two loves: the cowboy life and Western art. They speak out as a fresh voice in the teddy bear world.

Pooh-type *Bung Bear*. Made from redwood bungs. 1983. *Photograph by Marla Shelton Murphy, courtesy of Jim D. Clark.*

Bung Bear made from redwood bungs. 1983. *Photograph by Marla Shelton Murphy, courtesy of Jim D. Clark.*

Tasting Bears by J. D. Clark. 1983. *Courtesy of Jim D. Clark.*

Bung Bear With Fish. One-piece bear. 1983. *Photograph by Marla Shelton Murphy, courtesy of Jim D. Clark.*

BARBARA ISENBERG
(North American Bear Company, Inc.)

He sat motionless near the window, blue eyes peering under the brim of a brown fedora. The December light played on his classic trench coat, revealing a wine-colored ascot. Others were gaudier, more colorful, more beautiful. But when I held him in my arms, I knew *Humphrey Beargart* was the bear for me.

They evoke strong emotions, the audacious technicolor bears manufactured by North American Bear Company, Inc. *Humphrey* and his friends were designed by New Yorker, Barbara Isenberg. In fours years, they have changed the way Americans look at bears.

Barbara's sophisticated designs combine unexpected colors (blue, green, mauve, pink, lavender, red) and fabrics (velour, satin, velvet) with punning monikers (*Chef Bearnaise, Scarlett O'Beara, Green Bearet*).

"I felt that if the bears had humor and were attractive —were on their level — they would be acceptable to adults.

Barbara Isenberg and some of her designs. She holds *Albert,* who started it all. *Photograph by Gary Degnan, courtesy of North American Bear Company. Inc.*

When you give a bear to an adult, it's a compliment. It's saying, 'I recognize your sense of humor and the child in you. I recognize that you're like a big bear.' People are flattered that you feel you can give them a bear. It's nostalgic. It brings back childhood feelings."

It was children's feelings and reactions that guided Mrs. Isenberg's initial inspirations. In 1978, attracted by children's bear literature, which she describes as "strong and appealing," she designed a bear for her young son. It was he who had introduced her to bears. "I didn't have any when I was little. I just didn't know about them. And then when my son was born, I wanted to make him a big, soft, machinewashable bear." Her concept was original: the bear's body was actually a stretchy, bright green jogging suit, complete with removable hood. Its feet were white sneakers with laces. Its head and paws were made of the same jersey as the body. The bear was 20in (50.8cm) tall, so it could be cradled like a baby and wear infant-sized clothes.

But her son's friends did not like the green head and paws. "A bear needs to be furry. It doesn't look like a bear," they said. So she redid him with brown head and hands. The children liked him, but it was the adults who asked to buy

Running Bear for themselves. There were many more requests than she could accommodate, even with the help of the seamstresses who aided her in making the sample bears. This is how Barbara discovered that there was an untapped market — the adult bear buyer.

She decided to fill the vacuum. Armed with sample bears, she descended on the New York Toy Fair and showed them to a sales representative, who said he would carry them. All she had to do was fill the orders.

Mrs. Isenberg does not sew and she does not draw, but she has a good sense of three-dimensional design and a lot of classy good taste, which she credits to the year and a half she lived in France. So she put her concepts and confidence to work, got on the telephone, and prepared to fill her orders. She hired sample makers and set up shop in a "bombed out" New York factory that made carnival toys. She had the seamstresses redo bear heads until they finally resembled

her ideas. The face took a full year to develop.

Barbara's education was in English. She once wrote a column on hardware for the *New York Times*. And, although she enjoys inventing things, nowhere in her background was there pattern making or manufacturing knowhow. And no one in the fiercely protective, suspicious and competitive toy industry was open with information. So her crew of bear makers learned by doing.

They learned about toy industry and government codes, about bar tackers and grommet machines, about hand stuffing and machine stuffing and about how difficult plush is to cut.

A 20in (50.8cm) *Running Bear* was produced in four colors (red, yellow, blue and the original green) that first year. His body was made of stretchy sweat shirt fabric and looked like a jogging suit, with a pocket in front (one paw hole on either side) and a removable hood that fitted over a brown plush head.

Although she filled her orders and her bears were making a name for themselves that first year, Barbara's company made no profit. The carnival toy factory had neither the specialized machinery necessary for many of her processes, nor the resources for making necessary credit checks. They were stuck with a lot of bad debts.

It was then that her brother, who had a successful business, came into the picture. He became her partner and helped to guide and encourage her. "At this point," she recalls, "I would have sold the rights to my ideas on a royalty basis," had he not come along.

With his credit available, The North American Bear Company, Inc. began producing *Running Bear* and four of Barbara's other ideas: the first of the VIB's (Very Important Bears). They were *Chef Bearnaise, Douglass Bearbanks, Scarlett O'Beara* and *Sarah Bearnheart*. She began specializing. The clothing ws made in a Massachussetts doll clothes factory, which offered helpful suggestions on design simplifications. Parts of the bears were cut out in New York and sewn in Haiti, then were sent back to New York to be machine stuffed.

The first VIB's appeared in 1979. They were a daring concept: armful-sized bears in bright colors, of a soft veloury fabric. Lavishly dressed to visually carry out their punning names, they were aimed at adults. So different were they that some traditional teddy bear dealers were hesitant to stock them. One prominent bear merchant now laughs when he is reminded that he said, "Bears in colors? I don't know, Barbara, I don't think they'll go."

But they did. The den grew. However, the North American Bear Company, Inc. was still not making any money. So they decided to shift production to the Far East —at least in part. Negotiating and quality control at long distance posed problems, but costs dropped, and new avenues for design possibilities opened up.

Oriental fabrics and plushes, Barbara discovered, were superior to American products and less expensive, especially when they were sewn over there. Workers were eager to please and very flexible. They were also willing to hand-stuff bears, something American toy workers will not do, but which is a necessary process for the production of jointed bears. It also results in specially soft and huggable bears.

Designing long-distance was frustrating. Things went wrong. Bears were not stitched correctly. Designing long-distance was frustrating. Designs traveled back and forth in the mail for a year before they came out right. Barbara's brother convinced her that, if she wanted her company to be anything more than a hobby, she had to go to the Orient to have hands-on design experience.

"Here's Lookin at You, Kid." *Lauren Bearcall* and *Humphrey Beargart*, both 20in (50.8cm) tall. *Lauren Bearcall* has Chinese red velour body; mink-like coat and veil. *Humphrey Beargart*, beige velour; fedora; trench coat; corduroy pants; ascot. 1983. *Photograph courtesy of North American Bear Company, Inc.*

Bear Mitzvah. Designed by Barbara Isenberg. Deep blue bear. Tallis, vest, yarmulke. Carries gift pen; undressable. *Photograph courtesy of North American Bear Company, Inc.*

Bearman of the Board, 20in (50.8cm) tall. Designed by Barbara Isenberg. Unjointed cinnamon-colored plush bear. Pinstripe pants; striped suspenders; white shirt; bow tie. 1983. *Photograph courtesy of North American Bear Company, Inc.*

Vanderbear Family. Designed by Barbara Isenberg. Classic jointed teddy bear family. Made of light gold plush with felt foot pads. Left to right: *Cornelius Vanderbear, Alice Vanderbear,* (dressed, then bare), *Fluffy* and *Fuzzy.* All wear black velvet clothing. 1982. *Photograph courtesy of North American Bear Company, Inc.*

the Orient to have hands-on design experience.

A friend of his who speaks Korean scouted 40 factories for them in Korea and selected two with potential. In 1982, Barbara traveled to Korea. In two weeks, working day and night in the factories, she accomplished a year's worth of designing.

She would think of a concept and work with the factory on the spot until her ideas matched theirs. This is how her *Message Bearers,* new in 1983, came to be. "They would put six bear heads on sticks and I could say, 'I like this look, and this nose, and something about this one is just a bit off,' and we'd come out, in a surprisingly short time, with a realization of my ideas."

In Korea, she found that, if she wanted, she could have a fabric designed to her specific needs, that tiny bear sweaters could be rapidly produced to her specifications, that people were eager to please. She returned home with sample fabrics and bottomless possibilities.

Along with *Odl Bauer,* who helps design the bears' garments and patterns, she plans a logical extension, from designing bear clothes to designing children's clothes (to match).

The North American Bear Company, Inc. now numbers six. Each person has his own area of expertise, risk and responsibility. Its main offices are in Chicago, Illinois, but Barbara still works from her Greenwich Village location. She credits her success to her being in New York. "Here you see every new idea two years before it hits the market. You have access to the garment center, to raw materials for precise things. The cotton council, the lace council, plush manufacturers are here. I found a hat factory that would make 2000 tiny hats to my specifications. The right velvet for *Shakesbear's* pants, the precise flower for *Sarah Bearnheart* — everything's right at hand. Now that I know the business, I could work from anywhere. But I never could have done it initially from anywhere but New York."

She works 12 hours a day, every day at her business, and does extensive research into the background of each bear she produces. The bear's personality must mesh with the historical personage he repbearsents. Should *Bearthoven* wear a wig? What kind of dress should Queen Elizabear wear? How about *Cornelius Vandebear* — what would a prosperous Victorian bear wear? And what kind of trench coat should *Humphrey Beargart* have?

As new bears are added (four new VIB's each year), some are dropped, so that only 12 different styles are available each year. "It's easier for shopkeepers that way. And it makes them more collectible."

Barbara bought the rights to produce *Aloysius,* the *Brideshead Revisited* bears from the Waugh estate. A nostalgic, shaggy bear, he departs sharply from the VIB's.

Other designs, such as the *Vandebears,* an "old fashioned" teddy family of four, the 6in (15.2cm) tall message bearers (who carry sayings such as "Happy Bearthday" and "This Bears my Love to You," and appropriate props in their clip-on hands), and the *Baby Grizzlies,* were new for 1983, the result of Barbara's Korean trip.

Where does this leave *Running Bear?* He is bearing up very well. He now has a first name, *Albert.* He is the protagonist of a juvenile picture book, *"Adventures of Albert, the Running Bear,"* published on Good Bear Day (October 27th, Theodore Roosevelt's birthday) by Houghton, Mifflin, a collaboration of Barbara Isenberg and Susan Wold. Illustrated by the well-known aritst, Dick Gackenbach, it tells of *Albert's* adventures in a marathon and of how he acquired his running suit. To match the book, in which he originally appears naked (bare), he now sports a removable jogging suit (and sewn-on sneakers). A 12in (30.5cm) tall model, with sewn-on suit and a 4½ft (1.37m) tall model with removable suit are also available. *Albert* is still North American Bear Company, Inc.'s best seller.

But my heart belongs to *Humphrey Beargart.*

KAREN WALTER

Karen Walter's childhood bear was called *Teds*. He arrived on Christmas 1944, when she was two.

"I've had that bear all my life," she confesses. "I have loved bears all my life. When I got married I thought it was time to put my bear away (22 years ago who liked bears?). So I removed the stuffing from him amd put him in a suitcase so he would not take up very much room. Of course, he's been restuffed since and is still my favorite bear. He's a non-jointed dark brown (one) about 12in (30.5cm) high. He's no doubt one reason I became involved in bear making."

The Oregon bear maker began in 1974, to experiment with teddy bear designs years before bears became "big." A mixture of nostalgia for teds and the discovery of an elderly bear got her started.

"When I saw a small antique bear in a shop in 1974, I fell in love with him. He was so old, but the beauty and personality were still there. I thought, 'what a shame one can no longer buy bears like this!.' I became determined to make one as near like him as possible.

"After some research, I learned that only bears made before 1907 had humps. I knew the only way I was ever going to have another bear like this one was to make one and so I did. He had to be jointed, I had to figure out how to do it....

"My first attempts were terrible, but I was so determined I kept trying. It took several years to really accomplish what I had in my head, but wouldn't come out."

She felt alone; few bear makers dotted the landscape and fewer still were sources of information. "At that time I knew of no one who made handmade bears. The craze had not caught on. Even though my first bears were funny little things, I sold them all. I had to. The house was filling up with "attempts." I joined them with nuts and bolts and made them from old coats from thrift stores."

Karen Walter with her original bears. 1983. *Photograph courtesy of Karen Walter.*

"The first step, after cutting, is sewing the bears together, I stack the pieces and sew all legs first, then arms, then bodies and heads, etc." *Photograph courtesy of Karen Walter.*

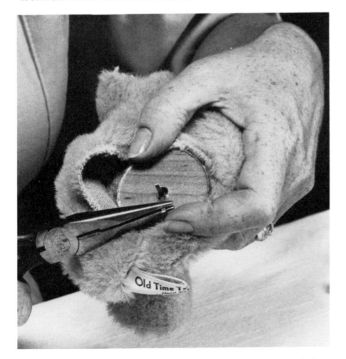

"After the head is complete, arms and legs are joined on the body. A disc is placed over the pin and bent down." *Photograph courtesy of Karen Walter.*

"The head is the first part to start with after sewing. Head is stuffed after eyes are put on, ears sewn on and then the mouth. Lastly, the discs and pin are put in place. It's ready to be put on the bear." *Photograph courtesy of Karen Walter.*

"Now for stuffing the bear. I use a stick to make it easier." *Photograph courtesy of Karen Walter.*

She calls her teds *Old Time Teddy Bears* and has succeeded in recreating, using her own original designs, the nostalgic look of "antique" bears. "All my patterns are my own, developed over the years, with trial and error, with many changes. They are all copyrighted." The range in size from 4in (10.2cm) to 3ft (91.4cm). In all, she has designed a dozen different bears. The 10in (25.4cm) bear is by far the most popular. But this term is relative, since Karen's bears have been wildly successful, so much so that she has had to acquire helpers to produce them. In her first nine years in business, her output topped 5000 bears. In 1983 she made 1300.

A combination of appealing design, high quality and attractive prices tells the story.

The bears are made in both plush and (the more popular) mohair, with shoe button eyes or English glass eyes. Paws are felt or leather, noses and mouths are embroidered. They are jointed with wooden joints made by Karen's husband (no more nuts and bolts).

Most *Old Time Teddy Bears* are recreations of old bears because this has become Mrs. Walter's specialty, and most are bare. But occasionally she designs an unusual limited edition, like the *Uncle Sam* bear, or the *Skier,* which proved to be the most popular of all. However, she had to discontinue the latter when the source of miniature skis dried up. Sometimes Karen will do special orders.

"I made a silver satin bear for a circus performer." Karen stated. "He (the bear) has some regular part in his act. I have also had people request that I make a certain bear for them that I've had to make a pattern for. Many times it is a bear they had as a child and want duplicated. This is always a welcome challenge. The circus bear was one of those."

The 10in (25.4cm) ted most often is garbed — somtimes with ice skates or roller skates, dresses or coveralls. "I've made about 700 of them," Karen reports. "Also clown collars and hats for the 18in (45.7cm) size bear."

Because of her enormous output, Karen does a bundle of bears at a time. "I cut about 25 to 30 bears at a time, then sew all legs, all arms, etc. So I'm working on all of them at once," she says.

In all these years, the Oregonian has not tired of her task. "If I were to start making bears all over again, I can't say I'd do anything differently. Everything has worked out beautifully. Seems I was meant to make bears. It has given me more satisfaction than anything I've done in my life. My family is very proud of my bears and my husband loves them all. He says 'There are no ugly bears.'

"I hate to say this, but I sometimes talk to the heads before they're joined on the bodies. They seem so alive. Some look pleasant, some sad, others happy and some downright mean. I enjoy making all the bears. I love them all."

Old Time Teddy Bears bear sewn-in labels reading:

Old Time Teddy Bears
Hand made by Karen Walter
Copyright 1981.

They come with circular tags with the same copy, tied on with black yarn. Some are signed on the foot, when this is requested; none have been numbered.

When asked why her bears, and bears in general, have become so popular, Karen Walter replies: "In recent years the bear has become more popular, but I believe there were many closet collectors before that; because I was one of them. I'd never dream of telling anyone how much I liked bears. I thought no one over a certain age was supposed to like bears anymore. Thank goodness we can still retain some of our childlike qualities (through bears) and escape."

I am sure, as he oversees production, that *Teds* approves.

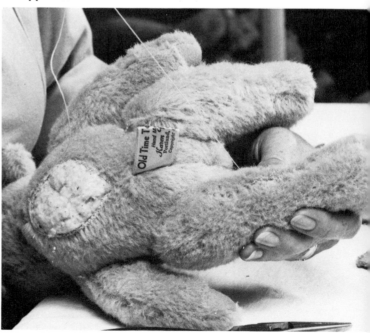

"Lastly, the bear is sewn shut with strong thread." *Photograph courtesy of Karen Walter.*

"Here is a 13in (30.5cm) mohair bear. He was the first mohair bear I ever made. I have made about 550 since." 1983. *Photograph courtesy of Karen Walter.*

"This is a 10in (25.4cm) mohair *Ski Bear* in matching cap and sweater. I made about 200 *Ski Bears*. Skis have been discontinued. The outfits were made from sweaters and wool bought at the Mill End Store. My mother knitted the scarfs and some caps. She made about 15 sets." *Photograph courtesy of Karen Walter.*

Gruff, 22in (55.9cm) tall. This Walter bear won first place in the jointed bear contest in Minneapolis-St. Paul, at "Teddy-n-Friends" in 1981. He is the exact color of a real bear, has long fur and feels and looks like a real animal; leather paws. *Photograph courtesy of Karen Walter.*

WHIM C. BEAR

Dean Hansen
Sandra Haroutunian (Hansen)

Dean Hansen with *Horton #1.* Antique shoe button eyes; leather paws; growler; velvet nose (*Horton*, not Dean). *Horton* is named for a teddy collector named D. A. Horton. Sandra Haroutunian (Hansen) with Whim C. Bear #1, *Buttercup.* Sherpa fur; velvet eyes and nose. "The Heart and Growl of Whim C. Bear." *Photograph by Village Photography Studio, courtesy of Whim C. Bear.*

Out in Napa, California, (land of bear makers, if there ever was one), two allegedly adult bear artists are being held hostage by bears. I make this statement based on the evidence at hand.

One day, not long ago, a postcard dropped into our mail chute. On the front of it was a graphic depiction of two dejected looking humans, bearing bears, with a rope around their necks. At the other end of the rope, seven bears were leading them away.

The message on the other side reads: "Stop the press! Yes, we Whim C. Bears have taken over the Sandy-Dean fiasco and are taking charge. WE had to answer your questionnaire and at this moment we have Sandy's mom locked in a room typing it (we don't have fingers or we'd do it)....Bear Hugs, Whim C."

These mysterious goings-on are, come to think of it, in character for *Whim C. Bear*. For, he was named for Dorothy L. Sayers' sleuth, Lord Peter Wimsey. Yet, there is something a bit disconcerting about receiving information acquired in this manner. On the other paw, this is the only information I have received directly from a bear. Since the circumstances of its acquisition are peculiar anyway, I am presenting my findings in the form of an interview.

*   *   *

Carol-Lynn Rössel Waugh (CLRW): Where were you born?
Whim C. Bear (WCB): I was born in the Napa Valley two years ago (1981). My parents, Sandy and Dean, are third and fourth generation Napa Valley folks; that makes me fifth generation.
CLRW: Where did you go to school?
WCB: I teach at Vintage High School with Sandy. She and Dean both went to schools in the valley. Sandy graduated from Lone Mountain (now University of San Francisco) cum laude in Fine Arts (painting). She also took pottery and porcelain classes at Napa College as well as doll making. Dean has studied drafting and classical painting.
CLRW: Did you have a bear as a child?
WCB: Well, I've always been partial to bears, but personally I have a stuffed bunny. Sandy has her childhood bear — looks just like Radar O'Reilly's (M.A.S.H.). Dean has his bear, too, but both say I'M their favorite bear.
CLRW: When did your people start designing bears?
WCB: I was started on June 7, 1981, but I was perfected (?) a couple of months later. I began making other bears immediately. Sandy and Dean made their first Teddy Bear Picnic Music Box in October of 1980.
CLRW: How did this come about?
WCB: Sandy wanted a Teddy Bear Picnic Music Box more than anything in the world. Dean complied. They made lots of bear and non-bear things. I AM the BEAR artist. I make only BEARS.
CLRW: How are the stuffed bears made?
WCB: The stuffed bears make themselves. After each bear was made, there were always extra parts left over. Those parts became the pattern for the next bear and so on. As a result, the bears have evolved all by themselves. They've also grown a lot.

Sandy does the faces by poking and pinching, nipping and tucking. The faces are always different. Dean is the official love tester. He makes their ribbons and kisses and hugs each bear. He tests their big bottoms for love pats and speaking of pats, he makes sure their arms are long enough for a good round of pitty-pat.

Personally, I'm embarrassed by the whole thing.

Incidentally, Sandy makes all the Fimo bears, the real tiny ones, 1/4in (.65cm) and less!!! They are made on her thumb nail. She uses acupuncture needles and specially filed fingernails as tools. Dean and I are in charge of timing their baking (Sandy forgets). Dean makes all the things they go in.

Dean is in charge of making "bear stuff." That's stuff like chairs that look like bears and boxes that have bear heads or springs in 'em (Bear in a Box)! He does all the wood things that hold all "bear stuff."

I direct.
CLRW: What size bears do you make?
WCB: We do whatever moves us. I make bears that started out 16in (40.6cm) and have grown to 20in (50.8cm).

Sandy and Dean haven't progressed as much as me and they're still doing bears that range from 1/8in (.31cm) to 3in (7.6cm) out of Fimo clay.
CLRW: What are bears best known for?
WCB: I am known for our MUSICAL stuffed *Whim C. Bears* and Sandy is known for her funny little Fimo bears. Dean contributes a dynamite candy house, 1in by 1in (2.5cm by 2.5cm), in which Sandy puts a whole family of the *Three Bears*! We just might make the smallest bears ever! Dean made a wagon 1/16in by 1/8in (.15cm by .31cm) and Sandy put a bear with a candy cane inside!
CLRW: What is your favorite bear?
WCB: The bear that is being made at the moment is the one we enjoy the best. Sandy likes doing the clay bears because she has complete control (?) and contact with the medium.

She gets frustrated with stuffed bears because she has a running argument with the sewing machine and she's always stabbing herself with needles. On the other hand, it's hard to hug something 1/4in (.65cm) high and stuffed teddies don't disappear with the wag of a doggie's tail.

Dean loves his wood critters because he loves the sinuous (?) nature of wood.

CLRW: Can you tell me how you were made?

WCB: Sandy will answer this.

Sandy: I made Whim C. out of maize lamb-type fur that everyone said was a dumb fur for a bear. He was one of the first bears I made and he is silly, floppy, soft, squishy and very sassy.

I named him *Buttercup* and he thinks he's very literary. When he's not writing to Carol-Lynn or the *Teddy Tribune*, he directs the Fury Folk Choral Society from atop Dean's piano.

He goes to all of our miniature shows and has made friends with every child (big and little) who comes to see us. Dean lets *Buttercup* drive the Volkswagen. He's not too bright, though, as he thinks going for a spin in the dryer is real "hot stuff." *Buttercup* loves our cats and dogs and is always sneaking his tummy under their heads while they're snoozing.

CLRW: Are bears "people" to you?

WCB: Wait a minute! Are you implying that there are bears that aren't people?

CLRW: Whence comes your inspiration?

WCB: Dean and Sandy like to look at old childrens' books for inspiration. They also rely on customers for ideas. Since they think they can make anything, people are always trying to challenge them. Sandy is always designing and constructing bears — in her mind. Before she actually makes anything, she goes over and over each step in her mind. Sometimes she does this so many times she thinks she has actually made the item and starts something else.

CLRW: Do you dress your bears?

WCB: We feel that the "bear makes the clothes." In our case, if we wee bears don't make our own clothes, we don't get any. Instead of clothing, Sandy and Dean create environments for us, gorgeous candy houses or hollow trees or miniature birthday parties that go on forever!

CLRW: What are the best and worst parts of bear making?

WCB: There are two wonderful moments in bear making, when they are thought of and the moment they are done. The worst moment is putting them in boxes and sending them away. Sometimes we will do an order over and over again and then have the customer say the magic Whim C. Bear chant so that we are sure to send the most perfect item to them.

CLRW: Do you exhibit your bears?

WCB: We find exhibitionism in bears to be in dubious taste. Most bears can handle it, but Whim C.'s tend to carry on; they are such hams!!!

CLRW: How are your bears sold?

WCB: WHAT DO YOU MEAN, SOLD?

Sandy: Whim C. Bears are not aware that they are actually sold. They thought they picked their new homes and an exchange of love only took place. We advertise occasionally. We started a mail order business one year ago. Prior to that we did (and still do) about ten miniature, craft and/or teddy shows a year.

The most unusual technique is that we send a poem to folks who have ordered our stuffed *Teddy* and on packing day at a designated time, they are instructed to chant so that the right bear will go to the right person. We have had 100% success with this method.

CLRW: What is your philosophy of bear making?

WCB: A cup of hot chocolate
    A cookie or two
    We'd love to make
    A Whim C. for you.

CLRW: How many *Whim C.*'s have you made?

WCB: Whim C.'s go out as quickly as they are made. We have made several hundreds, maybe thousands, of miniature bears: every one different. We have made about 100 stuffed teddies. We were using a treadle sewing machine. Now we have a computerized electric machine. As soon as Sandy learns to sew, things should go faster.

We have a question for your, Carol-Lynn. Are you, or have you ever been a teddy bear? Or is teddy bear just a state of mind?

CLRW: I refer you to *OOP*, my press agent. I think this interview is over.

Two jointed clay bears, approximately 1½in (3.8cm) tall. Front bear pulls wagon with tiny Whim C. Bear in it.

Low-fire clay Whim C. Bear holds dolly and wagon with tiny Whim C. Bear holding candy cane.

Jack-in-the-box bear. Low-fire clay head; wooden box.

Tiny Whim C. Bear in bear rocker holding red heart.

Bear chairs with designs painted front and back on wooden chair bodies. 1983.

TOMMY AND PATSY LEWIS

Tommy and Patsy Lewis with the *Prince*, 23in (58.4cm) dressed, undressed and in pieces. *Photograph courtesy of Louisiana Bear Co.*

In the window of the Louisiana Bear Company sits a realistic 65 lb. (29.4kg) stuffed bear. The owners of the emporium. Patsy and Tommy Lewis, insist he is a display model. They love him too much to part with him.

So, the three of them tend shop, watching the magic that happens when the civilian customer wanders into the place, emerging, smiling, a newly-converted artophile. Lots of bears are crammed into the Bear Company, but the most special and the real focus of it all are the original artist bears, some of which are the work of the proprietors.

The Bear Company is a second career for the Lewises, an outgrowth of a hobby, perhaps an obsession. Its roots were in Patsy's retirement and rapid dissatisfaction with inaction.

"I took an early retirement to bake bread for Tommy and had every intention of writing a book on the adventures of all the wonderful and zany people I had met in the business world," she says. She did not like being alone, though, and took up doll collecting to fill up the time. A doll collector friend lent her a bear pattern to make bears for a Christmas fair. After the first bear, Patsy was hooked. Soon, she was making piles of bears and designing her own. Orders backed up. Patsy was out of retirement.

So was her husband. The bear making, which had its genesis October 1980, coincided with his retirement from the Shreveport, Louisiana Fire Department. Soon he joined his wife in her newfound passion, devising unusual methods of putting the bears together — metal joints — and of making them stand on their own wooden inserts in the footpads. He started working on a mechanized teddy. Bears had captured the pair.

Neither had a ted as a child. Bears seem to have had zero impact on their development. The Shreveport, Louisiana, couple's initial interaction with teddies, to their recollection, was as parents.

"Our first experience with a teddy bear," Patsy says, "was when our first daughter, Julie, was 18 months old —December 1956. We bought her a 22in (55.9cm) mohair, mechanical yes-no bear. He cost $18, the equivalent to two weeks of our grocery budget. We definitely could not afford

him. We definitely could not resist him. He is still in mint condition and her pride and joy."

But teddies had low priority for the Lewises until Patsy started making them. Immediately, the furry critters became the new focus of their lives.

"We started to collect bears about three months after we made the first one and they multiplied like rabbits. I think we bought 30 the first month. Our real passion is for all the bears made by the American bear artists. We feel these are the real treasures of today and the heirlooms of tomorrow."

Lewis bears could easily fit the above description. The result of collaboration and experimentation, they utilize the complementary skills of their creators.

Patsy is an excellent seamstress. "As a child I divided my affection between my dolls, cats and my mother's treadle sewing machine. She allowed me to experiment with fabrics and that wonderful old machine from a very early age. By the time I was a sophomore in high school, I made most of my own clothes and by the time I was a mother, I was happily engaged in making lined coats and bonnets for Julie and Leita. I spent many happy hours making *Barbie* clothes for their dolls and then sat down in the middle of the floor and played with the girls and their dolls. It would only follow that I must dress the bears with great detail. Many of them wear lined velvet bonnets and coats."

Her husband has other talents. "Tommy cut his teeth on car parts. His father encouraged him to be mechanical and constructive. Our bears have metal joints that work very well for us. We are developing a mechanical bear and I want him to be very special." Patsy says. "Tommy has talked with some engineers and we will probably have this "mechanical genius" off the drawing board and in production sometime next year. Or the next?"

The bear makers share duties. The process is slow, painstaking. A small bear easily needs 12 hours of concentrated labor. A costume might need two or three days.

Patsy is meticulous in dressing the bears. "If the bear is getting a new costume," she says, "the pattern is made by fitting the pieces directly to his particular portly form. We search out the best fabrics and trims for their clothes. I press

51

Julie Lewis O'Daniel, 28 years old. *Yes/No Bear*, 26 1/2 years. *Photograph courtesy of Louisiana Bear Co.*

each seam in their garments as it is sewed. In our opinion, there can be no shortcut taken in making the quality and style of our bear. This is what our collectors are paying for."

"Virtually all the work, except the main seams, is done by hand." Patsy says. "I ruined my first sewing machine stitching bears. I use needle-nosed pliers, heavy needles and we insert saftey-lock eyes for child safety. While many of our bears go into collections, we make them all safe for children."

"Time and the telephone are our worst enemies," she continues. "We are both slow and methodical in each phase of constructing our bears. Tommy cuts out each piece, very carefully and one at a time." ("I watch football on TV and cut out two bears per game," he explains.) "I do all of the machine and hand sewing and we work together in stuffing and jointing them."

Two *T.C. Bears*, 14in (35.6cm). Fully-jointed. *Sailor T.C.* beige acrylic plush fur; felt collar and hat with navy soutache braid trim; red broadcloth tie. *Aaron Boatman Collection.* Standing *T.C.* made of oyster white acrylic plush fur. Tag reads:

T.C. BEAR
by Patsy Lewis
Louisiana Bear Co.
Photograph courtesy of Louisiana Bear Co.

"Tommy makes thin, smoothly sanded plywood innerfeet so that our bears stand firmly without assistance of a doll stand and they pose easily because of their firm footing. We use the finest polyester fluff and stuff it in very firmly. We trim all the plush away from the seamlines before stitching begins. Our bears have so many time-consuming features and one I haven't mentioned is hand-clipped snouts.

"I am very content chugging away at my own pace in my workroom when we have no deadline to meet, but get me under pressure and I'd rather go fishing. Sometimes I get up at 3:00 a.m.; sometimes I work late at night. Sometimes I HAVE to."

The Lewises have narrowed down their production to a few styles which they can transform with clothing. Their names are marked on the printed labels sewn into the back seam. The labels read: *T.C. Bear, Wiffy, Mikey* or *Lei-Lei.*

Patsy describes the bears.

"14in (35.6cm) *T.C. Bear* was the first. He is named after Tommy and the earlier ones reflect my great admiration for Steiff. *T.C.* is always chunky and is rarely dressed in more than a hat and collar — usually sailor or clown.

"14in (35.6cm) *Wiffy* came next and has a rather pointy, turned up nose, a whimsical half-smile and usually is costumed in feminine attire. Many of them are dressed in elaborate velvet costumes — some Victorian *Wiffy* has been costumed as Little Lord Fauntlebear and Little Red Riding Hood.

"16in to 18in (40.6cm to 45.7cm) *Mikey* is named after our son-in-law who insists on being called Michael but owns the original and has won a photography award in the local newspaper for a picture of *Mikey* peeking out from behind their woodpile. *Mikey* is rarely dressed and I can only recall one dressed as a girl and he did not fit the image at all. It was a birthday gift purchased by a grandmother and the little girl promptly named him *Bar* and won't even let me touch him now to straighten the ribbon in his hair.

"One of our most original and sought-after designs is *Mikey* made in red plush with velvet paw pads, horns on his head and a pointy tail. He is not meant to be satanic. He carries a dinner fork rather than a trident and encourages everyone to eat all the chocolate chip cookies they can stuff in their tummies. Viewed from the side, it is noticeable that he has stuffed quite a few of the delectable little morsels himself.

"*Mikey* most often is made of dark brown plush with a light beige snout. He has been popular in this area, waving a Confederate flag and his music box plays "Dixie."

"12in (30.5cm) *Lei-Lei* is our version of a jointed chunk of a panda. He is named after our daughter, Leita (my mother's name, too). *Lei-Lei* is seldom costumed and never more than a sailor collar and hat or a clown ruff and cap.

"*The Prince* is our 23in (58.4cm) bear that we created last year in honor of the new little prince that was born in England. He has an air of aristocracy about him and very large feet. He wears an elegant red felt uniform jacket trimmed with much gold braid and gold buttons. He has gold-leafed Bearhead insignia on each side of his collar. Every prince must prove his valor and he wears a medal of valor that he was awarded for fighting the Battle of the Bees. His uniform is completed with a royal blue satin sash tied in a rosette."

Occasionally, the Lewises do special editions of their bears for shops, like *Elizabeth Bearet Browny,* an over-dressed Victorian lady Wiffy bear. They never produce more than fifty of any costume; some are limited to maybe five.

Before the shop opened in August 1983, Lewis bears sold through word-of-mouth; this is still the case. Shopkeeping eats into bear making time, so Louisiana Bear Company bears are not readily available; there is always a waiting list.

Artist bears are time-consuming to make, especially if constructed with the care that Tommy and Patsy invest. But customers usually understand. There is a magic to them, different from that in any other bear. You can see it in the smiles of their owners.

If you have any doubts, just ask the big bear in the window.

RIGHT: *Mikey,* 16in (40.6cm) tall. Fully-jointed; brown acrylic plush with beige, hand-clipped snout; brown felt paw pads. This is the original from the *Michael O'Daniel Collection — Mikey's* namesake. Tag in back seam:

Mikey
by Patsy Lewis
Louisiana Bear Co.
Photograph courtesy of Louisiana Bear Co.

ABOVE: Little Red Riding Hood (*Wiffy*), 14in (35.6cm) tall. Fully-jointed; oatmeal beige acrylic plush fur; red felt cloak; separate hood trimmed with embroidered braid, pink gingham check pinafore with matching braid trim; red hearts printed on white cloth in basket. *Tommy and Patsy Lewis Collection.* This bear won first place ribbon in novelty toys at the Louisiana State Fair, October 1982.
Tag:

WIFFY
by Patsy Lewis
Louisiana Bear Co.
Photograph courtesy of Louisiana Bear Co.

ABOVE: *Bee-L-Zee-Bear (Mikey).* 16in (40.6cm) tall. Red acrylic plush; fully-jointed; red velvet paw pads, horns and tail. This is the original from the *Celia Sawyer Collection.* Celia provided him with an antique oyster fork and this verse:

If you like candy cakes, or fudge
From this sweet Bear you'll get a nudge.
"Bee-L-Zee-Bear" is quite a riot;
He'll always make you Bear your diet!
Tag:

Copyright 1982
Mikey by Patsy Lewis
Louisiana Bear Co.
Photograph courtesy of Louisiana Bear Co.

RIGHT: An original one-of-a-kind 18in (45.7cm) tall *Sweetheart Bear* created as a special order for Valentine's Day gift to Celia Sawyer from her husband, Ronnie. Fully-jointed; oyster white acrylic plush; red velvet Victorian gown with train; red velvet bonnet with heart shaped brim; white pantaloons and petticoat with tucks and lace; umbrella of white broadcloth printed with red hearts and edged with double lace ruffle; umbrella opens; wig of brown long curls. Tag: Copyright 1983. Handmade by Patsy Lewis Louisiana Bear Company *Photograph courtesy of Louisiana Bear Co.*

SUSAN L. KRUSE

Sue Kruse and her bears. *Photograph courtesy of Sue Kruse.*

Sue Kruse's logo.

"Bear making is so much a part of me that I wouldn't stop making them even if I never sold another bear." Sue Kruse is speaking of her work, which is sometimes more like play. At its best, it combines aesthetic, intellectual and emotional challenge.

"The thing I most enjoy about bear making is the creating. When I really think about it, the creating is so exciting that I can't begin to describe what I actually get out of it. I will stay awake till early morning working out patterns mentally. When I am really charged, the beds do not get made, dinner isn't cooked and I swear sometimes the roof could cave in and I would never notice. Fortunately, I have a very patient husband who indulges me and a six-year-old daughter who is usually so busy with her own projects that she forgets what's going on, too."

The California bear designer has an extensive background in art, and has had experience working in many media. She credits a sympathetic high school teacher with instilling the feeling that "I could create anything I put my mind to with the help of a little research and the right materials and skills."

With this attitude, she taught herself bearmaking, following the directions in Margaret Hutchings' book, *Teddy Bears and How to Make Them*. It was 1976, and her first child was due.

The clone-bears sold, and, after a year of "making someone else's bears," she designed her own. "I worked for a week from morning till night to come up with a bear that looked old-fashioned — a hump, button eyes, jointed, etc. I was so pleased with the results that I have never looked at someone else's patterns again. I think I learned the necessary bear making skills from the Hutchings' book and later, armed with the confidence gained from selling bears and the design skills from art school, I was able to make up my own patterns."

Sue's bears have an antique air; they do not resemble her childhood bear. She describes him: "When I was a child, I had a typical 50's brown teddy bear and a panda bear, both

of whom I practically loved to death. Then at one point either my mother or I decided that I was too old to play with such creatures and they were packed up and relegated to the garage, poor dears. I really regret that now because later when I decided the bears should return from their exile, we discovered that there was a family of spiders living with them. My mother tossed them out; I guess she didn't realize that bears can be cleaned and fumigated. I nag her about this from time to time and I think she regrets it, too, as she has developed an interest in bears through my involvement with them.

"I do have a few small bears that survived that ordeal, however. When I was in the fifth grade, there was a classmate of mine who owned a small panda bear. Through a great deal of badgering and persuasion, I finally convinced her to trade the bear for a ratty old purse I had. To this day I can't understand why she finally traded. I'm sure to her the trade is long forgotten, but not to me. I still am the very happy owner of the bear, whose name is *Buster*.

"*Buster* is a non-jointed panda bear. He is 5½in (14cm) tall and is excelsior-stuffed. He has one clear glass eye and one amber-colored glass eye. *Buster* proudly sports a t-shirt and hat that I made for him from one of my brother's socks. I'm not sure my mother appreciated her then ten-year-old daughter doing this, but *Buster* seemed to like it, as 22 years later he's still wearing his hat and t-shirt."

Sue is best known for her traditional jointed "character bears." Her first original bears, on which her reputation was made, were old-fashioned "hump-back" bears. "I enjoy making jointed character bears best," she says. "This is because of the challenge and research involved. For example, I created an Elizabethan bear. This involved researching the types of clothing that would have been worn during that time. Then there is the matter of deciding what materials to use and working out a pattern that will fit a bear. The final result is a bear that is as close to authentic as I can get it and still have it be appropriate for a bear.

Bill Shakesbear, 11in (25.4cm) tall. Fur fabric; button eyes; wool tapestry yarn nose; lace ruff; red velvet doublet; black velvet short-stuffed breeches; white hose, brown leather shoes with black velvet inserted in the slits; metal sword held in place by a black leather belt. Tag sewn in back seam of bear's body. *Photograph courtesy of Sue Kruse.*

20in (50.8cm) bear. Fur fabric; button eyes; wool tapestry yarn nose and mouth; faux suede paw pads; growler; scarf not original. Fabric Tag in back seam of bear's body. This is the only Kruse bear of this large size in existence. *Photograph courtesy of Sue Kruse.*

"My favorite bear is my Elizabethan bear followed closely by *Blackbearrd*. The time of Elizabeth I is a favorite of mine in history so I have a feeling that this is what endears him to me. That, plus I am a devoted Anglophile. The bear is affectionately referred to as *Bill Shakesbear*. I started out to see if I could make a lace ruff that was authentic looking and the bear took off from there. After several aborted attempts and many references to theater costuming books, I finally hit upon how to make the ruff. It took five hours to complete; each fold of lace is individually stitched. The rest of the bear's costume consists of red velvet doublet with black velvet epaulets. The doublet's sleeves are trimmed in lace. He wears black velvet short stuffed breeches and trunk hose. On his feet are leather shoes with slits on top that are filled with black velvet. He wears a black velvet cap with plumes and carries a sword."

Other character bears include *Paddy*, the *Irish Bear*, whose genesis was some green plush Sue did not know what to do with. He started them all. She is slowly working on a series of authentically costumed pirate bear, starting with *Blackbeard*.

Although some stand as large as 20in (50.8cm), most Kruse bears range between 10in and 12in (25.4cm and 30.5cm); some are as small as 6in (15.2cm). "I have found that 10in to 12in (25.4cm to 30.5cm) is a nice comfortable size not requiring the intricacies of a small bear nor the volumes of stuffing, material, etc. of a large bear. Also, I make all my own joint sets on a drill press and the large joint sets are a horror to me to make. To paraphrase Goldilocks, 10in to 12in (25.4cm to 30.5cm), is just right!"

Her methods and motives for bear making have evolved. "I began making bears for my daughter. Today, however, the impetus is completely different. It's more the challenge to create something new from scraps of 'nothing' and the 'fire' that sets up inside me as a result of the creative juices flowing....

"The medium I began with was fake fur, non-jointed polyester fiber-filled bears with embroidery floss eyes. I am still making fabric bears, but they have gotten a great deal more sophisticated since the first ones. I use mohair, wools and the best fur fabrics I can find. I also use old coat fabric from time to time. For eyes, I now favor glass eyes or button eyes to achieve an old-fashioned feel. The bears are still stuffed with polyfill, and I am playing with stuffing some of them with some excelsior that I have acquired. I only make jointed bears now as this is my favorite type of bear. I find it pretty exciting to make all the body parts and then assemble them. The bear emerges before my very eyes; it's almost magical."

How does she design a bear?

"My bear designing takes action one of two ways,. I am either spurred on by an old bear whose essence I try to capture (as in the case of my *Bearhop* bear), or I work with a specific picture in my mind as to what I am trying to achieve. Sometimes I make many sketches in my sketchbook and I never put it down on paper before I begin working.

"Next I work out the patterns on brown butcher paper. I draw the pattern pieces and then cut them out of inexpensive fur fabric. From here I sew the bear and put him together.

Bearhop, 11in (27.9cm) tall. Fur fabric; wool felt body; gold metallic braid trim; button *eyes*; wool tapestry yarn nose and mouth; felt paw pads. Suitcase not original to bear. Cloth tag in back of bear's body; paper hang tag tied to red satin bow. *Photograph courtesy of Sue Kruse. Barbara Trego Collection.*

"I usually put the head on the body and one arm and one leg — no finishing details. From this I can tell what needs correcting. I will then draft new pattern pieces and start over.

"I keep going this way until I end up with a bear that is right. It usually takes four to six bears to get one that looks like what I have in mind.

"When this part is complete, I make a whole bear in the inexpensive fur. Then the finishing details are tried. Eyes go on next. I like to put the eyes in after the head is stuffed and attached because I can really sink them into the head which makes them tight and defines the eye-nose area better. Then the nose is stitched on with either perle cotton or wool tapestry yarn. What I use depends on the bear.

"After the bear is constructed, if it is to be dressed, I begin whatever research is necessary for the clothes. After the type of clothing is decided upon, I use inexpensive felt to design the clothing patterns. The bear essentially becomes a pin cushion as I pin felt to him, molding it in shape to fit his body. For example, if I need a shirt for the bear, the felt is pinned to the upper torso and then I use a pen to draw on the felt where the armholes and other cutting lines will be. This becomes the pattern, which I then cut out of another piece of felt and sew up, try on, and then correct what's wrong. I repeat this process until the pattern is right.

"After all this is completed. I then make up a bear in the materials that I decide the final bear will be made in. Sometimes these have been selected before I design the bear and other times not until the patterns are complete, as a full picture of how the bear should look forms in my mind while I am working on him."

Bear making for Sue is self-fulfillment. "My intended audience is first and foremost myself. The bears are always created to fill a void that exists for me. After that consideration, I would suppose that I would have to say collectors are the intended audience. I do not do various bears for different audiences as I cannot and will not work on something whose *sole raison d'etre* is to please someone else. I hope that doesn't sound too egotistical, but I learned long ago that it must please me, set a fire under me, in order for me to want to do the work. For those reasons, I have made it a point not to accept a commmission with restrictions other than price range."

Boswell, 15in (38.1cm) tall. Gray fur fabric; glass eyes; growler; wool felt paw pads; wool tapestry yarn nose and mouth; red plaid bow. Cloth tag in back seam of bear's body. This bear is not numbered. Edition of six. *Photograph courtesy of Sue Kruse.*

11in (27.9cm) tall bear. Grayish fur fabric body; suede paw pads. Bear side of head has glass eyes, wool felt nose and mouth. Doll side of head has porcelain doll head with glass eyes and small mohair fringe-type bangs. Cloth tag in back of bear's body. This is one of only two bears of this type in existence, both of which are prototypes and are marked "AP." *Photograph courtesy of Sue Kruse.*

Designing, for Sue, is the best part of bear making. Repetition is the worst, and her "editions" of bears are growing smaller and smaller because of this. But it is the challenge of creation, the pleasure derived from artistic statement, that keeps her at it.

"My philosophy in bear making is to have fun," she says, "I hope that doesn't sound too hedonistic, but they're such terrific little creatures I'm sure that's what they're here for." Nary an arctophile can argue with that.

Bearheart In Disguise, 11in (27.9cm) tall. White velour costume with hood; pink satin lined ears; white yarn "cotton-tail" attached to back of suit; pink satin ribbon about the neck; Easter basket attached to left paw containing assorted silk flowers, green velvet leaves, moss, tiny eggs and a small bird. Cloth tag in back seam of bear's body; paper hang tag attached to bow. *Barbara Trego Collection.*

PAT MARRISON

Pat Marrison and son Ryan. *Photograph courtesy of Pat Marrison.*

"Bears for interior design" might be one way to describe Pat Marrison's work.

"My intended audience/public is not children, but adults who like to use bears for decoration," she says.

Pat's bears are made of brightly colored felt and are different from traditional teds. They evolved out of yuletide decorations.

"I started designing my own Christmas ornaments in 1977, because they didn't make and weren't patterns for the type of ornaments I wanted," she explains "I designed a few ornaments for that Christmas and continued to design more Christmas and holiday decorations. I now make mostly wired, posable dolls and animals, frequently dressing or decorating them for holidays and special occasions. Bears are a big part of my overall production."

The Michigan designer began bear making in November 1982, with 8in (20.3cm) flat, wired, posable bears. They were an outgrowth of her dolls and other animals. "I make all kinds of little (and a few big) felt people and creatures: country girls and boys, turkeys, ducks, chickens, a Father Christmas, tree-top angels, owls, leprechauns, scarecrow boys and girls, rabbits, lambs and a few others. I started making bears because teddies are so lovable and sweet and because everyone begged me to do them!" she says. "I make bears today because they serve as a good creative medium. They are fun to do and my customers demand that I make them."

Her customers are treated to a wide variety of unusual teddy concepts. Pat describes some.

"I make an Irish bear: green body with a white collar and bib with a shamrock on it. For Valentine's Day, a red bear with a ribbon around his neck with a small heart on the ribbon. A cupid bear with wings holds a bouquet of flowers with ribbons streaming down. For Christmas, an angel bear with wings and halo. I also do country bears."

In August 1983, Pat introduced a line of larger, more rounded, wired felt bears perfect for centerpieces. Among them, a sailor bear and *Father Christmas* are outstanding — full of personality. This word sums up the character of Pat's critters. She builds it into their design.

"Everything I create has a definite personality to me" she explains. "I love people and find all kinds of people interesting. I had a somewhat lonely, isolated childhood, so meeting and appreciating people is part of my present exploration of a world that I didn't experience much of as a child. I suppose creating something with 'personality' is what every true artist does. When one works with intensity, a bit of 'you' shows in your work. I always end up talking to MY work as though all my little creations were good friends.

"My bear designing and making procedures are quite different from any I've ever seen. In the first place, I don't design bears as children's toys. They are designed to be friends for older children and adults. They are meant to be "played with," but only a decorative way. So far, all my bears are wired so they are posable. They do not have attached arms and legs, but rather, the body, arms and legs are all cut together. This allows the wire armature to fit into the body better.

Father Christmas, 12½in (31.8cm). Camel-color felt body with wire armature; crimson velour robe; gray fur trim; white false beard attached with hooks behind ears; crimson velour hat with gray fake fur band and pompon and sprig of holly; key on chain at waist; sack of toys with teddy on top. 1983.

"The bear loses its flat appearance after it is stuffed and positioned. Right now I only work in felt. I do not make "furry" bears. My bears are made only from wool-blend felt, wire and stuffing."

Positioning is important for the bears' impact. "I am trying to make bears that will hold almost any pose, so that the owner can achieve almost unlimited effects by posing the bear and having it hold that pose."

Pat devised her own methods. "I learned most of what I know from studying construction of clothing and stuffed animals. When I couldn't find a technique to fit my need, I invented one. I suggest that others do the same: take time to experiment and explore."

The designer works at home, where her family serves as insbearation. "They will never know how much I use them as models for what I do," she confides. "My step-son, Kirk, and my nine-year-old, Christopher, are my bear models. This is a SECRET! SHHH."

Pat puts in long hours at the sewing table with her bears. But she finds her work fascinating. "I enjoy taking my basic small bear and giving him clothes, accessories and a "setting," and making him into a one-of-a-kind bear decoration. This is so challenging, creative and fun, I could do nothing but!," she says.

Intended for adults, her bearish decorations appeal to the child in everyone: "Teddy bears are that bit of security and silliness that we all need to stay sane in a crazy world," Pat explains. As the world continues to get more complex, people like to know there is something/someone who retains the simplicity of times-gone-by. Teddy bears love you no matter what and they are always there to listen but not to judge. At the end of EVERY day they can give you a smile and a bit of joy — no strings attached."

These art bears, which are marketed under the name, "Beanie Pie" — Pat calls them "pieces of Beanie Pie," may look different from the traditional ted, but, she feels this is a mixture of progress and artistic statement, and all for the good.

"Most of today's teddy bears are very different from antique bears, unless they are intended to be copies. The difference reflects the changes that have occurred in available materials, new techniques and new machinery.

"The difference also reflects a changing attitude in 'How things should be.' Today's artist/designer no longer has to stay within very limited boundaries. A teddy bear today doesn't have to look just like a real bear. It can be just what the artist wants it to be — fat, skinny, hairy, hairless, etc.

"Most of today's bears are aimed at the same audience as the first bears — adults and children. What joy! Finally a TOY adults can brag about owning instead of hiding away for secret play."

Pat's customers have no intention of hiding her bears. They buy them with every intention of displaying them to all comers. What else does one do with a teddy bear for interior design?

Close-up of *Father Christmas.* Note hooks attaching beard to ear at left.

8in (20.3cm) green felt bear; wire armature; white bib with shamrocks; camel-colored face.

LORI GARDINER

Lori Gardiner and her bears. Left to right: *Gold Klina, Ellen* with balloon, *Prince William, Baron von Grinit* and *Moe*. All bears have label behind left ear. *Photograph by Ken Bannister, courtesy of Lori Gardiner.*

Lori Gardiner is hooked on nostalgia. She calls her bear business "Echoes From the Past."

"My bears appeal in the same way an old song appeals to you," she says. "It makes you remember something or someone from your past."

Probably the best example of this is *Rick*, a ted she designed in 1983. 12in (30.5cm) tall, made of black velvet with gold glass eyes (they have eyelashes — a Gardiner hallmark), he is fully-jointed and wears a white 1940s dinner jacket, white collar and a black bow tie. Concealed in his back, a music box, when wound, plays "As Time Goes By." She has designed a special setting for him, one she terms "a Casablanca-style archway with a handmade fan hanging in the center." It has shiny tile, a "Persian" rug and green plant for atmosphere. Humphrey Bogart, watch out.

Most of Lori's teddies are less flamboyant but they are all designed to tug at one's heartstrings a bit, especially if the viewer has celtic ancestors. She explains, "At first the names we used were influenced by the German quality (for teddy bears) but we realized immediately that our command of cute German words was grossly limited. We decided to use family names on them in the future. Except for *Klina, Buttons* and *Q. Phinney* (there is a family story connected with that one, too), we will be using good old Irish names."

So the bear maker named her Grandma bear *Bridget Mack*, after her grandmother. "She is the perfect grandmother and perfectly loving," Lori says. Her Grandpa bear is *Padrick*, "named after a great uncle but now married to *Bridget* bear — I hope this does not cast doubt on my ancestry. He has a mustache and if there ever was a Grandpa, he's it." *Vernie* is named after her husband. "He is also a big teddy bear and the *Vernie* bear fits his personality to a "T."

She enjoys making "character" bears. "I hope my bears are best known for their originality," she says. "I dearly love the old bears but I would get no pleasure from copying one. I admire originality and aptness of thought. I like to be surprised and I think other collectors do, too.

"I do bears WITH character most often. The character I planned is not always the one that comes out in the finished bear. In fact, many of my patterns have one name on them and end up being someone else. The *Fat Baby* ended up

being *Franklyn* because he was really a short fat gentleman bear, and he could not have been anyone else. *Old Fashioned Bear* turned out to be *Joseph, the Urban Cowbear* because his fat little legs looked like chaps."

Lori has been making bears since 1981, but was not inspired by childhood bears. "Alas," she says, "I didn't have a bear to love until my thirties. My daughter, Wendy, who now assists me in bear making, bought a *Winnie-the-Pooh* for me at Disneyland. It was my special friend before I knew anything about teddy bears. He is the only bear permanently ensconced in my bedroom. Well, except for some tiny teddies that don't even have names — just "Tiny."

She made her first bear — a large, unjointed sitting one — for her daughter, Wendy's 25th birthday, from a commercial pattern. They named it *Peaches*. As with many bear makers, something snapped and she became addicted.

"Making that bear inspired my interest in making a jointed one. I sent for a kit for a jointed bear and soon started designing my own style bears." The bear kit did not work out well. "I felt that it had been designed to drive me mad so I started improvising and finally adapted some methods that went faster."

Designing has a particular order.

"When I get an idea for a bear, I write out a numbered list including the points I want to include. It starts: "*WILLIAM*: 1. About 18in (45.7cm) tall. 2. Real snooty. 3. Mink eyelashes," and so on until I have a clear picture of what I'm going to make. Then I sketch a pattern (I use big old grocery bags), select the material, cut one out and sew it. Wendy joints it and I put the features on. If I feel that it needs some changes, I list the changes, make a new pattern and remake the bear.

"I usually show the bear around before I make too many changes. It's amazing how different people respond to the same bear. I have followed the same procedure since I made the first *Lacey*.

"I sometimes get negative reactions on a bear, but being stubborn, I refuse to change it and it still becomes a real favorite, as is.

"On the other hand, I have a couple of bears I personally liked, but others have suggested a mercy killing. HOW RUDE! I still have them here — ugly, but alive and well. In fact, I think I have the only *Luden Cough Drop Bear* in the world. He is the color of a Luden cough drop and his body is shaped just like a very large Luden cough drop. I have never put eyes on him because I don't want him to know what he looks like. I don't think he could forgive me.

"On the other hand, *Gerald* is kinda strange looking. When he was done, we fell to the floor laughing and *Gerald* is our top seller. Of course, he has learned to stand on his head and you know the world loves a clown."

Lori does not exactly design her bears for adults, and is delighted when her critters find their way to children's arms. But adults, especially men, seem to be seduced by them, and this pleases her. She feels that men need teddies.

"The recent popularity of bears, I feel, came about because more men felt that they could collect without generating feelings that are associated with "men who play with toys." They (bears) now have a real history and are highly collectible as antiques and this frees a large segment of collectors, men in particular, to collect bits of history, even if they are teddy bears.

"I am delighted to see grown men and women wanting my bears. My husband, who is a gorilla — 6ft, 3in (109.4cm), 230lbs (104.3kg) — got a teddy bear from me for Valentine's Day this year. I made him a blue bear, from the *Buttons* pattern, and put a Dodger hard hat on him. It is his *Dodger Blue* bear and he took it to work today. He is an executive at a huge international company.

"It never occurred to him that gorillas don't carry teddy bears around. And he gets calls from his main office in San Francisco, from other executives asking where they can see the bears in that area. It appears that bear lovers are really coming out of the closet. He is really proud to own the only *Dodger Blue* bear in town. (By the way, you do know about the baseball team, the Dodgers. I am taking for granted that their fame has reached Maine.)"

Ahem. Dear Lori, the Dodgers were from my home town — they called them "the bums," I recall — a long time before they were from yours. Up here, in New England, however, it is safer to root for the Red Sox.

Lori makes about 30 different bears, but only offers a dozen or fourteen on a regular basis. She has done few limited editions, aimed directly at the adult collector, but those she has done have been popular and appeal to the sentiments.

William, Prince of Wales, a commemorative edition, was one of these — *Rick*, another.

"I enjoy the limited editions," she says, "because you can really let your imagination run rampant. You are not limited by other people's expectations and I delight in surprising people with something they hadn't even thought of. *Rick*, for instance, or *William*, a little Prince of Wales. I had to research the question of rights. Did I have the right to make a bear and offer it under that title? My lawyer thought "yes," as long as it was very limited, homemade and in good taste. Also, the little prince is not the first William, Prince of Wales. There have been several before him. I am still expecting to hear Princess Di let out a howl of protest because I immortalized her baby in bear form. Thank goodness for the press in Europe keeping her busy.

"I'm looking over my shoulder as I approach the end of the edition — only 15 left and then on to another worry. Will

Rick, 12½in (30.5cm) tall. Black velvet bear; gold glass eyes; lashes. Label behind left ear. Music box concealed in his back plays "As Time Goes By." *Rick* wears a white 1940s style dinner jacket; white collar; black bow tie. He stands in a Casablanca-style archway with a handmade fan hanging in the center. He is held by a stand and is standing on a "Persian" rug. A plant (handmade) of green leaves balances him. The floor is shiny "tile." Each setting is marked with a brass plaque which states the number of the bear, the edition and the manufacturer. Signed on folder attached to setting. Produced in 1983. Limited edition of 50. *Photograph by Ken Bannister, courtesy of Lori Gardiner.*

Everett as a clown, 14in (35.6cm). Amber glass eyes; lashes; soft beige fake fur; dressed as a clown with organdy ruff and red decoration; organdy hat with liner, red tassel and red ribbons. Sometimes comes dressed as sailor with sailor hat with blue or red anchor, white collar and red or blue anchors at corners of collar; red tie. Label behind left ear. First made in 1981. *Shana Routhan Collection. Photography by Ken Bannister, courtesy of Lori Gardiner.*

Shannon's First Christmas, 16in (40.6cm). Soft beige fake fur; velvet foot and paw pads; velvet muzzle; amber glass eyes; mink lashes. Label behind left ear. Signed on tag. Red velvet ribbon with moss green ribbons and gold bell. Red and green custom-made bread dough ornament — new one made each year. She can be placed in crawling position or lying on tummy. Has "Mama" cryer. Music box plays "Jingle Bells." Issued each year at Christmas. *Photograph by Ken Bannister, courtesy of Lori Gardiner.*

Pilgrim, 15in (38.1cm). Glass eyes; gray plush; Pilgrim hat with gold buckle; white felt collar; black tie; black belt; gold buttons. Signed on tag. Label behind left ear. Made especially for Pilgrim, a toy store in Monrovia, California. 1983. *Pat Shiner Collection. Photograph by Ken Bannister, courtesy of Lori Gardiner.*

anyone connect Bogart and *Rich*??? Will they care???"

Rick, who takes about ten hours to make, is Lori's most heavily-dressed bear. Usually, clothing is just suggested.

"*Everett,* as a sailor wears a gathered ruff and clown hat. The other bears that have any clothing wear only hats, shawls, vests, and so forth. In other words, anything they might find in their natural habitat. Although, I shudder to think what might have happened to the clothing's original occupant. But, since they can't shop at Sears, they just wear what they find in the forest or my sewing room, and, of course, very little of that.

"It must be obvious that my bears are really little furry people. I never leave sweaters on them if it is too warm and I don't leave them in uncomfortable positions. Yes, I do talk to them."

There is a lot of emotional satisfaction for the California designer, in bear making. "There's something about completing a bear," she says, "when his ears are sewn on and his personality is finally apparent that is completely satisfying to me. I have to set him (or her) up in full view, usually on the antique trunk facing the end of my bed, so I can admire him."

She wants her bears to be just as satisfying to their purchasers.

"A teddy bear is more than a toy. It has gained a reputation over the years for being a great companion. I have tried to offer companions in many different forms. But they have to be more than a stuffed animal to talk to; they also have to be apparently and obviously sympathetic, the face of an interested listener. After all, it wouldn't do any good to tell your problems to a bear that had something else on its mind.

"Early bear makers were forced by society to appeal only to children. It would not have been seemly for an adult to enjoy a toy. Since we have kicked over the traces it is not only o.k., but healthy to let the whole world see that adults still love toys, especially those that evoke memories."

Lori Gardiner is hooked on nostalgia. A world without it would, for her, be unbearable.

TEROL REED

Terol Reed and some of her porcelain designs. 1983. *Photograph courtesy of Terol Reed.*

"If I could use one word to describe my dolls, the way that they look, the way I feel about them, why they are, it would be FANTASY!"

Terol Reed is a Colorado doll artist. Member of ODACA, the Original Doll Artist Council of America, she sculpts visions and dreams: fairies, jesters, children — and teddy bears. All of them combine sculpture and materials in unexpected ways. Her fairy has a "pearlized art nouveau style" hat and wings; its clothing is made from antique millinery. Her jesters are porcelain heads painted with art nouveau designs and flowers, set on dowels, wrapped with ribbon. Their hats are made of cotton velvet, decorated with bells, ribbons and feathers. Her teddy bears are a mixture of porcelain and fur.

She began making bears in 1982 as an offshoot of her doll work. She has designed one original bear at this writing, but he has gone through stages of development. His name is *Jonathan B.* 16in (40.6cm) tall, he has a porcelain masque face and porcelain patent leather shoes/lower legs. The balance of him is what she terms "mingled high quality brown synthetic fur." Fully-jointed, equipped with growler, *Jonathan* wears two different outfits, both quite dressy: a navy blue woolen sailor suit with gold anchor buttons and a red satin tie around his neck, or a reversible velvet vest (solid on one side, flowered on the other) with burgundy satin bow tie. "He's a very sophisticated bear," Terol says.

Jonathan started out with an all-porcelain head, but gradually evolved into a bear with a porcelain masque face, the balance of his head made of synthetic fur. Perhaps this is a result of childhood experiences.

"I got my first teddy bear at seven months on my first Christmas and I still have it," Terol states. "I have one other teddy bear from my childhood, *Teddy Freckles*. He's quite large. He has a masque face, is fully-jointed and growls. This is my favorite. I remember him as being an integral part of my childhood."

In 1983, *Jonathan*'s face evolved into a textured porcelain masque face, using the central section of his old head. The combination of porcelain and fur plays well together. Perhaps this is because of Terol's painting technique.

"I begin with white porcelain and begin to stroke each hair on individually. I use five different colors of brown with a firing between each color which gives a layered depth."

Terol's bear making techniques stem from her doll making, except that she has added plush to her list of materials. But, basically, the skills used are the same. Perhaps her working conditions are a little unusual. "I make my dolls in the kitchen on a high stool with a crying baby hanging on my leg. If I could use one word to describe myself, it would be TIRED!

"The part of doll making that I like best is, of course, sculpting and the painting. These are the areas where my creativity can flow. No matter how many times I paint, or sculpt, I always get a warm feeling inside just thinking about it. I love making dolls, having them and feeling that I have created them."

Her feelings about her ted are similar. "What I enjoy most about making my bears is, as always, all the most creative aspects: the sculpting, the painting, drawing and making the pattern for the body and designing the clothes — implementing the concept — the ideas are so exciting.

"And then there is work involved — making the mold, sanding the porcelain and sewing. I hope I get better at my sewing and change it from a chore to a joy."

Terol's bear is designed as an art object, and has been exhibited in a Glenwood Springs, Colorado, art gallery, as well as at the Denver Museum of Natural History. He is the first of a planned series of bruins. The next will be smaller, about 10in (25.4cm) tall. "This has been one of the most fun endeavors I have undertaken and I can't wait to try some more ideas I have," the doll maker states.

Whatever they are, Terol's ideas are bound to be offbeat and original and her bears are certain to embody ursine fantasy.

Jonathan B. Second version, 1982. 16in (40.6cm) tall. Textured porcelain masque face; balance of head fur-fabric; porcelain lower legs and patent leather shoes; balance "mingled high-quality brown synthetic fur;" fully-jointed; growler; wearing reversible velvet vest (solid on one side, flowered on the other); burgundy satin bow tie. *Photograph courtesy of Terol Reed.*

Jonathan B. Second version, 1982. 16in (40.6cm) tall. Textured porcelain masque face; balance of head fur-fabric; porcelain lower legs and patent leather shoes; balance mingled high-quality brown synthetic fur; fully-jointed; growler. *Photograph courtesy of Terol Reed.*

Jonathan B. First version, 1982. 16in (40.6cm) tall. Porcelain head; porcelain lower legs and patent leather shoes; balance synthetic fur; fully-jointed; growler. *Photograph courtesy of Terol Reed.*

Jonathan B. First version, 1982. 16in (40.6cm) tall. Porcelain head; porcelain lower legs and patent leather shoes; balance synthetic fur; fully-jointed; growler; wearing navy blue woolen sailor suit with gold anchor buttons; red satin tie around neck. *Photograph courtesy of Terol Reed.*

"Teddy Bear time capsules" might be an appropriate description of Marianne Anderson's teddy bear paper dolls. "Each paper doll represents a sentimental spot in my heart and my paper dolls are really a small history of my life, as I have been drawing them since I was very young," she states.

The Oregon artist loves and collects paper dolls, and she still has one of her first paper dolls — one of Queen Holden's bears, cut from a set in the 1930s and 1940s. She made pages of clothes for the bear and colored them with crayons. For years they have been safe, carefully glued into a book.

The summer Marianne was 12 years old, she found a 6in (15.2cm) tall teddy bear in the basement of a house in Canada where she was vacationing. *Samantha*, aka *Sam*, became a favorite. Marianne created an extensive wardrobe for her out of favorite bits and pieces of laces and charms she had collected. Sadly, *Sam* was lost somewhere during a move and her owner hunted far and wide for another bear to take her place. "My good friend, Gladys, gave me a much worn and loved teddy bear and I drew her and drew *Sam*'s clothes as I remembered them so I could keep her forever in my heart. When *Sam II* came to me by mail, she was packed with her head in a paper cup and as I opened the package and took the cup from her head, I actually cried as she has such a sweet face. Although she is not *Sam I*, I know they must have been good friends and I finally feel satisfied again."

Marianne's *Samantha* paper doll is a very personal artistic expression. "When I drew her from my memory, I never planned on showing anyone as she is really a part of my past. She is not drawn for the best reproduction quality — just a labor of love."

Other paper dolls are equally personal. *Mama Prego and Baby Freedom* came about as the hostages were freed from Iran, as Marianne was watching their release. This paper doll set includes a pregnant Mama Bear with tummy flap, maternity clothes, a suitcase, baby basket, baby clothes, a shower gift and birth announcement. And, of course, a cub-in-the-tummy to be cut out, with a back glue-on panel so he can be inserted and removed. All are surrounded on the page by ribbons, which one is instructed to color yellow.

When a new panda was born, the artist drew a new paper doll of the event.

And *Moth Bear* is "a tiny teddy I own and love. He was purchased at a flea market and I've always wished he had moth wings as he is so worn and loved."

Marianne Anderson's paper dolls are busy, full of witty detail and clever ideas. She works in pen and ink, black and white, seldom coloring her work, because she is colorblind. Occasionally, she will use colored pencils or watercolors.

In high school, Marianne majored in art and sewing and took color and composition. By profession, she is a cosmetologist, beautician and manicurist.

Most of the bears she draws are from her collection, as she knows them well. "Bears are very much people to me —dear friends, indeed." Sometimes, though, she invents her characters.

Marianne Anderson and her bears. *Moth Bear* is right, front, next to paper doll page. *Samantha* is next to her. *Photograph courtesy of Marianne Anderson.*

Moth Bear. © 1980. *Courtesy of Marianne Anderson.*

If she had to pick a favorite bear, it would probably be "a small stuffed bear my brother gave me for Christmas when I was about nine years old, during World War II, and we were away from home spending Christmas with my father, who was in the army. My brother was about 13 years old and bought me the bear with his own money."

There is a special, intimate quality to Marianne Anderson's paper dolls. They are drawn with love and exhibit all sorts of fond details and surprises, nifty little things to be cut out and put together and played with.

Perhaps this is a reflection of the circumstances in which they are created. "My paper dolls just happen," she says. Some of the best things in life are serendipitous.

Samantha by Marianne Anderson. Sheet 1. © 1978. *Courtesy of Marianne Anderson.*

Samantha, sheet 2. © 1978. *Courtesy of Marianne Anderson.*

LOIS BECK

Lois Beck once made a 5ft (1.52m) tall bear. *Big Bear* was, truth be told, the product of a bad buy.

Always on the lookout for unusual fabrics for her bear designs, Lois lighted one day upon a bolt of lovely, long-pile beige fake fur. So she bought a wad of it and took it home for experimentation.

Beauty often proves temperamental and the fur fabric was disaster from the start. It was very tightly woven and a challenge (to be euphemistic) to sew, since the presser foot on Lois' sewing machine only came within 1/2in (1.3cm) of the sewing surface. That job completed, Lois discovered that the bear skin was difficult to turn, even at 30in (76.2cm) size. With much stress and sweat, the cub was completed, reflecting none of its birth pains. He soon found a home, and a military career, proudly sporting the medals his new owner pinned to his chest.

Obviously, the long-pile beige fur was not the ticket for bear making, but Lois had so much of it and had paid cold cash for it, so she wanted to use it up. The solution was to use it all for one phenomenal bear. When a collector said, "I'll take it," she cut out a bruiser of a bear, stitched it up and stuffed it. *Big Bear* stood about 5ft (1.52m) tall and was fully-jointed.

Lois wrestled him into the front seat of her car and delivered the critter to the collector at a meeting, where he was a big hit. When it came time for *Big Bear* to go home, it was 10:30pm and he had to be once again wrestled, this time into the collector's car. They made quite a show for passersby, all the way downtown.

Most of Lois Beck's bears are smaller: between 16in (40.6cm) and 18in (45.7cm) tall. They go as small as 6in (15.2cm). Made of many materials and combinations of materials, they are fresh and original in their concepts. Sometimes they sport porcelain faces or hand-painted portrait faces. Fabrics range from fake fur to real fur, as well as mohair. They are always jointed strongly enough for a child to play with.

The Beck menagerie boasts a wide diversity of characters. *String Ben*, a 24in (61cm) bear with long thin arms and legs and *Twin Delight*, a plush bear featuring two porcelain faces: a teddy face with set-in glass eyes and a brown child's face with open mouth and inset teeth are two examples. All Lois' bears, by dint of excellence of construction, and variety of concepts, give evidence to their creator's career as a doll artist.

Lois Beck's bears were among the first of the current generation of artist bears. An offshoot of her doll artist work, Lois' teddies began appearing in 1976 on her sales tables as companions to her original porcelain dolls. As virtually no one in her area was offering original bears, she was soon so swamped with orders that dolls took a back seat.

But they were not forgotten; the techniques and discipline required for doll work were transferred to mixed-media bears.

She designs with the collector in mind, doing different bears for different audiences: various sizes, getups, char-

Lois Beck and Beck bears. *Big Bear* is to the right. *Photograph courtesy of Lois Beck.*

String Ben, 24in (61cm) tall. Fake fur. When he is made of European mohair, he is 18in (45.7cm) tall. Jointed; tagged; red bow. *Photograph courtesy of Lois Beck.*

acters, even mechanical bears. One of her critters turns his head when his tail is waggled. She makes hand puppets and paper dolls and, to date, has probably completed 2000 bears.

Each bruin takes roughly one and a half hours to construct. Any clothing adds to this. Lois is not convinced that clothing adds to the charm of the bear, anyway. Construction time can be cut by assembly-line techniques.

One serendipitous discovery the artist made was that, if she cut her pattern pieces out of felt, they would cling to the plush fabric and she did not need to pin the two together to cut out bear parts.

Lois feels that something would definitely be lost if her bears were commercially produced, indicating that the collector tends to buy a certain "look on the face" of the bear. This is the part she enjoys most, sewing the expressions that bring the bears to life. "Surely completing the face is like bringing out the personality," Lois says. "If the maker does not do the faces individually, him or herself, surely that 'look' is lost. It's like the brushstroke of an artist, a signature."

Lumpkin He and *Lumpkin She*, 18in (45.7cm) tall. Jointed; tagged; fake fur; little tuft of fake fur between ears; sculptured mouth; red bows; bow in hair of girl. *Photograph courtesy of Lois Beck.*

Mrs. Beck paints portraits of children, bears and dolls and restores old oil paintings, old teddies and old dolls when she has time, but she finds that the bears have taken over her production and she has to make space for other artistic outlets.

There is nothing particularly difficult, Lois claims, about making bears.

"I am the eternal optimist so I don't look at any part as being difficult or easy — just a process to an end. The procedure to make them has remained the same. I draw my own pattern from ideas in my head and draw the pieces to go together to create the 'look' I'm striving to achieve," she states. "The bears do not take thought because I've done so many they are pretty much automatic (except the face). I work out of my home. My business could be full-time so by combining it in my home with other duties, I'm busy from 7:00 a.m. to 11:00 p.m. I do have a girl who cuts and sews for me and a daughter who helps."

Beck bears are made from many materials. Lois started with fake fur and leather paws, then switched to felt for paws. "As the field of makers increased," she states, "I also added wool and mohair (new and old), real fur...then was able to get some gold half-mohair from Europe. I used felt for paws on the wool and mohair and on the half-mohair bears. Real fur bears will be found with both felt and leather paws."

Beck bears are labeled with a tag sewn into the back reading, "LOIS BECK ORIGINAL," and the date.

Mrs. Beck is a member of the Good Bears of the World, but does not enter competitions of any kind nor exhibit her

Wilbur, 18in (45.7cm) tall. Fake fur; jointed; tagged; knit sweater and hat; glued-on papier-mâché boots. *Photograph courtesy of Lois Beck.*

bears except at shows. She advertises in national bear magazines and *The Doll Catalog* and is listed in the *Teddy Bear Lovers Catalog* and *The Teddy Bear Catalog*. This has evolved into a mail-order business, with both commercial and private customers in the United States and abroad.

"I receive my satisfaction from the enjoyment the collectors gain from the different 'looks' and bears I produce," the Washington State artist says. She has no favorites among her bears. "I enjoy all of them," Lois says. But she has never made another bear 5ft (1.52m) tall.

Baby Bear, 12in (30.5cm) bear. Fake fur; jointed; cryer. Tag reads, "LOIS BECK ORIGINAL" — year. Wears diaper. If sold at Christmas time, the diaper was red. *Photograph courtesy of Lois Beck.*

Jester Bear, 18in (45.7cm) tall. Fake fur; jointed; tagged; shoe-button eyes; jester costume; felt hat; neck ruff. *Photograph courtesy of Lois Beck.*

Night Guardian, oil painting by Lois Beck. 12in (30.5cm) x 18in (45.7cm). *Photograph courtesy of Lois Beck.*

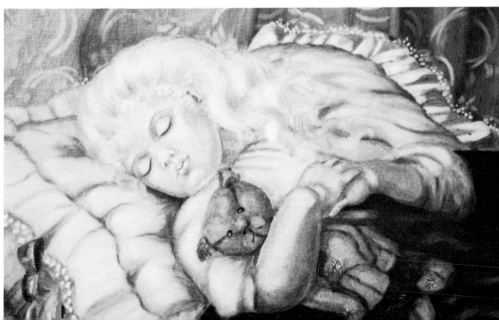

REBECCA IVERSON

Rebecca Iverson with a selection of her bears. *Photograph by W. Barry Iverson, courtesy of Rebecca Iverson.*

"Rebecca Iverson • Needlesmith. This card accompanies each of Rebecca Iverson's bears. *Courtesy of Rebecca Iverson.*

Rebecca Iverson calls herself a "needlesmith." A fiber artist who specializes in cloth dolls with distinctive hand-painted faces, she began designing bears as an adjunct to them in 1978. "It was a natural progression to transfer the technique of hand-painted faces from dolls to bears. I was curious to see the effect — if it would work," she says.

Rebecca's dolls are unusual. She calls them "primary all-cloth dolls." Gentle, slightly attenuated, with wistful, introspective expressions on their sometimes needle-modeled faces, they seem visitors from another world — a parallel world where all is peaceful, like the one often depicted in illustrations in certain children's books. Indeed, this may be their provenance.

"My bears," says the Wisconsin artist, "are an outgrowth of REAL bears, my dolls and illustrations from old children's books. I also wanted bears for my dolls to hold. A cloth bear seemed a natural match for the cloth doll."

More doll than ted, Iverson bears are made of atypical unbearlike combinations of materials that somehow complement each other. Some are velour, some velvet, felt or even corduroy. This is usually combined with a hand-painted leather face, sometimes leather (or deerskin) ears and/or foot pads. Their limbs are jointed. Shapes vary, but seem more doll-like than bear-like (in the tradition of both animal dolls and the critters in juvenile book illustrations), and they love to wear clothes. In fact, Rebecca does not refer to her bears as teddies. She calls them "bear-like figures," or "bear

Christopher Robin, 10in (22.9cm) and *Friend*, 4in (10.2cm). All-cloth "primary dolls." January 1980. *Photograph by Rebecca Iverson.*

dolls." She says, "I strive to make appealing, well-formed, bear-like figures, each with a 'presence' of its own."

It is hard to say which comes first, the clothing or the bear. Rebecca describes the way she designs her creations:

Velvet Bear, 12in (30cm). Old velvet, brown with golden highlights, complementing the deerskin foot pads and hand-painted face. One made. 1983. *Photograph by W. Barry Iverson, courtesy of Rebecca Iverson.*

"My procedure is to visualize a bear, invent a pattern, make up the bear (sew), and then make changes until it's something I like, (not always what I'd initially visualized). Sometimes the clothing idea comes first and I design a bear to fit the concept; sometimes I costume a bear. The clothing makes the bears seem playful or dignified or reserved (etc.). It adds to their personalities much as our clothing does to ours. I enjoy outlandish un-bear costumes: roller skates and ballet slippers, tutus, lace collars and bonnets."

Her favorites are the highly-costumed ones. "I enjoy *Tessie*," Rebecca says, "because I like costuming her."

Their distinctive hand-painted (mostly) leather faces evolved slowly, with experimentation. Sometimes feedback from customers proved instructive. "I began making cloth bears with flat hand-painted cloth faces. The newest bears are cloth with dimensional (with a muzzle) painted leather faces or dimensional cloth or felt faces. When I was making my first flat-painted-face bears, I had people too often asking, 'What are they, bears or cats?' One woman approached me with (what I thought would be) the usual question. She asked, 'Oh! What are they, CATS OR DOGS?' This made me re-evaluate and come up with the current muzzle-like face."

The muzzle-like face, using a different medium from the rest of the bear, may have its origins in memories of one of Rebecca's childhood companions. "I've always loved both dolls and bears. *Algy* (so named because he was BIO-ALLERGENIC!) had a charming molded vinyl face and I loved him in spite of his yellow and aqua plush body. Several years ago I made a new body for him of brown corduroy and he's living with a young friend. Collectors will be aghast, but aqua was never his color."

Bears often go through stages in design, sometimes ending with unexpected personas, as Rebecca works. "My first bear was *Ted*. He evolved into a sitting bear with a muzzle (no longer made). *Little Bear* went through four or five versions and gradually became *Benjamin*. My early *Roosevelt* has become my *Honey Bear*."

Possessor of a B.S. art degree, Rebecca is an accomplished artist in other media. She once took a year off and designed and made unusual quilts combining trapunto, embroidery and quilting. Her drawings are simply delightful. Occasionally, she designs original paper dolls and she has drawn one especially for this book. Her work is brimful with good humor and whimsy, and she feels that its many aspects are "all extremely inter-related and constantly add to each other."

Bear making is a learning process for Rebecca. "I'm constantly 'starting all over' each time I begin a new bear. I love CLOTH and prefer it. I'd like to try wool mohair. My bears are didactic in that I learn from them while I make them! Most I enjoy working out a new concept and pattern, because of the excitement, suspense and challenge involved. Least pleasurable would be making 'production line bears' so I don't." Every Iverson bear, even if nominally a part of a series, is one-of-a-kind.

The artist currently spends about 25 percent of her time at bear making. "The time spent varies with bear demand."

Tessie Bear, 13in (33cm). Gold velour; leather foot pads; hand-painted face; co-ordinating brown and gold calico dress, bonnet and its lining; ribbon and old lace trim. One made. 1983. *Photograph by W. Barry Iverson, courtesy of Rebecca Iverson.*

Sleepy Baby Bear, 5in (12.7cm). Tan wool felt; leather ears and foot pads; hand-painted cloth face; unbleached muslin christening gown and bonnet trimmed with ribbon and old lace. He sleeps on a pastel blue calico quilt. One made. 1983. *Photograph courtesy of Rebecca Iverson.*

She does not forsee commercial production of her designs. "Given today's 'common' standards of quality and materials, I would find it difficult to have my bears commercially produced. 'Quality control' could make it a possibility."

Bears are signed on the bottom of the left foot:

REBECCA IVERSON

© date

The doll artist describes her work and her intended audience: "The bears are sturdy enough for play. They are unique, creatively conceived, and made in small numbers, which makes them appealing to collectors looking for hand-made originals, or persons in search of fine toys."

Rebecca Iverson, needlesmith, thinks of her bear-dolls as "personalities with character." When asked what is the most appealing part of her process, she replies, "I enjoy dreaming up an idea and then holding the reality in my hand." Their hand-painted faces and unusual combinations of media make Iverson bears stand out in any collection. It is fortunate that Rebecca's dreams and their reality mesh so pleasurably.

Rebecca Iverson holding *Honey Bear. Photograph by W. Barry Iverson, courtesy of Rebecca Iverson.*

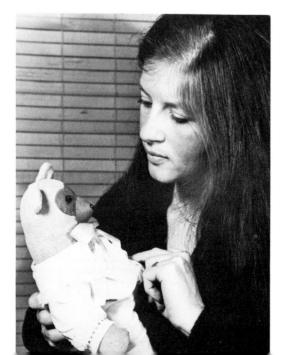

Honey Bear, 13in (33cm) and his pine pony. White percale shirt trimmed with pearl buttons, laces and ribbon embroidered with pink, green and blue; pale blue neck bow matching his panne velvet pants; white cotton stockings; black-ribboned slippers of patent leather. The pine pony was made by W. Barry Iverson. One made. 1982. *Photograph by W. Barry Iverson, courtesy of Rebecca Iverson.*

Early *Tessie Bear,* 13in (33cm). Beige corduroy with a hand-painted face; pink taffeta dress; bonnet trimmed with pink ribbon and old laces in shades of ecru; hand-knit pink sweater. All *Tessie Bears* are different fabrics and colors and have varied costumes. Begun 1980. Less than 12 made. *Photograph by W. Barry Iverson, courtesy of Rebecca Iverson.*

PENNY NOBLE

"I just love my bears!"

Penny Noble's enthusiasm for her teddy bears is infectious. These vivacious, mischievous characters seem to spill from her fingertips, in just about every bear making medium imaginable. Clay, fiber, metal and paper all have been turned into bears, almost as rapidly as Cinderella's pumpkin turned into a coach.

From an artistic family, trained in advertising design, Penny is well-versed in many artistic media and seems to have plunged head first into a vat of them and come up with fistfuls of teddies.

A doll artist, miniaturist and bear collector, Penny started, in January 1983, applying her talents and enthusiasm to teds as an experiment. "I began to make them to prove I could and they turned out to my satisfaction so I wanted to share them, and give other people the pleasure they gave me," she says.

The operative word is "pleasure," for Penny obviously derives joy from her work. And it shows.

Her first modeled bears, made of Sculpey, (a low-fire synthetic clay compound) view the world with self-satisfied mischievous miens. Derived from dolls, they usually combine sculpted heads and limbs with posable stuffed bodies. Approximately 4in (10.2cm) tall, these character critters are just right for doll houses, miniature settings or any place else.

All share their maker's humor and energy. She concentrates on fabric bruins, which generally stand 11in (27.9cm) high. "I enjoy the cloth, mainly because they are the most creative for me," she says. "I like looking for different fabrics and wonderful furs. I also like looking for accessories and accent pieces for the bears. My designing is simple. I tend to find the fabric or fur first, then the ideas just seem to come."

Indeed they do. Penny's 11in (27.9cm) bears range from *Terry Beary, the Fairy Bear*, made of plush, to *Delma*, who is sewn from violet wool, with purple pads and a straw hat.

Penny Noble and her bears. 1983. *Photograph courtesy of Penny Noble.*

Delma, 11in (27.9cm) tall. Violet wool; purple pads; straw hat with small silk daisies; cotton fabric shawl; lace trim; white pearl button heart at her neck. She is named after Delma Peery, who owns "Wind Bells Cottage." Delma loves purple, thus a purple bear. Edition of 25. 1983. *Photograph courtesy of Penny Noble.*

Penny's doll house-scale bears. Sculpy heads, hands (arms) and legs; cloth bodies. Approximately 4in (10.2cm) tall. First bear is in pajamas, holding felt bear. Second is *Daddy Bear* wearing green coat, brown check pants, gold buttons. *Mom Bear* wears flowered dress with white apron and bonnet. *Santa Bear* is last; velvet red pants, red knit shirt, rosebud pillow and removable beard, velvet hat with fur trim. 1983. *Photograph courtesy of Penny Noble.*

Terry Beary, the Fairy Bear, 11in (27.9cm) tall. Yellow acrylic fur; yellow and orange silk flowers. Named for Penny's sister, Terry, whom she used to call "Terry Beary." Edition of 25. 1983. *Photograph courtesy of Penny Noble.*

Wilson, 11in (27.9cm) tall. White fur; tan pads and feet; red felt vest overstitched with black stitching; gold buttons; dark green satin ribbon. Limited edition of 25. 1983. *Photograph courtesy of Penny Noble.*

She ranks high on my list right beside a gent called *Wilson,* of white fur with tan pads and feet. He wears a red felt vest.

All are christened for special people. "I tend to name my bears after friends and members of my family," she says. "*Garnet* is named after my mother and is a garnet stone color. *Delma* is after my friend, Delma, that has a wonderful bear and antique shop and adores purple, thus *Delma* is a purple bear. My neighbors helped me name some of them and I have a teddy named *Terry Beary, the Fairy Bear.* We used to call my sister, Terry Beary. Around Christmas there will be a *Nicholas* and *Noell Bear* after my children."

Most of her cloth bears are done in limited editions of 25. "I don't tend to totally dress my bears," she says. "I love laces and trims. Hats and lockets also change the bear's personality." Each is marked with a tiny penny — sewn to its chest. These bears are intended for collectors; Penny does not use safety eyes or washable fabrics.

Collectors are the audience she seeks with all her work, whether in three dimensions or two.

Penny's acrylic paintings of bears, approximately 11 by 14in (27.9cm by 35.6cm), range from family portraits to lively character pieces.

Her sculpted bears, though, to me, have the most pizzazz. Whether they are clay, stationary, cavorting in perpetuity atop music boxes or are cast metal with movable limbs, these teds transmit an infectious liveliness.

Few bear makers work with metal. Penny explains the origin of her metal teddies. "My metal bears were first made of Sculpey. I met a man, George Smith, of Hawthorne, California, who did metal castings. We worked together and perfected my small flocked metal bear. The bear is held together with elastic and then glued together. I paint it first with metal primer, then acrylic paint, flocking and finally put it together. The one that isn't flocked is similar in technique. I dress them in many ways: ballerinas, clowns, bows, vest, skirts, etc. Their names are *George* or *Georgina.*"

Every bear is named. "Of course they are people," Penny says. "But special people. They don't talk back and are good listeners. My philosophy of bear making is to make a wonderful bear with a great personality and charm that is contagious."

She succeeds in so doing. Maybe it is because Penny Noble loves her bears.

Metal bear, 1¾in (4.5cm) tall. Jointed at arms and legs with wire; heavy; painted brown; blue coat. 1983.

Motley, 11in (27.9cm) tall. Brownish gray fabric; beige wool pads and feet; red plaid scarf; gold teddy bear stick pin. Limited edition of 25. 1983. *Photograph courtesy of Penny Noble.*

Flocked metal bear, 1¾in (4.5cm) tall. Jointed at arms, legs and head; brown flocking over metal; red ribbon at neck. 1983.

Top of music box. Tan bears on brass bicycle. Bears are made of Super Sculpy, as is pad. Small brown paper lunch sack. 1983. *Photograph courtesy of Penny Noble.*

Sandy Williams sewing a 2in (5.1cm) bear. *Photograph courtesy of Sandy Williams.*

The bear world is relatively new to Sandy Williams. For years she has lived with dolls. The Washington, D.C.-area artist's name and work are well-known to doll collectors. Her paper dolls, patterns for making cloth dolls and her dressing old and new dolls highlight many issues of *Doll Reader*™ magazine. She has also designed doll giftwrap.

Dolls were her first love. She had no teddy as a child. A pair of dolls were her companions; she began her doll making career fashioning fanciful clothing for them. "I had two dolls that I kept designing and sewing clothes for," she says, "even to the extent of removing the larger doll's wig and gluing white yarn, strand by strand, on her head in a colonial hairdo to go along with a new period dress that I had sewn for her."

Bears had to wait until Sandy grew up. "When my first boy was born," she says, "he received a teddy bear as a gift. That started me looking for teddies (which were rather scarce to find) and making teddies from patterns. Most of the patterns I made up I did not care for (for one reason or another) as they turned out too skinny, neck too long, head too narrow, so I began designing my own from 1in (2.5cm) jointed ones to my favorite teddies of 11½in (29.2cm) tall."

Sandy's teddies are heirs of her skills as a doll couturiere. They are furry fashion plates. She calls them *Bearsons*, recreating, with them, legendary characters in teddy bear form.

Madame de Pompabear seems the most direct descendant of her childhood efforts. Designed in 1982, she has a tan fur head, paws and feet, tan ultrasuede inner ears and foot soles. Her head flirtingly tilts to one side. Dressed in a pink moire gown trimmed with ivory lace and pink satin ribbons, she lacks the plump tummy of Sandy's other bears. Instead, a somewhat tapered waistline is pushed in by a moire satin "stomacher." Her low neckline, adorned by blue flowers, covers a modest swelling bosom. White muslin lace-trimmed "pantalettes" form her legs which end in largish tan fur feet.

Madame de Pompabear, 11½in (29.2cm). Photograph courtesy of Sandy Williams.

All of the *Bearsons* are constructed with clothing as an integral part of their bodies. Usually the only "bear fur" skin showing is head, paws and feet. They stand and pose well, but are not jointed. Rather, the edges of the legs and arms are sewn into the bodies, affording limited movement.

Robin'Bear, designed in 1982, is constructed in this way. His body and arms are made of forest green velour. His vest and hat (with a green feather) are rust suede. On his back perches a suede quiver.

Santa Claws' body is berry red velour trimmed with white fur. Black satin boots form "feet." He carries a canvas sack. Like all of the *Bearsons*, he is identified with a cloth label with Sandy's name printed in blue, sewn into his center back seam.

Most ubiquitous of Sandy's bears are her ultrasuede critters. She describes them.

"These tiny ultrasuede teddies are completely handsewn with tiny stitches, approximately 28 per inch (2.5cm). They are jointed at the shoulders and hips. Usually a red silk ribbon with a big bow is tied around their necks. The tiny bears come in tan, white and dark brown.

"I started making the small bears in felt but found that even though I was using the same pattern over and over again, each bear turned out to be a different size. The reason was that felt manufactured today is much thinner and more subject to stretching (resulting in a rather fat, distorted bear) than the thicker felt of yesterday. Finally, I gave up making bears in felt and now prefer to sew them in ultrasuede, instead."

Robin Bear, 11½in (29.2cm). *Photograph courtesy of Sandy Williams.*

Miniature bear making offers one big advantage. "All of my tiny bear making supplies are easily carried around in an old straw purse, ready to be brought out at a moment's notice."

In all her work, Sandy Williams' skills as a cloth doll designer are evident. A flair for materials and a touch of whimsy help her teddies bridge the gap between doll and bear. A little of both, they live in the best of both worlds.

Sandy Williams sewing 2in (2.5cm) jointed bear. *Photograph courtesy of Sandy Williams.*

Santa Claws, 11½in (29.2cm). *Photograph courtesy of Sandy Williams.*

2in (5.1cm) jointed bear by Sandy Williams.

1in (2.5cm) jointed bear by Sandy Williams. *Photograph courtesy of Sandy Williams.*

THE MEREART BEARS

(Suzy Stewart and JoAnna Meredith)

Suzy Stewart (left) and JoAnna Meredith (right) with Mereart bears. *Photograph courtesy of Mereart Bears.*

Bear makers derive insbearation from the strangest places. In the case of Suzy Stewart and JoAnna Meredith, producers of the Mereart (pronounced Merry-Art) bears, it came from an old stuffed monkey.

The sisters, who are bear collectors, played around in early 1982 with the idea of designing an original bear. After buying a book and learning the basics of bear making, they began to search for a calling card — an idea that would make their work immediately recognizable.

About this time, the novice bear makers chanced upon an old stuffed monkey made of mohair and velveteen with painted sleep eyes and nose. The monkey was "nothing at all like our bears we make today," Suzy Stewart explains. "But, we realized that we had not seen bears with painted eyes on the market so we proceeded in that direction and copyrighted our design."

They chose the name Mereart for their product as it is a combination of the names MEREdith and StewART.

Both Texas natives have degrees in art and education. In addition, Suzy is a wildlife artist. They have worked in many art media, mostly two-dimensional, but the bears are their first three-dimensional soft-sculpture, a logical extension of their talents and inclinations.

Collectors themselves, the sisters are highly attuned to desirable bear qualities and they aim to produce bears with the high standards they admire.

"We were aiming at the collector market, but we seem to appeal to a variety of buyers," JoAnna reports. "We want our bears to be well made, durable, professional looking, with high quality materials — a bear we ourselves would buy."

Suzy and JoAnna divide up the bear making tasks, each contributing her strengths. "We have both shared in the design and the construction of the bears, JoAnna working with pattern design and Suzy with the hand-painting of

features. We like making the bears with hand-painted features because each one comes out a little different and seems to take on its own personality," they explain.

Mereart bears with acrylic-painted features are instantly recognizable. Their bodies are made of high quality plush fur fabric with velveteen trim and faces. However, Mereart also produces a traditional bear with glass eyes.

Some of the sisters' favorites include an almost blonde mink-like fabric bear with matching velveteen paws and face. Its eyes are turquoise to brown color. Another special bear is of shaggy red fur fabric with a clipped muzzle and glass eyes.

After working in sizes from 3in (7.6cm) to 34in (86.4cm), the team has settled on a 17in (43.2cm) bear, which "seems to be a nice size to handle and display." They are constructed in sections: head, body, limbs, on a sewing machine. The actual assembly is done by hand, as are the joints (wood and metal discs, and cotter pins).

It took some time, however, to perfect the current model. "Our first attempts at bear making turned out rather funny, with heads anywhere from weasel shape to E.T.," Suzy Stewart explains. "One of the most amusing things happened at a doll show. Our display was totally bears that we had made. We had a family grouping dressed as *Papa, Mama* and *Baby*, and we overheard a mother explaining to her small child, 'I think they are beavers!' "

There is no mistaking bears for beavers anymore. Mereart bears have reached and appealed to their target audience, the adult collector. The bear makers report: "It is interesting to us that of all the bears we have sold personally, only a very few have been for children. One couple bought a bear for him, a bear for her, and one for each of their mothers. Another couple, he the bear collector, she a doll collector, proceeded to have a rather animated discussion about his bears and her dolls and if she would buy him a bear, he would buy her a doll. Another lady purchased a bear to act as a guard to her doll collection. Still another lady bought

Mereart bears, both 17in (43.2cm) tall. Fully-jointed; plush fake fur. 1983. *Photograph courtesy of Mereart Bears.*

Mereart bear, 17in (43.2cm) tall. Jointed; fake-fur; trimmed muzzle. *Photograph courtesy of Mereart Bear.*

Bearlin, the Magician. Fully-jointed white plush; velvet wizard's garment; peaked hat. 1984. *Photograph courtesy of Mereart Bears.*

Mereart bears: *Bear Lancelot* and *Ex Calibear.* Fully-jointed; plush; medieval knight costumes. 1984. *Photograph courtesy of Mereart Bears.*

Bearilyn, 17in (43.2cm) tall. Fully-jointed; white plush; painted face and paws; fake eyelashes; satin gown with brooch; marabou boa; earrings. 1984. *Photograph courtesy of Mereart Bears.*

a whole set: *Mama, Papa, Baby,* for her daughter, who turned out to be a college coed."

The sisters are only part-time bear makers, as Suzy is a full-time artist and JoAnna, a teacher, but they have not considered having their designs commercially duplicated. "In our case," they explain, "it would be difficult, if not impossible, to reproduce the features. The most esthetic effect (of the bears) is that they are different. They seem to speak to you with their eyes and appeal to you to pick them up and love them."

So the bear makers work at their own pace, producing "three bears tops" a day, ensuring that, by dint of quality and limited production (the bears are signed, dated and numbered), Mereart bears will be treasured collectibles. They are represented by Eric Hahn and Associates of Texas, who wholesales their work — all they can make. It is a good thing Suzy and JoAnna enjoy working together. With two full-time careers each, the sisters have little free time to "Monkey Around."

MARGORY HOYA NOVAK

Margory Hoya Novak with some of her bears. 1984. *Photograph courtesy of Margory Novak.*

When Margory Hoya Novak told me she was designing original teddy bears, I was surprised and pleased. This meant we would have one more thing to share.

"Sharing" is an apt word to describe my California friend. In the decade I have known her, she has sprinkled the world with love and optimism, eliciting the best from those she encounters. This is the goal she sets for her bears. Marg intends to use them in a new career as a psychologist dealing with terminally ill patients, and hopes that "teddy bear therapy" will help ease her clients' stress and strain. "Eventually, when I get into practice," she says, "I want to be able to use the bears to help people to feel cuddled and loved, to be able to talk to the bears if they can't talk to people."

To reach this goal, at the halfway point in her life, the doll-artist-turned-bear-artist has returned to school, studying with students young enough to be her children, and enjoying every moment of it, as is her style. Sonoma State University reaps the benefits of her presence. And the bears are helping to pay her tuition.

We met at our first doll convention, in Reno, Nevada, in 1973 — a peculiar place to begin a bicoastal friendship. Neophyte doll artists, we discovered together, and separately, the rites of porcelain doll making, sharing our findings via Ma Bell. Eventually, we joined ODACA, the Original Doll Artist Council of America, under whose aegis we displayed our work. I always thought Marg's dolls were delightful. They somehow managed to capture her spirit.

Someone once said that every ten years you are another person. Ten years down the road from Reno, Marg is on her way, with one foot still in the doll world. She is designing dolls for a commercial firm, but has put production work on a back burner, concentrating, instead, on school and BEARS.

Marg has the knack of rapidly internalizing craft techniques, and has taught over 120 different art and craft related subjects for about 15 years in San Rafael, California. When she decided it was time for teddy bears, the aptitude and attitude were well-honed for production. Typically, her methods and materials are a bit offbeat.

"I began with real lamb fur in brown and off-white," she says. "They are all hand-sewn because the leather is so thick. The bears are sturdy and the fur is soft. It takes about three days to make one bear and my hands do take a beating when I have completed it. I use fish line to sew with."

As in any Novak designs, sources for inspiration are unusual. "What inspired me was the real fur that I use; it is so soft and cuddly. I used my dog, Chou-Chou, as a model for the bear's legs. I kept drawing a design, cutting the pattern, using some old material as a model, sewing and stuffing until I finally was satisfied with my design."

Novak bears range from 10 to 20in (25.4 to 50.8cm) in height, and are cut from the two shades of fur. "The fur," Marg says, "can be cleaned with a foam canned dog shampoo. So they can be played with. They are very sturdy."

Some have music boxes; all have growlers. Their distinctive long snouts give them "a very shy, bashful, baby look." All are identified with a leather tag on the back side.

Besides her basic bear, Marg makes character bears.

"I do a *Patches Bear* that is entirely made of patchwork design, also a *Santa Bear* and a *Jester Bear*." But, for the future psychologist, her first teds are the ones with personality.

"The real fur bears are my favorite. The brown ones are named *Lambeart* and the off-white ones are named *Woolsley*. Their last name is *Woolington* and they live on Hob Nob Hill in San Francisco. I am writing some children's

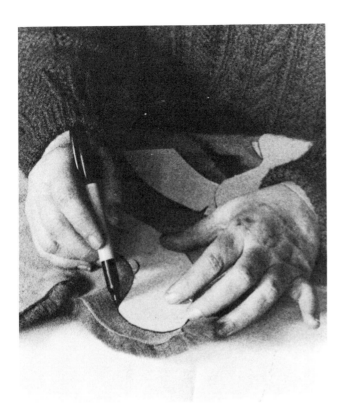

Marg Novak tracing bear body pattern onto lamb fur. *Photograph courtesy of Margory Novak.*

Marg Novak hand-stitching lambskin bear body sections with fish line. *Photograph courtesy of Margory Novak.*

books about the adventures that the *Woolington* bears have together in San Francisco. These bears are alive to me and they help people to respond and bring out the magical fun child in themselves."

Like the bears, the books will have a gentle, didactic purpose: to teach children to be positive thinkers. Marg remembers how, when she was young, bears and stories played an important part in her development.

"I liked bears as a child but there were not many of them around during World War II. I had only one favorite bear and it was a panda. I was about ten years old when I got him and I loved to cuddle with him. He was so soft and had the most beautiful loving face I had ever seen. He was easy to talk to and I told him all my stories."

It is this quality of trustfulness and ursine approachability that Marg intends to utilize in her work. "I think that teddy bears represent the need to hug and be hugged. It is a simple means of communication between people bringing lots of joy and laughter. The time is right for this as people are so serious and need props to help relieve stress and tension. What better way to relieve stress and tension but to hug your teddy?"

She has encountered numerous testimonies to the healing power bears embody, for grownups as well as children, and recounts this story: "One doctor told me that he has a collection of over 40 bears and recently when he was hospitalized for several weeks, he had his wife bring two of his favorite bears to stay with him in the hospital so he wouldn't get lonesome. He said his wife was rather embarrassed as she worked as a nurse at that hospital and she didn't want her friends to see her hubby there with his friendly childhood bears."

Lambeart, 20in (50.8cm). Brown lamb's fur; jointed at neck, shoulders and hips; hump on back; growler. Novak bears tend to be shy. 1984. *Photograph courtesy of Margory Novak.*

Though she has just started her bear making career, Marg Novak is already sharing, through teddies, her love and optimism with the world. "It is turning out that people have a real love affair with the bears and the communication between bears and people is open, warm and loving," she reports. "I like the connection that it makes between people. The bears are so cuddly and adorable that people can't help but pick them up and hold them. I'm in love with the work that I do and I love to share the love with others."

As her bears reach out and touch her patients, there will be many more who, like me, are pleased that Marg Novak has chosen something special to share.

Jester Bear. Fully-jointed; jester suit part of bear's body. 1984. *Photograph courtesy of Margory Novak.*

Santa Bear. Fully-jointed; Santa suit part of bear's body. 1984. *Photograph courtesy of Margory Novak.*

Woolsley, 10in (25.4cm). Off-white lambskin; jointed at neck, shoulders and hips; hump on back; leather nose. 1984. *Photograph courtesy of Margory Novak.*

82

MARIA KWONG

Maria Kwong's card. *Courtesy of Maria Kwong.*

Before original bear artists proliferated, Maria Kwong was one. Her business card reads: "Maria Kwong Bears. Since 1971." To date, she has produced over 4000 handmade bears.

Maria's bear making evolved naturally. Both her parents are artists. Her mother encouraged her, at age 13, to design a line of original cloth dolls. These proved so successful they appeared in gallery shows and were used in two books by noted fiber-arts chronicler Jean Ray Laury.

The young designer's first bear making foray built upon this foundation occurred in 1964, when, as a gift for her sister, she improved upon a commercial teddy bear pattern.

"I...modified the features and shape of the pattern... Periodically (the bear's) flannel skin would wear out, and after the patches were patched, the time would come for a new skin.

"The transformation would occur on Christmas Eve, when (bear) would disappear from his owner's bed and reappear under the Christmas tree with his old skin neatly stuffed inside his new one. I think he is in his third skin.

"After awhile, his life became a bit quieter. He is, however, a very well-traveled bear. He even went to Smith College."

In 1970, the discovery of Peter Bull's *Teddy Bear Book* changed a sometime bearish outlook to an obsession and a profession.

"Bears didn't really come into my life until 1970 when I read Peter Bull's *Teddy Bear Book*. I had a panda and a koala which survived my childhood, but I had no REAL teddy bear. That same year I sent for my first bear, a 10in (25.4cm) Steiff from F.A.O. Schwarz. Between Hershel's arrival and Peter Bull's book, my future in bears was sealed.

"On my 19th birthday my friend Beverly gave me a bear kit from the London Design Centre. After carefully following the pattern on the first bear, I started improvising a series of bears for friends and family. The first bears traveled as far as Bali and Ireland. If I met new people that I liked, I would send them a bear as a reminder of our meeting. My mother used to say that what I couldn't express in conversation, I would put into a bear."

Kwong bears have a distinctive body language. They seem to express and embody all sorts of ideas and sentiments through the magic of, basically, the way they are "dressed." But the original bears were bare, descendants of the original 1964 bear.

Maria Kwong wearing T-shirt designed by Gary van der Steur. *Ursula* bear sits in background. She is a life-size velveteen bear Maria Kwong made in 1979. *Photograph courtesy of Maria Kwong.*

"The bear that started me off in 1971 was a 3in (7.6cm) high standing bear made of felt. For many years that was the only kind of bear that I made.

"I moved from 3in (7.6cm) to 10in (25.4cm) around 1974 and then made a 5ft (1.52m) bear in 1978. The 5ft (1.52m) bear started me using velveteen. It was also the first bear that I did not sew completely by hand."

Gradually, Maria's bears began to evolve into art concepts. She considered them not only as bears, but as conveyers of ideas. They were developing into sculptural statements.

"In 1978, I started a project intended as a fine art piece. It was a calendar, a personal diary depicted in bears. I made a different 3in (7.6cm) bear for every day of that year. They were decorated or embellished according to what happened (or didn't) to me that day. The resulting collection of bears were exhibited by the month in plexiglass cases. The exhibit appeared at the Barnsdall Municipal Gallery in Los Angeles, California, in December of 1978. Each week in December I would add new bears. The piece was shown on the CBS news with Ralph Story as the interviewer. It was after that TV spot that I started on the line of bears that I am most well-known for today."

Maria sold out of 11 of the 12 months. She kept October. She and her husband met in October that year.

Interest in Maria's work grew, "But only if it had to do with bears," she says. This was before bears had achieved their current popularity. But her bears were time-consuming to produce and the market was limited, so she needed to come up with an idea that would grab the public imagination.

"Eventually I came up with the idea of making a bear one could wear. I shrank my bears down to 2in (5.1cm) and put pins and ribbons onto them so they could be worn as

20in (50.8cm) velveteen bear with 14in (35.6cm) Jr. velveteen bear. Stock item sewn by machine and assembled by hand. Not jointed; embroidered faces; velveteen noses; felt paw pads; hand-stitched on larger bear; machine stitched on smaller; light brown, dark brown, rust or charcoal velveteen; polyester stuffing. Marked with red felt heart with the letter "M" embroidered on it. Heart is appliqued on left side of chest and does not show in illustration. *Photograph courtesy of Maria Kwong.*

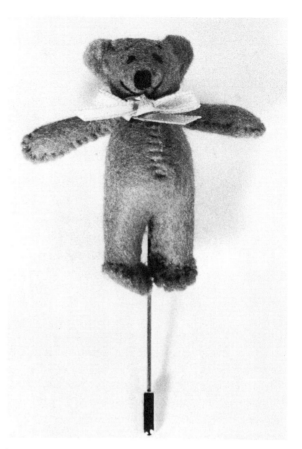

Stickpin Bear. Stock item in assortment of colors. Handmade, hand-stitched felt. Size: 2in (5.1cm) bear alone. This bear is red, but they are made in dark brown, light brown, gold, rust, red, orange, yellow, green, blue, purple, light pink, lavendar and turquoise. *Photograph courtesy of Maria Kwong.*

jewelry. I dressed some as ballerinas and superbears and left some bare, and, voila, Bearware was born!"

The Bearware bears include stickpins, fancy and embroidered designs, neckpieces, regular pins and all sorts of inspired "regular" bears. But there is nothing usual about any of them. They feature bright colors, a lovely sense of design, a dollop of whimsy and an inspired incongruity that gets to the basics of bearness. Most of them are felt.

"My original medium was felt, but I have also started using cotton velveteen for larger bears. I like my bears to have a sort of sculptural smooth look. I want them to maintain the tactile quality of a warm, fuzzy fabric."

Designs include silk flowers with bear faces peeking out of the centers, rainbow neckpieces consisting of six rainbow-hued bears on a black velvet cord (which also double as belts), baby bears dressed in Dr. Dentons with embroidered or appliqued bibs or bears with decorated shirts. Bear colors are bright: regular bear colors, certainly, but also lavender, purple, red, orange, yellow, green, blue and pink. The light pink bear has dark pink embroidered facial features. All others are done in black. The larger, 14in or 20in (35.6cm or 50.8cm) cotton velveteen bears are, of course, much harder to wear. They prefer to be hugged.

Kwong bears require extensive handwork. The felt bears, the majority of her output, must be entirely handmade.

"What I like most about my work is that it uses the simplest of tools and materials. Except for the larger bears which have to be sewn by machine, my work is extremely portable. Needles, thread (I only use DMC embroidery floss split into single strands; it is the best for color stability and strength, and it seems to meld with the felt fibers, unlike polyester blend threads), sharp scissors and large bobby pins for stuffers all fit in a small plastic bag full of bits of felt and can be carried anywhere in my purse. I even work in the car if we are driving for any length of time."

But, one bear maker can only do so many handmade felt bears. Maria has hired some helpers for production bears, ones who will keep her quality high. She would never have her work mass-produced. "This has come up more than once and I have always been somewhat relieved that such plans have not been realized. I think there are artists and designers who have made successful compromises, but there always seems to be something lost in the commercialization of a bear. One of the problems with mass producing my bear is the time-consuming handwork. Even the Phillipines have rejected the work. And then there are the horror stories about even small-scale mass-production. The batches of ruined work, the lack of interest on the part of the helpers. I feel funny about hiring outside labor, so the only people who help me are either family or friends. The people who have stuck with me for the past two or three years are really special. They have as much interest in producing the bears as I do."

Maria looks upon her bear making as an art form. She has a degree in art, works in photography and graphic design, as well as bears, and she tries to produce enough special works for at least one gallery show a year of bear-art pieces. She has exhibited at the Memory Gallery, Freehand Gallery and the Craft and Folk Museum, all located in Los Angeles, California. She showed her Bear Feet series at the Pittsburgh Center for the Arts.

One recent brainstorm was a chess set Maria called "RUSSkies vs. USSkies." All the chess players were felt bears, dressed either as Russians or Americans. The American and Russian pawns wore star-emblazoned T-shirts (each side a different color). The American "king" and "queen" were Uncle Sam and a pie-toting Statue of Liberty-type bear. The American knights were cowboys and the bishops wore western clerical clothes. The Russian "king" and "queen" were a goateed, red-star-lapeled, suited Russian Premier bear and a sickle-wielding Matroushka. Cossacks were knights.

"My bears are sort of a combination of toy and art. I try to design and make bears that are safe for children and that will stand up to handling by children over the age of three. As a matter of fact, I never send bears to friends with newborns. The nature of the materials I use makes it difficult to create an indestructible bear. Synthetics and fun furs are stronger, but I prefer to work with more natural fibers."

She really aims her bears at the young-in-heart. "My audience has always been primarily in the adult demographics. I really get a kick out of seeing kids who really like my bears, though, especially when it happens to be a child who recognizes the art involved and doesn't think of a bear as a brown Smurf or a furry *Barbie* doll."

Maria Kwong has been a bear artist longer than just about anybody. She finds she can make a living at it. The hours are flexible. The work is artistically challenging. But what is the real reason she has been at it so long?

She explains: "I have continued to make bears mainly because it is one of the few occupations I've found that incorporates the problems of design with total pleasure."

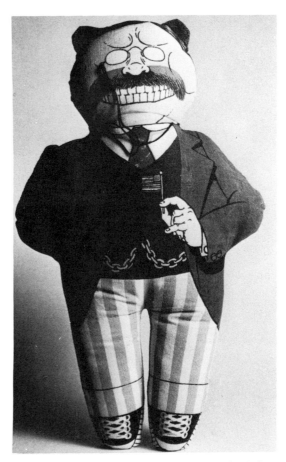

T.R. Bear, limited edition of 260. Printed in 1979. Designed with illustrator Gary van der Steur (Maria's husband). Printed with four colors; three additional colors hand-applied (red and blue for flag, skin tone are air-brushed); pince-nez string separate. "All in all, a major production." Sold in kit form and finished form. Printed on muslin, 13in (33cm). *Photograph courtesy of Maria Kwong.*

"RUSS-kies Vs. U.S.-kies" chess set, 1982. U.S. side. American bishops are Presbyterian ministers; knights are cowboys; rooks are wooden beehives with metal globes; colors are all red, white and blue. This illustration shows a close-up of *Uncle Sam* and *Statue of Liberty* (with pie) — the king and queen. *Photograph courtesy of Maria Kwong.*

Ice Cream Necklace/Belt (above). Rainbow Necklace/Belt (below). Bears, 2in (5.1cm) high. *Photograph courtesy of Maria Kwong.*

HERTA FORSTER

Herta Forster and *Jonathan. Photograph courtesy of Herta Forster.*

Herta Forster is in love. She has finally succeeded in bringing to life her childhood bear. After most of a lifetime of "on and off" bear making, the NIADA (National Institute of American Doll Artists) artist has come up with a design which, for her, makes time stand still.

"The recently-made bear has the face so much like the one I lost as a young girl (at least that is the way I remember it) that I loved him the moment I had the face (nose, eyes and ears) finished."

Herta grew up in Darmstadt, Germany, just before World War II. For a while, it seemed to her that she was destined to be bearless. "For some odd reason," she says, "my parents never gave me a teddy bear. Our best friends (parents' friends) had a daughter six years older than I. The moment we entered their house, I would drag her teddy around for the time we stayed. I was about three years old. I remember he was a medium brown (probably a Steiff) short plush bear of medium size, with a pointed snout and a surprised (and for my then-feeling, slightly hurt) look.

"After years of only visit-owning him, the family finally broke down and gave him to me. (I was, of course, not allowed to ask for it all these years!) From that moment on, he was the brother or sister I never had. I never went to bed without kissing him "Good Night."

"He burnt with the rest of our things on September 11, 1944. Needless to say, I still pine for him."

Herta comes from a long line of artists. "My grandfather and father were artists, sculptors, painters and restorers, as well as art collectors. It was a 'foregone conclusion' I should try my hand at some form of art," she says. In the fire, it was not only her bear that burned. "I was 14 when the war in Europe started and in 1944 we lost our house, studios, collections and all." Her family was displaced and Herta found herself making stuffed animals, including teddy bears, out of donated old velvet drapes to trade for food. "But my heart was not in it," she admits. Thus began the process, involving the creation of countless bears that led to the recreation of Herta's teddy.

For a while, inspiration flagged. But a book got her going again. "The big push I got was when I bought some of Dare Wright's books about the *Lonely Doll*," she says. "The bear in these stories woke up all the feelings about my lost bear. I just started my own designs and made some bears of various sizes."

Herta is accomplished at making up designs, and is well-known for her charming dolls, which have found their way to the shelves of many doll collectors and NIADA patrons. The bears are a more private project.

She describes her progress: "My very first bear was made of some kind of thick cloth. Since then, I have used mostly fake fur, preferably stiff plush like some coats are made of. (I used to go to second-hand stores and buy old coats in good condition and cut them up. Some of the material used for coats cannot be bought.)"

She describes how she makes a bear.

14in (35.6cm) *Jonathan* - beige color; glass eyes. "I mark my bears (since 1980) with a piece of material with the mark: '*HF*' sewn into their 'bottom' seams." — Herta Forster. *Photograph courtesy of Herta Forster.*

"The procedures I use are rather common. With cardboard, metal washers and cotter pins in all joints, kapok stuffing...I bought a huge amount (of kapok) 20 years ago, and almost dropped dead when they delivered it. It was a sack as big as a piano. At the time my husband was ready to commit me to an institution but now (I have half left over) I am more than happy I have it.

"I have used plastic eyes (the ones that look like glass eyes) but I would never make a good bear, or one to be sold, with plastic eyes. The dust will dull them eventually. Eyes make so much difference, people and bears alike. Only the best glass eyes will do. And I take great care with the nose and mouth embroidery."

Because of her memories of her childhood bear, Herta is insistent that her original bears have expressive faces. She describes one of them.

"I have made a bear to be used in a children's story (not published) over wire, as a bendable character. His nose was black leather and the eyes were exchangeable (for whatever mood was needed) made of white felt (overbuttons) and a black felt pupil. It is unbelievable how one can change a face with different eyes (position and size) and different color nose, mouth and size, also the positioning of same.

"Sometimes I trim the fur around the nose; other times I don't, depending on the expression I want to achieve. When I make an especially likable (to me) bear, I make smaller or larger patterns of the same pattern with my pantograph. Though some changes may be in order, as size difference sometimes changes the expressions."

In general, she likes bear making. "Almost everything is enjoyable for me except making the joints. And, of course, the fact that most materials one can buy are not to my liking. There is very little (or none at all) plush in the right colors available. If anyone knows where I can get this material, I would be delighted to know about it," she says.

Eventually, her attempts grew closer to her childhood friend. And then an adult friend's gift gave her the inspiration she needed.

"A puppeteer friend of mine gave me two 'old bears' many years ago. There was no talk in these days of values (antiques), etc. I did make a marionette for her (for the bears). She had tried to use these two bears as marionettes and (heaven forbid) pulled the joints loose to make them movable like a puppet. They are still in this condition. One of the "antiques" is an old Steiff bear. I love him in the limp condition and forego making new joints."

The antique bear's wobbly head gave him the imploring, perhaps, expression, the life-like look that Herta was seeking. She knew now how to design her bear.

"The way I attached the head leaves it a little more loose than the other joints. That gives him a tilt which most bears do not have. It makes him come alive. I think I will make any future bears this way. He has that innocent, surprised and slightly hurt look of my lost bear," she wrote in 1983. "I am 57 years old now, but I love him as if I were a child. If this makes me a nut, so be it."

Herta's teddy was made out of an old coat. She uses many materials for her bears, but not many garments. "In the stages I'm in now I rather see BEAR instead of too many clothes. On one of my Herta Bears I made a little German peasant smock, short, of blue material (tulip-blue). And two Christmas bears I made last holiday I used green and red fake furs transposed like on a chester. They have just a red cap and a neck ruffle. For my story-bear, of course, I would need some kind of clothes for character identification.

She does not make many bears for sale. She does not have a lot of time to spend making them, and her time is divided among dolls, miniatures, bears and family responsibilities. "As long as I have so little time, I'll probably have to do what I have done so far: grab every minute I can for something that wants to be made (bears — dolls)," she says.

Herta's bears come in about 20 different styles and sizes. "Many of them are made from the same pattern in different

Felix, 14in (35.6cm) high sitting. Not jointed; limbs and head sewn to body. 1984. *Photograph courtesy of Herta Forster.*

materials, which makes almost for a different bear." As bear making is, basically, a memory project for Herta, the only bears she has sold to collectors are her Herta Bears. She describes their origin.

"When I joined NIADA in 1970, I was terrified of flying (though I had flown before). So I made for myself a little (6in [15.2cm]) bean bag bear for good luck (believe it or not). I called this type *Herta-Bear.* It caught on in NIADA (at the convention) and I made many of them for collectors in various colors and in two different sizes. They are still one of my favorite bears."

Her other bears are very time-consuming. "They could be playbears, but for the time and care of workmanship involved, I would only sell them for collector prices." So, in general, she does not.

She has definite ideas about bears today, especially about their care and nurture. These seem to stem from personal experience. "The early bears were a treasure to a child who received them as gifts. Today they are made by many thousands, and are by far not treated as lovingly as they used to be. Any trip to a Salvation Army or Goodwill store will show how many of them are literally vandalized.

"I think this is not because children are worse today, but mainly because they are given things too easily. I told you at the beginning how I got "my" bear. There WAS no other. Today, if a child ruined the toy or lost it due to negligence, the parents buy another. The cost and quality is not such as to make it an irreparable loss. This is not lost on a child. It will not be as precious."

Herta finds this quality, most often, in the work of teddy bear artists. "There are some made by individual artists who have the innocence (the bears, that is), because the artist puts much of his or her own feeling into the making. I think you really put a great deal of yourself into the bear you make. In fact, I would almost say, "Show me the teddy you designed and made, and I can tell you a little bit about yourself."

To the California artist, teds are very important. "For an "animal" that does not exist, it has a powerful influence on children and adults. It must somehow fill a psychological need. It certainly did for me. And to be able to create your very own personal bear, what could be more pleasing?"

ELAINE FUJITA-GAMBLE

In the last couple of years, Elaine Gamble has mailed me a number of nifty items. All of them had direct bearing on this book. For a while, unbeknownst to each other, we were simultaneously compiling bear artist information. With uncommon generosity, one day, Elaine shipped me all of her research. I was astounded. Thank you, Elaine.

More recently, she sent a carton of visitor bears. It will be difficult to send them home.

Elaine's bears have a charming, antique look to them. They ought to. Antique bears were her inspiration — especially those in her collection.

"I have collected bears since 1973," she says, "but have always like them. I had a large collection of stuffed animals as a child. Beverly Port was a big help getting my collection started, as I had only collected current bears until meeting her.

"One day I was going through my collection and began studying the Hermann teddy. I decided the lines didn't look too difficult so I got some paper out and started to draw a rough pattern. To my luck, the first bear fit together without any adjusting. He was 5in (12.7cm) tall, and called *Baby Brother*. I have always enjoyed handwork and after studying

Elaine Gamble with one of her favorite bears, *Vinnie*. He is an early Steiff with gold plush mohair. *Photograph by Glenn Morita, courtesy of Elaine Gamble.*

Three Gamble bears visiting Maine. Left to right: *Snoots,* 14in (35.6cm), *Junior,* 13½in (34.3cm) and *Bernie,* 8in (20.3cm), dressed as a sailor.

the bear, I didn't think it would be difficult to make my own, so off I went. I enjoy it."

Since 1979, Elaine has made original collectors' bears, incorporating into them characteristics she, as collector, desires. "I try to make my bears look like the antique bears — old Steiffs," she says. "Old Steiffs with long snout, long curved arms, shoe button eyes and embroidered nose. I have different styles that tend to appeal to different people, but mostly when making bears, I try to please myself. If I don't like a particular style, I discontinue making that bear even if other people still want it made."

Elaine designs by observing the salient characteristics of the old bears, and recreating them, always adding her own interpretations. She describes how she works.

"I use notebook paper or paper bags to draw my patterns on. My husband pins and cuts all the pieces out for me. I do as much sewing as I can by machine, the rest by hand, then the finishing stuffing and stitching. I try to do as much by machine as possible and work out an assembly line process."

All of Elaine's bears are jointed fabric bears, none larger than 15in (38.1cm). "I tend to like the smaller bears," she explains. "I am best known for my smaller bears probably. I have sold the most of my bears in the 5in to 7in (12.7 to 17.8cm) sizes."

But working on this scale has drawbacks. "The most difficult (part) to me is working with the small bears' little pieces. I tend to grasp them too firmly and my fingers begin to ache."

She tries to cut the pieces out of apt materials. "Fabric has a lot to do with the way your stuffed bear turns out," Elaine explains. "I try to use as much of the same fabric as I can because I can perfect a style after making a few."

The Washington State physical education teacher squeezes bear making into corners of her schedule. She has designed about 15 bears, and completes about 200 teds a year, selling them at shows, primarily. Most bear making is relegated to vacations. "I try to spend as much of the summer making bears as I can," she explains. "Other than that, it's only a few nights a week."

Demand for her bears is sometimes more than she can handle. "I would like to slow down," she says. "I have too many orders hanging over my head, so I'd rather just sell at shows where I can make whatever I want to take rather than have particular bears on order. Orders seem to keep me from designing, also, as I fret about getting my orders out instead of creating. A few times a year I just have to get away from the sewing machine for a few months."

Still, Elaine does not feel that mass-production of her teds is the way to go. "I would like to carefully oversee the production if that were to ever happen. I feel the personal touch of the artist becomes somewhat compromised in mass producing. However, it does make the product more available and more affordable."

Elaine's personal touch is evident in innovations such as a musical bear with a key concealed in his tail. This bear is popular with collectors and doubles as a baby gift.

This popularity stems from the charm of Fujita-Gamble teddies. Elaine feels that the audience her bears is reaching is similar to that at the beginning of the teddy bear's popularity — the first decade of the century.

"I think the audience of today is much like that of 1907, where there were teddy bear items of everything you could imagine. Many of the bears have taken on a more cuddly, "cutesy" design, but many bear artists and manufacturers are going back to the old-style bears. My bears appeal to the child in all of us."

Elaine's preferred ted seems to. "My favorite bear I make is called *Junior* and I like him best because I have several outfits to fit him. He is the only one I have designed a lot of clothes for. Clothing changes bears' personalities into child-like qualities. I like overalls the best, but also have vests and suits, and have also made a clown and sailor."

One of the visitor bears is an adorable little 9in (22.9cm) cub dressed in a sailor suit. His upturned nose makes him seem snooty and uncomfortable in his duds. Tomorrow he goes back into the carton, with his two friends, and returns to his maker in Washington State. A souvenir or two of his spring vacation in Maine will come with him. It is time Elaine Gamble got something nifty from me in the mail.

Junior joins the circus. *Junior*, 13½in (34.3cm) is dressed in a clown suit made of pink and green. The bear in the box winds to play "Send in the Clowns." *Photograph by Glenn Morita, courtesy of Elaine Gamble.*

Junior, 13½in (34.3cm) and *Snoots*, 14in (35.6cm).

Bernie, 9in (20.3cm) tall. Fully-jointed; bright blue sailor suit; white piping; red tie; hump back; felt pads; black button eyes.

BALLARD BAINES BEAR COMPANY
(Karin Mandell and Howard Calvin)

Karin Mandell and Howard Calvin, with Ballard Baines bears. "Each one-of-a-kind, with generally good dispositions, the bears like us." *Photograph courtesy of Ballard Baines, Esq.*

Ballard Baines, Esq., 15in (38.1cm) tall. Age undetermined. Position: Chairman of the Board, Ballard Baines Bear Company. Disposition: Bearable. *Photograph courtesy of Ballard Baines, Esq.*

Few companies have the distinction of having a teddy bear as chairman of the board. *Ballard Baines*, an elderly bear found in an antique shop by Karin York, not only is chairman (chairbear?) of the board, but the company is named after him. He is even pictured on its brochure.

This honor came, really, by default, because nobody else wanted it. Besides, the Ballard Baines Bear Company sounded like a good, distinguished name for a business.

It began in June 1981, when Karin York and two of her friends, artists Gini Close and Nedra Argo, decided to make old fashioned teddy bears. For a year they developed patterns and sold to private collectors and a few shops.

At the end of the year, Gini and Nedra tired of making bears and decided to paint, and Karin found herself a displaced homemaker in search of a career.

She showed a guidance counselor photographs of her bears, and she tried to convince Karin to continue the business. "The next thing that happened was one of those amazing things that happen only rarely. I met Howard. I may have mentioned to him a few times about the bears but received little response, so on his birthday, I took a chance and made a bear, put him in a Snoopy Red Baron outfit, wrapped him up and gave him to this 6ft 1in (1.85m) very male person and, scared to death, waited for a response. Well, he was delighted. In fact, he said that I couldn't have given him anything more perfect. He named him *Barnstormer Baines* and on inspecting him closer, started making remarks like 'You should go into the bear business.' "

Five hours later, he had her convinced. At first, Howard helped in spare time stolen from his own business. One and a half years later, that business was shelved, as bears turned into a full-time job. Howard now runs the business and participates in every aspect of bear making, including designing.

"We have a wonderful partnership," Karin says, "and the added plus of good people working for us, especially Marie McEwan who has a real feeling for our bears as individuals."

Ballard Baines bears are elegant and aristocratic and are designed for the collector who appreciates the bear as an art form. "We feel every bear is a sculpture," Karin said. "Our philosophy of bear making is to build a quality bear everyone will love and enjoy. They are aimed more at adults; we think maybe they need them more in this world we live in."

Ranging in size from 12in (30.5cm) to 42in (106.6cm) tall, most are fully-jointed and are made of plush and/or velvet. The firm is known for its character bears. Perhaps the most famous of them is the first, *Dorian Grey*, an 18in (45.7cm) tall bear of short gray fabric. He has black foot pads, wears a black top hat and ribbon, a rose and carries a cane. Like all Ballard Baines bears, he bears a gold metallic heart. Only 100 were made of this limited edition.

Other character bears appear to be dressed, but actually their "clothing" is built-in. "Most clothing hides the wonderful bear shape, so we make the clothes the bear body and he seems dressed without losing his shape." *Santa Bear*, 18in (45.7cm) tall, is made with a red plush body and the rest of his costume is various types and colors of fur fabric. The *Jester Bear*, 18in (45.7cm) tall and jointed, is of various colors of velvet with built-on hat, and is trimmed in elegant gold braid.

But the masterpiece, perhaps, of the whole collection is *King Ludwig*, 21in (53.3cm) tall, made of gold or brown short-nap fabric. His body is red crushed velvet and he wears a red velveteen cape, a crown and carries a scepter.

Somehow, this "dressing up" seems to have affected some of the bears. When asked about this, Karin replied, "Yes, (a bear's) personality changes. It's bound to when someone crowns you and tells you that you're *King Ludwig*, King of Bears. It does go to the poor little bear's head."

Barn Stormer Baines, a Ballard basic bear, 18in (45.7cm) tall. Short napped fur; jointed; 1981. This is the bear that started it all, made for Howard Calvin's birthday. This bear is made in all colors. Each has an individual name; it is of unlimited edition. *Photograph by Liz McCord, courtesy of Ballard Baines Bear Company.*

Dorian Grey, 18in (45.7cm) tall. Limited edition of 100, each numbered and signed. Short gray fabric; tagged; labeled; gold heart on chest; top hat; cane; red rose; black bow. *Photograph courtesy of Ballard Baines, Esq.*

Karin and Howard work a minimum of eight hours a day, five days a week at bear making. In 1984, they plan on making 1000 bears. In the first year and a half of business they designed 15 different bears. The most difficult part of bear making for them is the everyday basic sewing and stuffing. "The ones that are the most fun to make are the latest new models. We both would rather be working on new ideas." But the very best part of bear making for Karin is "putting on their ribbon, telling them their name and giving them each a kiss on the nose (every Ballard Baines bear gets a kiss on the nose and that's the truth) before they are shipped out."

Ballard Baines bears are identified by labels sewn on the back, tags with names and numbers, and a metallic heart attached to the chest.

For two latecomers into the bear world (Karin got her first bear at Goodwill when she was 32 and Howard received his first bear for his 43rd birthday), the response to their efforts has been gratifying.

"It came as a great surprise to us. When we first started out, we were optimists but never expected the response we got. It was overwhelming.

Karin claims, "A teddy bear represents plain old love to us, and we feel they bring out the best in people. I guess you could say making bears is a very personal thing; they really do have a feeling of aliveness. Maybe that is why a bear business is a very wonderful place to be."

As far as we know, *Ballard Baines*, the chairbear of the board, is in silent agreement with her.

Santa Bear, 18in (45.7cm) tall. Unlimited. Fully-jointed; very furry red fabric; gold trim; tagged; labeled; gold heart and two jingle bells on chest. Made since 1981. *Photograph courtesy of Ballard Baines, Esq.*

Jester, 18in (45.7cm) tall. Heads are all colors and bodies are of various colors of velveteen. Each jester has an individual name. Tagged; labeled; gold heart on chest. Unlimited edition. Made since 1981. *Photograph courtesy Ballard Baines, Esq.*

King Ludwig, 21in (53.3cm) tall. Gold or brown short-napped fabric; red crushed velvet body; velveteen cape; gold heart on chest; jointed; wears crown and carries scepter; sword; tagged and labeled. King is numbered but not limited. Made since February 1983. *Photograph courtesy of Ballard Baines, Esq.*

Viola and *Violet*, 14in (35.6cm) fully-jointed bears by Mary D. Olsen. *Photograph courtesy of Mary Olsen.*

Barbara Sixby's *Bernice*. Fully-jointed 18in (45.7cm) gray plush bear with hat, 1983. Doris King's *Lady with Hat*. White plush bear with "leopard" fur hat, muff and scarf, 16in (40.6cm) tall, 1984.

RIGHT: 14in (35.6cm) bear by Catherine Bordi. Honey-colored European fur; fully-jointed; shaved muzzle; green plaid ribbon at neck. This bear's name is *M & M*. 1983.

ABOVE: Kimberlee Port Originals. Two *Jester Bears* approximately 5in (12.7cm) at left. Left bear's costume (which is part of his body) is two shades of lavender. Second *Jester* is two shades of blue. Heads, paws and feet are honey-colored. © 1980. *Le Clown and His Jester*, 2½in (6.4cm) (third from left). Dark brown bear; white and maroon suit trimmed with lace and silk ribbon; fully-jointed. In his hand he holds a white hand-sewn jester trimmed with maroon silk ribbon. Far right is a 1in (2.5cm) *Clown Bear*. Fully-jointed; yellow bear; green suit.

Caramel and Vanilla Pudding by Sylvia Lyons. Fully-jointed plush bears with growlers. 1984.

LEFT: *Pawcahontas with Pawpoose,* 22in (55.9cm) tall, by Sarah McClellan. Fully-jointed brown plush; suede fringed top and skirt; "turquoise" necklace. *Pawpoose* on back has no limbs. 1983.

BELOW LEFT: *Bright Bear (B.B.),* 12in (33.5cm), by Cappi Warnick. Fully-jointed; camel-colored coat wool; beige velour paw pads; black glass eyes; plaid bow. Tag in back seam is hand printed. 1983.

BELOW RIGHT: *Bearbit,* 10in (25.4cm) (bear-in-a-rabbit-suit) by Cappi Warnick. Fully-jointed; white fuzzy plush fake fur body; pink paw pads; white removable hood with rabbit ears; pink inner ears; black glass eyes; embroidered nose and mouth; pink ribbon at neck. 1984.

NEXT PAGE: Doris King Originals, 1983. Left to right: *Hucklebeary* and *Threadbear. Hucklebeary* is the second of the "pre-loved" bears, an edition of 75. Dressed in overalls and a beat-up straw hat, 14in (35.6cm) tall, he is a big brother for *Threadbear.* With his paws stuck in his pockets, he is a picture of innocence. In his back pocket, though, he carries a slingshot. The right paw is reaching for ammunition. The first of the "pre-loved" bears (on the right), *Threadbear* is 9½in (24.2cm) tall and dressed in worn and faded overalls and a white sweater. He is a copy of a very old teddy. There were 25 in this (now closed) edition. He is pre-loved with some worn spots on his elbows and nose and on his clothing to simulate the kind of wear a teddy gets from a lot of loving.

1in (2.5cm) jointed bears by Helen Hull. Made of synthetic clays; jointed at limbs with wire. 1984.

Mitzi and *Moe*, 1½in (3.8cm), by Janna Joseph. Porcelain bisque; molded-on sailor suits; jointed at limbs.

Carol-Lynn Rossel Waugh. *Bearishnikov*, 6in (15.2cm) porcelain bear jointed at limbs; molded-on ballet suit and shoes. Also made in latex. 1980. *Bearishnikova*, 5½in (14cm) porcelain bear. Jointed at limbs, molded-on ballet shoes and costume; roses in hair. Also made in latex. 1981.

NEXT PAGE: *Jonathan* by Herta Forster. Fully-jointed; tan plush. *Photograph courtesy of Herta Forster.*

Two metal bears by Penny Noble, approximately 2in (5.1cm) tall. Jointed at limbs. Bear on right has molded-on jacket with buttons which is painted predominantly blue; body is painted brown. Bear on left is flocked in brown and wears red bow. 1983.

Time Machine Tiny Teddies, 2½in (6.4cm) tall, by Beverly Port. Hand-sewn. These are some of the first Beverly Port bears.

Bernie, as a sailor, 8in (20.3cm) bear by Elaine Fujita-Gamble. Fully-jointed; tan plush.

Gladly Gordon, 34in (86.4cm) by Deanna Duvall. Beige plush; jointed at arms and legs; acrylic safety lock eyes; black wool nose and claws. *Photograph courtesy of Deanna Duvall.*

Humphree, approximately 23in (58.4cm) tall, by
Barbara Sixby. Rush plush. Designed January
1984.

Jenny-Lynn Waugh with *Beverly's Big Bear,* © 1980. Beverly Port Originals. *Big Bear* is approximately 34in (86.4cm) tall. Creamy-white long mohair; black button eyes; brown embroidered nose, mouth and claws; fully-jointed; swivel head; suede paw and foot pads. He has a tail that when turned moves his head back and forth. There is a growler in his body plus a music box that plays "Teddy Bear's Picnic."

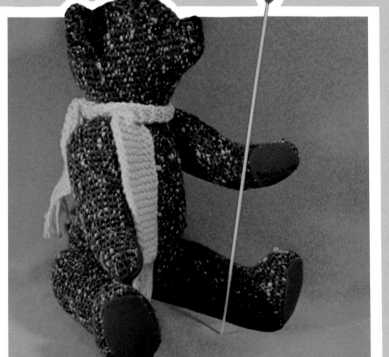

Bromleigh, 18in (45.7cm), by June Beckett. Fully-jointed; green Donegal tweed bear with off-white scarf; old shoe button eyes; corduroy paws.

NEXT PAGE: Barbara Sixby's goldish-copper color bear, approximately 16in (40.6cm) tall. Fully-jointed. 1984.

Le Jester and *Clown Bear* by Beverly Port.

ABOVE: *Teeny Tiny Teddies,* approximately 6in (15.2cm) tall by Barbara Sixby. Fake fur and upholstery material. Designed in December 1983.

LEFT: *Woody Bear,* 14in (35.6cm) by Bob Raikes. Fully-jointed plush; wooden face mask and foot pads. 1984.

2in (5.1cm) bear by April Whitcomb, held by reproduction Richard Steiff bear. 1984. Fully-jointed; gray short plush over hand-sculpted body parts; pink painted pads. Steiff bear is 1983 limited edition bear. Fully-jointed; gray plush.

Unjointed bears by Carole Bowling. *Photograph courtesy of Carole Bowling.*

Baby Victoria, Lindsay Purpus Bears. Photograph courtesy of Cheryl Lindsay and Joanne Purpus.

"Eric-Jon and *Oop.*" Watercolor painting by Carol-Lynn Rössel Waugh. 11in by 14in (27.9cm by 35.6cm). Painting depicts the artist's son and one of her favorite bears. February 1984.

NEXT PAGE: Billie Bear, Ballard Baines Bear Company. Unjointed floppy beige boy bears. *Photograph courtesy of Ballard Baines, Esq.*

ABOVE: *St. Nicholas Bear* by Pat Marrison, 14in (35.6cm). Felt; wire armature inside; crimson velour robe; gray fake fur trim; matching hat with "holly;" belt at waist holds silvery cord from which dangles a key; white rectangular pillow inside waist; bag of toys contains toy bear and other items and comes with bear. 1983.

RIGHT: *Baggy Bear* by Bob Beckett. Carved wooden head; fuzzy knitted stuffed blue and white striped overalls.

JUDY LEWIS

At the post office in Santa Ana, California, Judy Lewis is known as "The Bear Lady." A lot of people think of her that way. And she could not be happier.

"I simply can't imagine not being involved in the Bear World," she says. "It holds for me creativity and friendship. Through the bears I have met the warmest and nicest of people. Many have become new best friends."

Judy entered the Bear World in 1978, when she took a class on how to make the three bears using wool felt. The bears were developed by Mary Hardy, a San Diego artist about whom Judy writes: "She is a warm and wonderful lady who not only inspired my interest in making and collecting bears, but undoubtedly has touched the lives of hundreds of craft-oriented people."

Judy took to bears like the proverbial duck to water, and was soon adapting Mary's patterns. After a while she had developed a family of eight bears, and eventually sold over 1400 of them. It was time, she figured, to move on to her own designs.

Mrs. Lewis has a background in crafts that stems from her childhood. The daughter of a United States Army cavalry officer, she moved around a lot as a child. "By the time I graduated from high school, I had some 22 different addresses. I'd traveled the entire United States and lived in Panama and Japan," she says. "As a child, many of my

Judy Lewis with *Amy* and *Abbott, Tinker* and *Toy.* 1983. *Photograph courtesy of Judy Lewis.*

father's assignments were in isolated areas. I turned to crafts and projects I could make with my hands for entertainment and relaxation. This carried over into my adult life."

With an apprenticeship of 1400 bears and a lifetime of crafts projects, Judy Lewis was well-equipped to develop her own patterns. From felt she branched out into fur and other fabrics. She found that fabric combinations brought out unusual personalities in her creations.

"I started sewing with wool felt, but over the years have also used fur, velvet and textured upholstry fabrics. *Bear Elegance* (one of my designs) is a clown and a combination of all three. His head is of fur; his body is a textured and sometimes patterned upholstry fabric. His paw pads and hat are of a contrasting velvet. His collar is a wide lace ruff. He is complete with silk flowers of ribbon attached to one side of his velvet hat."

Judy's bears have always had names, life histories and particular clothing preferences. She prefers to make them 18in (45.7cm) and under because, she explains, "I have more opportunity to display that size in a showcase fashion."

With an eye to "display," Judy designs her bears for adults. "My bears have always been purchased by the serious collector," she says. "I am especially pleased with the number of men who have enjoyed my creations. I intend for my bears to be collected, loved and handled on the adult level. To be works of worth — the best of workmanship and lasting appeal."

This in mind, she presents her critters as objects for interior decoration. "I started making the bears thinking they

Judy Lewis cutting out future *Tinkers* and *Toys. Photograph courtesy of Judy Lewis.*

Judy Lewis discussing construction procedures with *Tinker. Photograph courtesy of Judy Lewis.*

Tarbuckle, the Sailor. Honey-colored wool felt; lighter wool paw pads; navy blue and white wool sailor suit; red tie; red pompon on top of blue sailor hat. Judy Lewis tag in back seam. 42 issued in 1982 and 1983. *Photograph courtesy of Judy Lewis.*

would make a cute table centerpiece for the Christmas holidays. Today I continue to make bears because I want a particular look for a spot in my home. I try to make a bear that will add to peoples' homes when set apart from a large collection; to be used as an accent piece."

She offers her residence as an example. It is decorated in a style that might be called Contemporary Teddy Bear. "My bears are displayed throughout my home and in my workroom-office. Each week brings a fresh group of bear-lovers to tour." An impromptu tour is always welcome. "My neighbor regularly brings little children to visit (sometimes big children, too). Before they leave, they are introduced to *Florabelle* in the dining room. She treats them to a chocolate teddy bear lollipop as a remembrance of their visit."

Florabelle, like all Judy's teds, is "real" to her.

"Bears are definitely alive characters to me," the designer says. "I enjoy making fur bears that I have also designed a costume for so that it becomes a particular character. I am probably known for the variety of bears I make and the stories about them rather than one bear in particular."

She tells about a series of five "character" felt bears: "*Arthur Twiggins III* carried a shiny penny in his vest pocket. He would purchase good buys in honey. *J.T. Thatcher* wore a burgundy coat that had a lodge pin in the lapel with the initials BYA. It stood for Bear Youth of America and he lobbied in Congress for them for the protection of betterment of beehives. *Thurston Tru-Heart* is simply a dear and sports a red heart. He's especially fond of Valentine's Day.

Bear Elegance. Fur face; body of textured, patterned velvet; contrasting velvet paw pads; pearl, brass or silver beads up front of body; full lace ruffs at neckline; hat of contrasting velvet with silk flowers and ribbon to one side. *Bear Elegance* bears can stand on their heads and balance their hat on one foot. No more than 14 of each fabric combination is made. Judy Lewis name tag in back seam. 74 issued in 1983. Also came with paper tag with issued number and artist signature. *Photograph courtesy of Judy Lewis.*

Bear Elegance balancing on his head. *Photograph courtesy of Judy Lewis.*

Tarbuckle is a honey-colored bear in a navy blue sailor outfit and looks snappy with his red tie. *Tee-Winkle* is a Victorian-dressed circus clown."

Judy Lewis bears definite opinions on ursine haberdashery: "Clothing brings a bear to 'life' and I prefer the Victorian look. I usually design a wardrobe for *every* bear."

She has plans for a series of stately lady bears dressed in "yesteryear finery. They will be known as the *Dowagers* and are truly characters," Judy says. But most of her bears are male. All are marked with cloth tags bearing her name and the year she started making the bruin. In addition, each ted has a paper tag hanging from the arm joint with his name and production number. More expensive bears are dated and hand-signed.

Which are her favorites? "My favorite bears are two 18in (45.7cm) fur-jointed and dressed brother and sister bears. *Amy* and *Abbott* are of the Victorian age. *Amy* is brown and dressed in white with a large bow at the dropped waist. She carries a basket of flowers. *Abbott* is honey-colored and dressed in plum velvet short pants and tam hat. He has a lace collar and black satin bow at the neck. It's not his favorite outfit but Mama has dressed them for a Sunday picnic and told them to stick together. *Amy* is in a snit because *Abbott* carries a sling shot in his hip pocket in case he spots a beehive. *Amy* doesn't want to get stung while out gathering flowers. Each has a music box that plays the 'Teddy Bear Picnic.' "

What is the best part of bear making? "After I have drafted a pattern, the most exciting time is when the first bear comes into being. When it is complete, I have to share him with my family and then find a special place in our home for him."

With her family's help, Judy produces from 300 to 500 bears a year. "I work reasonably fast but every step must be correct and perfect," she says. "The entire family has pitched in to help with shows, deliveries or just plain stuffing. Dad always joints my bears and keeps my books up to date. The bears have been fun for all of us. We all talk to them and are hopelessly in love with their endless variety and appeal.

Other people seem to feel so, too. "About a year ago," Judy says, "I walked into a cookie shop in a mountain resort. The clerk-owner was wearing a bear hat. I asked him if he liked bears. Indeed he did, and his favorite was in back of me and up on a shelf. I turned to look and there was one of my creations."

Now that she is firmly entrenched in the Bear World, the designer often gets this reaction to her critters. "People have been very warm and open with their feeling about my bears," she reports. At the Santa Ana, California, post office — or anywhere else, for that matter - Judy Lewis enjoys being known as "The Bear Lady."

Amy, a prim and proper Victorian young miss, 18in (45.7cm). Brown fur; ecru eyelet dress with plum satin bow at drop waist; carrying a basket of "just picked flowers." She is musical and plays the "Teddy Bears' Picnic." Judy Lewis name tag in back seam. Also comes with paper tag with bear's name, number of issue and artist's signature. 50 issued in 1983. *Photograph courtesy of Judy Lewis.*

Abbott, 18in (45.7cm) tall. Honey-colored fur; light paw pads; plum-colored velvet short pants with brass buttons; lace collar with black satin bow; matching hat. He sports a slingshot in his hip pocket in case he spots a beehive. He is musical and plays "The Teddy Bears' Picnic." Judy Lewis name tag in back seam. Also comes with paper tag with his name, number of issue and artist's signature. 50 issued in 1983. *Photograph courtesy of Judy Lewis.*

Tinker and *Toy*. *Tinker* is 18in (45.7cm) tall. Honey-colored fur; shaved nose; black shoe button eyes; light suede-like cloth paw pads. Judy Lewis tag in back seam. 50 in first issue of 1983. Also comes with paper tag with issue number and artist signature. *Photograph courtesy of Judy Lewis.*

Judy Lewis with *Amy* and *Abbott* in workroom. *Photograph courtesy of Judy Lewis.*

BONNIE HARRON

For Bonnie Harron, 20,000 hand-painted mushrooms led the way to a bear making career.

In the late 1960s, Bonnie and her three daughters found themselves in the hand built mushroom-shaped incense burner business when, after seeing samples of the teenagers' work, a shop owner ordered two gross of them, deliverable in two weeks.

This astounding initial success led to diversification. Bonnie joined forces with them, producing a line of over 40 hand built stoneware and low-fire clay items under the banner of "The Happy Mushroom."

After the defection of two daughters, Bonnie and her oldest daughter got serious about the business. They added wheel-thrown ware and began to work in porcelain. Dinnerware, honey pots and planters sprang from their fingers alongside the individually sculpted angels, castles, piglets, butterflies and frogs. Sometimes the creatures and vessels were combined, and the resulting products proved popular. But, people went wild over them when, in 1980, Bonnie began to decorate them with teddy bears.

The teddy bears are memory-likenesses of Bonnie's bear, *Cinnamon*, who has been an important influence in her life for over 50 years. "Probably the only inspiration was *Cinnamon*," she says, "because I had a mental image of bearness and did no other research. I just thought of the bear of my childhood."

Although *Cinnamon* now lives with daughter Debby and "is patriarch presiding over a couchful of bears in her living room in San Jose," Bonnie has fond memories of him. "I can't remember a time when a teddy bear wasn't an important part of my life, at least since I was three. *Cinnamon* was the authority figure among my favorite toys. There was a sheepskin sealyham named Snowball and a teddy-shaped cat named Cuddly Kitty and a large Effanbee baby named Lovums — my four friends. They were a great comfort to me. (I always thought *Cinnamon* and Cuddly Kitty had a thing going, but they were very reticent about it.)"

So, it was natural that, when Bonnie began to design bears, *Cinnamon* would be her model. "After I began making stoneware bears in memory-likeness of *Cinnamon*, I borrowed him from Deb to take his picture and when I held him again, it instantly flicked me back to those days when he was one of my stalwart companions. But he was no longer the erect commanding bear of my memory. Now he's aged just like a human. His chest tilts a bit to one side and I'm sure trembles a little. Alas, now he's an OLD, OLD bear. He has his work to do, though, keeping all Debby's young bears in line. This year (1983) he's 52."

Bonnie individually sculpts each little bear. Most of them are miniatures, from 1/2in (1.3cm) to 4in (10.2cm). Some, done in collaboration with her daughter, who wheel-throws them, sit almost 12in (30.5cm) tall. "The large wheel-thrown bears are properly sculpture," she says. "Because, unfortunately, they're not really huggable." She has lost count of the number of designs she has come up with.

"Probably my best-known bears are those several inches or less who are doing things — eating honey or porridge (my

Bonnie Harron at work on stoneware bear. 1983. *Photograph courtesy of Bonnie Harron.*

daughter throws tiny porcelain bowls which I glaze and fill with stoneware 'porridge' and white glaze 'milk'), fishing, playing blocks, riding ponies, reading, eating from a bag of popcorn, etc. Bears are very clever. I no sooner put together a catalog (Bear-a-log), than they learn new tricks and make it all obsolete. I have no idea of my production. Besides individual bears, many are used as handles on jars, etc. On my current price list I have about 27 styles, with five or six more since I made up the list, plus another dozen in my head. There is just no end to it! Bears, bears, everywhere, dancing in my head! I'm delighted that something I can make has become so popular. Sure beats planters."

I asked Bonnie if she had any special bear making techniques. "Procedures for making my bears are probably just standard for clay," she said. "My design procedures are mostly unconscious. I get an idea of something bears might enjoy doing and then think 'bear.' When I do their little faces, I hold a feeling of what they think. Usually I want them to have a sweet happy expression if they are children bears, a calm loving look if they are lady bears and a stalwart upstanding look if they are gentlemen bears. Of course, while bears can be mischievous, they're never bad, cruel or disagreeable. That's why they're so much nicer companions than many people. I've never watched anyone else do this sort of thing and have worked out my own system. My only 'trick of the trade' is to 'think bear' — to hold in my mind a

Cinnamon, Bonnie Harron's traveling companion. *Photograph courtesy of Bonnie Harron.*

And she is pleased.

"I'm delighted with the new (?) popularity of teddy bears. I think anything that allows adults to get in touch with their "childness" and their childhood is great therapy. And who doesn't need some of that now? More and more of the people I speak to at craft shows, etc. are 'into' fantasy. The real world is getting quite annoying and frustrating, perhaps because we are told not only of the villainy on our doorstep but of the villainy all across the world. Therefore, wizards, dragons, Star Wars, Snow White, miniature houses and teddy bears become a perfect antidote to pollution, nuclear threat, frustration at the govenment and a general feeling of impotence. Hurray for TEDDY BEARS!"

So, Bonnie has begun to make bear wizards and dragons. They have struck a responsive chord. "I enjoy doing...dragons, a much maligned species. Mine are all winged Welsh dragons and those from Ann McCaffrey's *Dragonriders of Pern* series.

It was a logical step for the bear maker to use her work in miniature scenes, since the bears already enact little dramas. "Soon after I began making bears," she says, "I made my first foray into miniature scenes, a Teddy Bears' Picnic. It's 18in (45.7cm) square and has 24 bears cavorting in it, and a tree with stoneware trunk, bushes, stream, etc. Another scene I'm proud of was a "peasant-style" kitchen with a stone corner fireplace, wrought iron candelabra; plate rail full of porcelain dishes, cupboard on top of flour-bin table, tole-

firm idea, as if I WERE the bear I'm creating. As, in writing fiction, you for a time become the viewpoint character."

Bonnie is familiar with the above literary technique. She's a writer. "I have the two world's greatest novels waiting for those finishing touches," she says.

For a while, demand for her work was so great that she hired helpers, but that was a wrong move. "One of the hardest things I've found is to turn my designs over to someone else. Only one of our employees was capable of reproducing my castles, etc., anywhere near how I wanted them. But after a while the quality would always slip, because she had no stake in the integrity of the design. They quickly became just so many 'things' with no thought as to whether they had the "feel" of what they were. You can't pay people to THINK what they're doing. Either they will or they won't. Mostly won't. I never have turned production of my bears to anything else. My daughter is reluctant to learn 'bearing' because she knows I'd be too exacting. So I guess I'll make as many bears as I can and leave it at that."

Mrs. Harron has definite goals for her bears. "The aesthetic effect I try for is that the essence of teddy bear-ness is pleasant reassurance, just as it should be with a stuffed bear. A teddy bear should be a best friend, a comforter, a companion, undemanding but constant, very much like *Harvey*. Perhaps a small stoneware bear can't be hugged or dragged about by one arm, but I hope the bear's personality makes up for his physical limitations and that he holds the 'essence of bearness.' Their only didactic purpose would be their good example in being constant friends."

Besides teddy bears, the ceramist enjoys making dragons. As with a number of arctophiles, Mrs. Harron enjoys fantasy. Indeed, the basic descriptions of fantasy fans and teddy bear enthusiasts seem awfully close. More bears every year seem to make it to science fiction conventions and fantasy fans to bear events. Bonnie has noticed this, too.

Drowsy *Papa Bear*, 5½in (14.0cm). Stoneware. 1983. *Photograph courtesy of Bonnie Harron.*

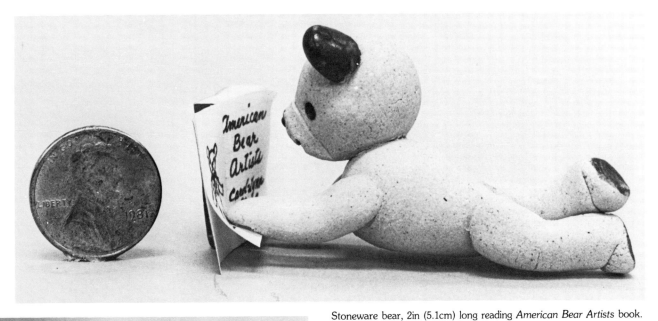

Stoneware bear, 2in (5.1cm) long reading *American Bear Artists* book. 1983.

Merlin Bear in blue robe and hat, 3½in (8.9cm) high and the *Sorcerer's Apprentice* get ready to study their crystal balls and cast a few spells. Stoneware. 1983. *Photograph courtesy of Bonnie Harron.*

Papa Bear, 2in (5.1cm) high plays with *Wee Wee Bear* while *Mama Bear* holds the new baby sister in a receiving blanket. Stoneware. 1983. *Photograph courtesy of Bonnie Harron.*

painted dining table and chairs — all of which I made. *Mama Bear* is carrying an "iron" pot of porridge to the table. *Wee Wee Bear*, sitting on books on his chair, is banging his spoon on the table and demanding food. *Papa Bear*, with his elbow on the end of the table, is reading the newspaper. The fourth place is also set, (bowls of porridge all around) and the room is entitled, "Goldy Locks Is Coming To Dinner."

Bonnie regularly takes her bears to shows. There she gets much-needed feedback from customers that keeps the den growing. Of course, since she has her own pottery studio, "The Happy Mushroom," Bonnie's bears are directly available from her. More and more, shops are stocking them, too.

Bonnie has an idea that her work will be remembered in future generations, but not, perhaps, thoroughly understood — especially the mushrooms, which got her started.

Bonnie sort of regrets that her bears cannot be comfortably hugged, but, since this is the nature of her medium, she has learned to live with this disadvantage. She has turned it into a plus. Because of it, she figures that her work will be long remembered, after her models, bears like *Cinnamon*, have disappeared. She explains: "Of course, stoneware is quite durable. After all, the only thing man makes that survives the millenia is stoneware. When metal, wood, everything else has deteriorated, they use stoneware to date archaeological sites. So these bears are my bid for immortality!"

MARY OLSEN

Mary Olsen likes bears that begin with "G."

It all began with a bear she made from a kit in January 1980. She named him *Grizley*. Contrary to her expectations, he was fun and fascinating to make. "Starting early that day," she says, "I soon became totally engrossed. Mistakes were plentiful, but after working into the evening, my new teddy bear was completed. I was thrilled to think I had made my very own teddy bear."

The Washington State bear maker collects teddies. She still owns her first ted, a first Christmas gift. Probably her favorite bear of all disappeared from home years ago — a little Steiff perfume bottle bear, a present from her father. "Makes me sad when I think of it." she says.

The bear area in her Graham, Washington, home, crammed with hundreds of teds, could be termed "Teddy Bear Heaven." Many are antiques, some thrift shop refugees. But Mrs. Olsen buys artist bears today. "I'm very fond of the modern handmade bears," she says. "I very rarely buy commercially made bears anymore. (I have around 450 bears, so I've become more particular about what I buy.) I feel that once a bear becomes 'commercially' made, it's lost that 'special something' that the designer-maker achieves."

She has become a bear artist herself. *Grizley* showed her how.

"I started wondering whether I could design a bear of my own. I wanted to get back to the look of old-fashioned bears that had shoe button eyes and distinctive bodies with long arms and short, fat legs with big feet.

"Pictures of old teddy bears in Bialoskys' *Teddy Bear Catalog* had me longing for an old-style bear. After looking through the pictures, I decided on the features of different bears that I liked most. Margaret Hutching's book, *How To Make Teddy Bears* was most helpful. By trial and error and some time, *Gridley* was born."

This was January 1981.

He was christened by a friend of Mary's, a retired school teacher, who howled at the sight of him, saying; "He looks just like my old principal, named Gridley."

When she showed *Gridley* around, requests poured in, and Mrs. Olsen found herself in business, with three sizes of *Gridleys* in repertoire; 11in (27.9cm), 14in (35.6cm) and 20in (50.8cm).

Gridley led to *Grindley* ("I wanted a bear that smiles," she explained), who is 16in (40.6cm) tall, and to *Gorgy*, the same size, for whom she sells a pattern.

All Olsen bears are made of fur-like material, are jointed and have suede or felt paws. They are signed, dated and numbered.

And all, even though from the same patterns, look different when she is finished. One of them, for the bear maker, stands out from the rest of the den.

"*Graham Gridley* is my absolute favorite. He is No. 176 and when I made him, I decided he was the one I liked the most of any I had made so far and, of course, since then. He is *Chairbear* of the company. He likes to be seen in his cowboy outfit, as he is, after all, a country bear at heart (we live in the country). He attends all functions with me and is

Mary D. Olsen and 20in (50.8cm) *Madame Rouge*, one-of-a-kind bear. Made from old white wool coat; beige felt paws; pearl and gold jewelry; red feather boa; red velvet ribbon and old red velvet flowers around head. *Photograph courtesy of Mary D. Olsen.*

14in (35.6cm) *Gridley, Viola.* Fully-jointed; beige fur-like fabric; beige felt paws; black (plastic) shoe button eyes; white cotton dress trimmed with lavender and purple ribbons and violets. *Photograph courtesy of Mary D. Olsen.*

accumulating quite a few buttons from his travels for the vest he wears. His cowboy hat is becoming quite tattered from travel and we are on the "lookout" for a new appropriate one for a bear of his position. He does wear glasses as it makes him more distinguished-looking."

Graham Gridley may be distinguished, but most of Mary Olsen's bears have a sweet, understanding, patient look to their faces. This endearing expression has made them popular with collectors, making it is the best part of bear making for her.

"I think I enjoy embroidering the faces on the bear most, as that really determines what he will look like. I never have been able to make two bears look exactly alike. They are each one-of-a-kind. People tell me they like that and for that reason, many buy more than one."

Although designed for collectors, she feels that her bears are also play bears. Her grandchildren test them out for her. The problem is, though, she cannot seem to make enough of them — for kids or grownups.

Bear making has mushroomed for the Washington artist. "I didn't intend for my bear making to become a full-time occupation," she says, "but it has. I usually spend at least eight to ten hours a day on them, four days a week.

"I have been making about 200 or 250 bears a year. I can do 20 bears a month easily, but have been doing closer to 35 a month to keep up with orders. Some days I can produce several bears and others I can only complete one.

"I never make a bear from start to finish in a day. I make them in stages. I will spend several days tracing and cutting out, then basting and machine sewing and next stuffing and completing them. My daughter-in-law, Shirley, does help me with cutting out the bears and doing the hand basting, which I find very boring. This has helped me to produce bears much faster."

The best part of bear making, for Mary, is seeing the completed bear. "It's always fun to see how it will look," she says.

After more than 700 bears, each one still offers excitement and surprise to its maker, but none has matched the impact of *Graham Gridley,* of Graham, Washington. To Mary Olsen, he is GRReat.

Graham Gridley, Chairbear of the Graham Gridley Bear Co. (No. 176), 20in (50.8cm). Dark gold fur-like fabric; suede paws; red felt cowboy hat; blue and white checkered shirt; beige suede vest; navy jeans; leather belt; white boots. Buttons are souvenirs from travels and from clubs he belongs to. Glasses came from Goodwill. *Photograph courtesy of Mary D. Olsen.*

Gridleys, 20in (50.8cm) and 11in (27.9cm) tall. Fully-jointed; beige wooly fur-like fabric; beige felt paws; black plastic shoe button-type eyes. *Photograph courtesy of Mary D. Olsen.*

Close-up of *Grindley. Photograph courtesy of Mary D. Olsen.*

Grindley, 16in (40.6cm) tall. Fully-jointed; gray fur-like material; beige felt paws; black (plastic) shoe button eyes. *Photograph courtesy of Mary D. Olsen.*

Kimberlee Port hand-sewing a teddy bear. Friend "Scamper" sleeps next to her. 1984. *Photograph by Beverly Port, courtesy of Kimberlee Port.*

In 1981, Hans-Otto Steiff proclaimed Kimberlee Port's *Bitsy Bear* the "biggest bear in the world."

Actually, Bitsy may be in the running for the smallest fully-jointed stuffed bear in the world. But that's big in a lot of people's books.

Kimberlee specializes in original fully-jointed teddy bears. Her biggest is 8in (20.3cm) high. Her smallest is near-microscopic.

Kim Port was born with bears in her blood. Daughter of artist Beverly Port, she grew up surrounded by dolls and bears — antique and handmade.

"During my lifetime I've had many favorite teddy bears," she says. "The first one was light tan with a music box in his body. He would lull me to sleep when I was a baby.

"When my brother was born I gave this bear to him. A couple of years ago I had the pleasure of opening a birthday present from my brother and finding my much-beloved old teddy bear inside.

"One of my other favorite bears is *Bitsy*. He was given to me by my Mom when I was about four years old. He is a 3in (7.6cm) tall, fully-jointed, light brown Steiff bear. I used to clutch him in my hand and sleep with him at night. Today when you pick *Bitsy* up from my bookshelf (where he sits with his wife and child) and look at his back, you can see the imprint where my fingers held him. When I was looking for a trade name for my miniature bears, I called them after him: "Bitsy Bears."

Kimberlee's "Bitsy Bears" have to be seen to be believed. Actually, they have to be handled for full appreciation. It is amazing that something so dainty, smaller than a finger digit, can combine such personality, imagination and also be fully-jointed.

Kim's bears embody flights of fancy. Flower bears, *Bearies, Bearlerinas,* jesters, leprechauns, muffs, babies, guardian angels: their personas are only limited by imagination. And Kim has piles of this.

"My bears are definitely an expression of the 'inner' me," the Washington State artist declares. She describes how she gets her ideas.

"Inspiration for my teddy bears comes from the world around me. It seems an idea for a bear can come from anywhere. Last summer I was sitting in our yard sewing a teddy bear. It was a glorious summer day. I was looking at our flower garden when the idea of a flower bear came to me. My initial idea developed into *"Fleur Bear."* Her head is the flower, with petals flowing out from her neck, and her body (stem) is long, slim and green."

At this writing (May 1984), Kim is 23 years old, a student at the University of Washington, working toward a double degree in International Studies and Business Administration. She squeezes bear making into her schedule, along with a part-time job. "I have a very small output of bears during the year," she says. "I also work slowly because I try to make each bear the very best I can."

She always has. She has been making bears this way for almost half of her life, for the last decade, at least.

"The first bear I made was in 1974, as a Christmas present for my parents. My mom had been asking me for a handmade bear to add to her collection. That was just the beginning. She now has over 30 teddy bears that I've made for her over a ten-year period."

In this time she has developed an amazing array of ursine characters. In 1976, Kimberlee designed the cover Winter Issue of *DOLL* NEWS — the Teddy Bear issue. Her mom was editor. The cover featured a Christmas scene with a *Santa* ted, a *Mama* ted and a bunch of bearlings. She was 16 at the time.

Most of her bears are characters and she has unusual ideas, like the 8in (20.3cm) tall *Mama Bear,* designed in 1977. She wears a bonnet and lace trim around her neck. When you unzip her tummy, two 2½in (6.4cm) tall fully-jointed babies — pink and blue — peek out. *Eau de Bear,* a 2in (5.1cm) tall bear has a removable head, which has a cork in it. The cork fits into a tiny perfume bottle. Her 2½in (6.4cm) tall *Bearterflies,* designed in 1978, boast multicolored flocked wings, which come in many shapes with different decorative patterns, and sport antennae on their heads. Then there is her "portrait bear," *A. Chris Bear,* copyrighted in 1983. This 2½in (6.4cm) tall grey bear wears glasses and a green visor. In his paws he holds a pen and list. He bearsonifies A. Christian Revi, Editor of the magazine, *The Teddy Bear and friends™.*

RIGHT: This is a gold *Mama Bear,* © 1977, 8in (20.3cm) tall. Bonnet; lace trim around neck. When you unzip her tummy, a 2½in (6.4cm) pink and a 2½in (6.4cm) blue baby peek out. All are fully-jointed and made of a short plush. *Photograph by Beverly Port, courtesy of Kimberlee Port.*

Clothing for many bears is an integral part of the design. Often, the body is made up of clothing parts, with bear fur showing at appropriate spots. "I use clothing to enhance the character of the bear," Kim states. "I don't dress bears that look like they'd be uncomfortable in clothes." Perhaps some of her inspiration for color and clothing comes from one of the favorite bears in her collection — one she didn't make.

"My absolute favorite teddy bear is *Miss Violet Lavender*. She is an antique Steiff bear, who has received a lot of love. I think she's dressed in her first prom outfit. Her outfit is tied around the waist with a lavender ribbon; at her shoulder is a bouquet of violets in which I put one of my old fashioned teddy bears. It was her face that first caught my attention. Her black shoe button eyes looked directly at me as she smiled her sweet smile. The wisdom of many years and happy experiences are behind her smile."

For Kim, "the expression on the bear's face is most important," and she strives to create in her own work the sweet, loving bear faces she seeks in others'. The eyes, noses and mouths are carefully stitched.

Nearly all of Kim's bears are hand-sewn from a short plush fabric which is no longer manufactured. Over 30 stitches to the inch (2.5cm) join the 19 to 27 individual pieces that comprise each ted. All are fully-jointed with wire and round discs: head, arms and legs are movable.

Larger bears are machine-sewn, as are her dressed rabbits, dressed cats, Puss 'n Boots and his Lady Cat, unicorns, rocking horses, horses, sheep, elephants, camels, lions, donkeys and pull toys (sewn animals on wooden platforms with wheels).

The tiny bears are distinctively marked and packaged. They usually inhabit tiny handmade "gift boxes" fashioned by Kim's father. Minute heart-shaped plastic labels which tell the bear's name, copyright date and Kim's name are made by her boyfriend and are attached, usually, to the outside of each box.

It is the bears on the inside of the boxes that are the most astonishing. And Kim feels a sort of magic when she makes them.

"To me, it is an amazing experience to make a bear," she says. "From a tiny scrap of material, a needle, some thread and stuffing I fashion something unique which has never been made before. Making teddy bears is a synthesis of my love for bears and the urge to create something uniquely my own. I make bears because I enjoy making bears. If it ever stops being fun, I'll stop."

This would be a sad day for arctophiles. These "You-gotta-see-it-to-believe-it" bears have graced the collections of many ardent, discriminating collectors. Like Hans-Otto Steiff, they will agree that Kimberlee's little teddies just may be "the biggest bears in the world."

Hans-Otto Steiff holds up what he proclaimed, "the biggest bear in the world," one of Kim Port's bears, to the crowd at the Frederick & Nelson store in Seattle, Washington, 1981. *Photograph courtesy of Beverly Port.*

Close-up of Kim port's hands sewing. 1984. *Photograph by Beverly Port, courtesy of Kimberlee Port.*

Old Fashioned Bear, © 1983, 2in (5.1cm) tall. Kim Port's version of an antique bear. Long arms; big paws; felt paw pads; large feet; hump on back. He is sitting on a thimble and holding one of Kim's teddy bear muffs, next to his handmade gift box.

"The Teddy Bears' Christmas," © 1976, created for the cover of *Doll News*, Winter Issue, 1976. All are hand-sewn of a fine gold plush. *Santa Bear*, 7in (17.8cm); *Mama Bear* 6¾in (17.2cm); *Brother* and *Sister Bears*, 2½in (6.4cm); Angel Bear, 1in (2.5cm). *Mama, Brother* and *Sister Bear* are wire-jointed; the rest of the family is fully-jointed. The artist also made the tiny rocking horse and rabbit on packages. *Photograph by Beverly Port, courtesy of Kimberlee Port.*

Bearlerina, © 1982, and *Clown Bear,* © 1981. *Bearlerina* is a beige "Bitsy Bear" approximately 1¼in (3.2cm) tall. Her tutu is made of dainty lace, ribbon and net. A crown adorns her head and on her feet are ribbon ballet slippers. *Clown Bear* wears a two-tone wine-colored outfit trimmed with silk ribbon and French knots.

I.M. Bear, © 1983, 1in (2.5cm). Fully-jointed hand-sewn felt bear; embroidered features. Comes in custom-made gift box with bow; plastic heart on box.

The 2½in (6.4cm) tall *Bearterfly,* © 1978, is standing next to her nest. She is pink with multicolored, flocked wings. A flower, ribbon and antennae trim her. A pink baby *Bearterfly,* © 1978, is riding his rocking horse in the nest. He also has antennae and flocked wings. *Photograph by Beverly Port, courtesy of Kimberlee Port.*

Two *Jester Bears,* approximately 5in (12.7cm) at left. Left bear's costume (which is part of his body) is two shades of lavender. Second *Jester* is two shades of blue. Heads, paws and feet are honey-colored. © 1980. *Le Clown and his Jester,* 2½in (6.4cm), is third from left. He is a dark brown bear in a white and maroon suit trimmed with lace and silk ribbon; fully-jointed. In his hand he holds a white hand-sewn *Jester* trimmed with marron silk ribbon. Far right is a 1in (2.5cm) *Clown Bear;* fully-jointed; yellow bear; green suit.

Baby Bear and her rattle, © 1983, are sitting on a silver filigree buggy. The 2in (5.1cm) tall baby is wearing a long dress and bonnet made of lace with silk ribbon trim. In her paw she holds a tiny teddy bear head hand-sewn rattle decorated with silk ribbon.

Bear Muffs, © 1981. A small bear or doll can warm its hands in these bear muffs. The legs are sewn into the muff body while the arms and head are jointed. The 1¼in (3.2cm) tall beige muff on the left has a red silk ribbon around her neck. The one on the right is a 1¼in (3.2cm) tall gold muff. *Photograph by Beverly Port, courtesy of Kimberlee Port.*

A. Chris Bear, © 1983 by Kimberlee Port makes his home with A. Christian Revi, Editor of *The Teddy Bear and friends*™ magazine. This 2½in (6.4cm) gray bear wears glasses and a green visor. In his paws he holds a pen and list. *Photograph by Betty-anne Twigg.*

MAXINE LOOK

Maxine Look and some of her antique bears. *Poor Mr. Lindsay,* with the bald spot, is seated on the white chair next to a friend. *1983 photograph by Barbara Kennedy, courtesy of Maxine Look.*

Every once in a while Maxine Look brings her bears down East. Their official destination is Harrington, Maine, but Winthrop is on the way. These two antique Steiffs decided to try out the local honey. Bear on the left is a pre-teddy Steiff circus bear. Blank silver button in his ear; circus collar around his neck; fully-jointed; leather nose, and is un-teddy; very long arms. The bear on the right is an early Steiff teddy. He looks to be a brother of the Margaret Strong Steiff bear. Red and black checkered bow tie; Roosevelt pin. *Photograph taken August 1983.*

For Maxine Look, the road to teddy bear creation took a long detour at restoration. The journey began with a doll collection — and a needle and thread. Maxine was born in Harrington, Maine. It was there she learned to sew.

The process, at first, was problematic, and dolls — or bears — were not of optimum interest. They came much later in her career. Maxine is a bit apologetic about it now.

"It would be interesting if I could tell of my love for teddy bears and dolls as a child and the interesting ones I owned. The truth is I was a tomboy as a child, having a brother 14 months younger than I. We were very close and I played boy games.

"The only time I remember playing dolls was when a neighbor friend came to visit for the afternoon. She was dainty, sewed, played dolls so Mom suggested I should sew for my dollies, with her.

"I agreed on the condition that my brother would also 'play dolls.' We were given needle, thread, fabric, lemonade and cookies to spend a productive afternoon. At the end of our sewing, my friend had beautifully costumed her doll. My brother had sewed his material through my celluloid doll's head many times in order to create a hat. When I had completed my costume, I discovered it was sewn tightly to my own dress as I held it in my lap to sew.

"I don't remember being encouraged to sew after that."

Eventually, she did learn, however. The family was filled with professional seamstresses; it was in her blood. Sewing led to doll collecting — via costuming. However, Maxine confesses that she has always liked bears better.

Early *Max* bears. Brown plush fabric; prominent long noses; shoe button eyes, dressed in old fabrics. *Max* is 15in (25.4cm). *Mrs. Max* is 13in (33cm); *Maxie* is 11in (27.9cm). Made in 1981. All carry Maxine Look's distinctive leather tag in the shape of a bear paw print, with the words, "Max Bear." *Photograph by Barbara Kennedy, courtesy of Maxine Look.*

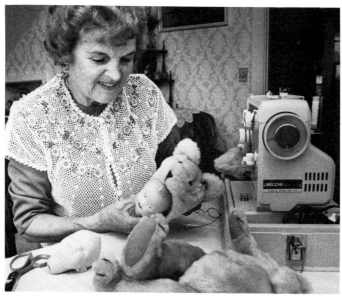

Theodora, 15in (38.1cm). Fully-jointed; pink satin tutu; flowers in ears; embroidered claws, nose and mouth.

Maxine Look sewing *Me Two*. She is inserting a reproduction Heubach child's head into the bear's head. An unpainted head lies beside the scissors on the table. Note the unstuffed body beside the sewing maching. 1983. *Photograph by Barbara Kennedy, courtesy of Maxine Look.*

Me Two, 16in (40.6cm). Light beige bear combining a bear body with a double-head. Under the bear's head, a reproduction Heubach doll's head is inserted. Fullyjointed; carries leather tag; wool scarf around neck; embroidered claws, nose and mouth.

The smaller Steiff bear with the Waugh honey pot. He wears a Roosevelt button, August 1983.

Maxine Look's bears. Left to right: *Me Two*, *Theodora*, *Flower Child* and *Max*. First row: *Flower Child* and *Maxie*. *Photograph by Barbara Kennedy, courtesy of Maxine Look.*

"As much as I enjoy dolls, I've liked teddy bears more and for a long time. As with dolls, my early interest in bears was to repair and restore them. My favorites sometimes come from their backgrounds. One of these being *Poor Mr. Lindsay* (all my bears are named and most dressed).

"I purchased *Poor Mr. Lindsay* from a dealer who cleaned out a house and found him there. He had been battered by a dog, thereby having a great opening in his skull, and no eyes. His nose was badly pushed in and he was missing an ear, due to his abuse. He needed T.L.C. and I knew I could give it to him.

"He came through all of his surgery fine, except that he must wear a hat 'till death do us part' to conceal his brain surgery. To compensate for his bleak past, he has traveled to Washington, D.C. with me to see the cherry blossoms, visited Maine and got a clearance from the guards at the Margaret Woodbury Strong Doll Musuem in Rochester, New York, to visit the dolls there."

Maxine's skills as a bear doctor are diversified. Besides brain surgery, she is adept at eye transplants. "Dr. Look" tells of one such operation.

"One day while out for a walk I saw a little girl sitting on her steps holding her teddy. I could see his eyes were missing, so I went up and asked if she would like me to take him home and give him new eyes. She was reluctant at first, but I assured her I'd have him back within a few hours, so she let me take him. When I returned him with new (shoe button) eyes, she came to the door and, beaming, she took him and hugged him with so much love and said, "Oh, teddy. Now you can tee the tun tine." What a reward I had."

Maxine finds bear making a rewarding pastime, also. She has not been at it very long, despite her passion for bears. She started inadvertently, again via the doll route.

"I made my first bear in the spring of '81 when a doll club president called to tell me that the teddy bear slide program we were planning to show at our next meeting a few days away hadn't arrived and could I do a program. I had a teddy hand puppet, so I wrote a dialogue for him and hid behind a screen while my teddy did his thing. I also created a teddy from a fur fabric and looking at a long-nosed early bear I owned.

"I was surprised that a few of the doll club members who were also teddy bear collectors thought it was an antique bear. I had dressed him with old fabric. I didn't know how to make the joints sturdy, so didn't joint the legs when I started.

"Since my bear was so well-received and people wanted to buy him, I decided to make a family for him. That is how the *Max Bear Family* was born.

"*Max* is 15in (38.1cm), *Mrs. Max* is 13in (33cm) and *Maxie* is 11in (27.9cm) tall. They are made of brown fur fabric, black paw lines. They have a leather bear's paw attached to their wrist with the date, my name, their name and number. All bears I make have an ID of a leather bear's paw and each is numbered."

She has progressed in her bear construction techniques since the rush job for the doll meeting.

"My early *Max* bears were fully dressed, partly because they were cute dressed and partly because the bodies weren't designed as well as the heads. Now the body and joints have been perfected. *Max* wears a top hat and a bow tie. *Mrs. Max* wears a lace-trimmed hat and a lace collar. *Maxie* wears a cap and a ribbon about his neck."

The *Max* bears are her most antique-looking teds. They share characteristics with the types of bears Maxine prefers.

"My favorite bears are those with humps, long arms and legs, big feet and a button in the left ear. But most of all they must have personality. Some poor old bears talk to me, while others that are nearly perfect say nothing."

The Massachussetts bear maker has had a lot of comments about her other bears; they are far less traditional. One of them, called *Me Two*, a light beige bear, 16in (40.6cm) tall, combines a bear body with a double-head. Under the bear's head, a reproduction bisque Heubach child-doll's face peeks out. "I ran a little contest to decide on a name for this bear," Maxine wrote. "My nine-year-old granddaughter chose 'Two heads are better than one.' Good thought, but it wouldn't quite fit on the leather tag."

Another design, a ballerina, won a bear contest in Boston, Massachusetts.

"I made an off-white jointed ballerina I named *Theodora*, 15in (38.1cm) tall and dressed in a pink satin tutu with flowers in her ears. She was voted the best bear at the show (by all the other bears) and received a $50 award. When a reporter interviewed me because of *Theodora's* popularity and she was being photographed for front page coverage in our local newspaper, she asked if my other bears weren't envious of *Theodora's* success, and I said, not at all. I was only concerned that she may become unBEARable. She asked what *Theodora* would do with her prize money. I informed her that she had ordered a gym set for the rest of the bears."

Theodora is not the only Look bear who is photographed. Maxine spends an inordinate amount of time photographing her bears, in all locations and positions.

"The comments I get are interesting," she writes, "They are more about the photographs of bears than the bears I make. During the past year I have devoted a lot of time to filming a family of bears on their travels around the country and in the Canadian Rockies climbing glaciers.

"When I'm laying on the ground in front of the Capitol in Washington, D.C. photographing bears, someone taps me on the shouder and wants to know if I'm writing children's books. Others have asked who pays me to travel so many places with the bears. They don't realize I was going to Tahoe, California, skiing and just took the bears along."

Maxine's journey to teddy bear design was circuitous, and serendipitous, with a long detour at restoration. But it gave her a background of knowledge from which to reap an intimate understanding of teddy construction. Her journey nowadays is not alone. Camera in hand, she brings the bears along.

LOIS CARLISLE

Lois Carlisle and friend. *Photograph courtesy of Lois Carlisle.*

All Tuckered Out, etching. 6in (15.2cm) by 4in (10.2cm). 1983. *Photograph courtesy of Lois Carlisle.*

Bears are relatively new in Lois Carlisle's ouevre. So is the medium in which she rendered them — etching. All this is relative, of course, because Mrs. Carlisle has enjoyed a successful art career since the 1940s. She has been a commercial artist and illustrator, a display artist, a technical illustrator, art teacher and gallery owner. Currently, the New Jersey native pursues a freelance fine art career, producing and marketing her own original etchings.

Lois' etchings explore a broad range of generally upbeat motifs: carrousel horses, Victorian houses of the Western United States, sea otters, whales and...teddy bears. She wants her art to be "a positive, wholesome contribution to our living, for people of all ages — (and) — bears are ideal for this."

Mrs. Carlisle's career as a bear artist began in the wake of a Christmas show held at the Santa Barbara Museum of Art in the late 1970s. From the community, over 450 bears were loaned to the exhibit — bears of all shapes, sizes, ages and conditions. From childhood Lois had liked bears, but she cannot remember a specific bear friend. The Christmas show revived her interest, suggesting the idea of producing a series of teddy bear etchings, a project enthusiastically encouraged by her grandchildren.

The bear etching project has become a very personal one for the artist and for her customers who will single out teddies that remind them of childhood companions. This resemblance is not accidental, for all her etchings are done "from life." They are portraits of bears borrowed from friends, even strangers. Occasionally bear owners bring

their teds for sittings. One day, a gentleman from Los Angeles brought his bear, *Fenwick,* to Lois. Finding him attractive, she agreed to do an etching of the bear, and the owner left him to model. When the portrait was done the gentleman ordered the first six etchings of the edition and subsequently brought *Elliot* for immortalization.

But not just any bear will do. First of all it must appeal to Lois artistically. "Most good ones do," she states. It must have a happy and lovable character. The character of the bear is especially important for effective rendering.

This insistence on character and a relationship between the artist and the bear produces a sensitivity, an understanding of what it feels like to be a bear, that is conveyed to the viewer. When asked if bears are "people" to her, Lois responded: "Yes, bears are 'people,' as is our Weimaraner dog. That is why you can have such a personal relationship with a bear."

Her public seems attuned to this quality and to her attention to each bear's personality. One of her etchings, "Perfect 10," depicts a grouping of ten wide-eyed, expectant, eager, floppy bears. At the artist's reception at its first showing, two people asked Mrs. Carlisle if particular bears had been done individually because her versions of them were identical to fondly remembered childhood friends.

Bears constitute about ten percent of Lois' output, and she is as serious about making fine bear prints as she is with her other subject matter.

She began with three bear etchings among her first 60 or so editions of all subjects. They proved so popular that she increased her offerings to nine and plans on six more. All are carefully and professionally designed and etched, at times incorporating aquatint. Lois describes her methods of production as "a limited commercial way" of working. This means that she individually produces each etching in an edition, and that an edition consists of a sizable number of prints. When the first nine print editions are done, she will have produced 1320 prints.

Although an edition of etchings consists of multiples, each is technically considered an original, since prints exhibit differences, depending on the order and manner of printing. Each of Mrs. Carlisle's images is hand-printed on her own press using 100 percent rag paper and inks selected for permanence. Watercolors (Winsor-Newton) used for highlighting areas of some prints are selected for color fastness and resistance to fading. Matting and framing are done to conservation standards.

The California artist's audience is "children of all ages" and her works are shown at art exhibits and in galleries, primarily in California. One of her designs is available as a note card and some have been transformed into needlepoint kits.

She finds word-of-mouth particularly powerful — fifty percent of her buyers have bought her work before or are friends of previous buyers. And it is easy to see why. She manages to transform teddies into universal icons begging for a hug.

It is difficult to stop with just one.

Panda, etching. 4in (10.2cm) by 2¾in (7.1cm). *Photograph courtesy of Lois Carlisle.*

Honey Bears, etching. 4in (10.2cm) by 2½in (6.4cm). 1982. *Photograph courtesy of Lois Carlisle.*

Perfect '10,' etching. 5½in (14cm) by 24in (61cm). *Photograph courtesy of Lois Carlisle.*

GARRETT AND JANET SAKAMOTO

The Sakamoto family, James Stewart and the *James Stewart Bear* (with *Harvey,* the Rabbit). 1983. *Photograph courtesy of the Sakamotos.*

James Stewart and the *James Stewart Bear* (and *Harvey,* the Rabbit). Mohair bear in golden color; white pleated bib; polka dotted bow tie; fully-jointed. 1983. *Photograph courtesy of the Sakamotos.*

A teddy bear portrait is usually a drawing or a painting of a bear. A portrait doll, on the other paw, usually approximates the subject's appearance. Janet and Garrett Sakamoto of Torrance, California, have created a teddy bear portrait that falls somewhere in between.

In March 1983, they presented the *James Stewart Bear* to his namesake. A fully-jointed golden-color mohair bear, he wears a white pleated bib and a red polka dot bow tie. He totes his rabbit friend, *Harvey.*

There seems to be a certain resemblance between them, the man and the bear, something about the way the eyes and nose come together, and the shape of the top of the head. Maybe, too, the angle of the ears, if one looks closely. It is more difficult to capture a likeness in fur than in porcelain. The idea, anyway, is nifty.

The Sakamotos have worked in porcelain. Some of their bears have porcelain mask faces, sculpted by Garrett, who is, as his wife, Janet, describes him "an artist in *every* sense of the word. He paints, sculpts, draws, etc. He even carved a carrousel horse which is about 12in (30.5cm) long and 8in (20.3cm) tall. He paints pictures, creates centerpieces, makes mechanical displays and is familiar with porcelain doll making. I enjoy cake decorating and crewel embroidery."

The couple makes a great team when it comes to bear making. Since 1982, they have been designing original teddies, the teddies they wanted to purchase but could not.

Bear collectors, they were most attracted to teds with "old, earlier bear faces." This was what they strove for in their early bear making attempts. But the first bear they sold had a porcelain face, the result of a porcelain doll making class the couple shared.

They shared the bear making process and use each other as springboards for new concepts. "We do a lot of talking/sharing with each other," Janet says. "Through this we talked a lot and decided to try making our own bear. We have inspired each other and have given constructive criticism to each other. We began using plush of various kinds/colors/weights, etc. We especially enjoy making the bears of mohair. Garrett and I do all the work ourselves so the number of bears we make is limited."

This partnership has resulted in some charming bruins. They range in size from 10in (25.4cm) to 16in (40.6cm). Among their best-known are a sorcerer, a magician, a jester and a ballerina. Most are named for family members.

Janet describes their designing procedures: "First we draw up our designs on paper and then we make a plush sample and then decide what changes we want to make. We talk, step back, talk, discuss, etc. Then we make our mohair prototype. We duplicate between 1 and 50 bears of each style. Many of our bears are one-of-a-kind.

"The most enjoyable part of bear making is creating the first of an edition, the least enjoyable part of bear making is repeating the bear over and over.

"We have designed between 18 and 20 bears," Janet wrote in 1983. "We work relatively slowly because only the two of us work on the bears.

"We do make clothes for the bears, but they are kept to the minimum, just to give us a way to create the character without covering up the bear. The clothing does not change the personality of the bear; it just adds to his/her character."

Janet's favorite bear is dressed. "My favorite bear," she says, "is a purple bear made of plush. Her name is *Delma,* named after a very dear friend. *Delma* has a tiara, wears a tutu and wears pink ballet ribbons on her feet. Her paws and feet are made of matching ultrasuede." The friend she speaks of, Delma Royce Peery, gave the pair "encouragement, praise and inspiration" as they developed their prototypes.

Scottie Magician, 12½in (31.8cm) tall. This bear is also made as a mechanical bear. The magician moves his head from side to side. The little bear appears and disappears from magicians hat. *Photograph courtesy of the Sakamotos.*

Wizard Bear and owl. Fully-jointed; gold mohair; blue peaked hat; collar trimmed in white. *Photograph courtesy of the Sakamotos.*

Ryan Jester, 11in (27.9cm) tall. Named for older Sakamoto son, Ryan. Golden and brown mohair; shoe button eyes; brown paws and feet; blue-green accented with golden bells and maroon ultrasuede; blue-green ultrasuede collar, maroon ribbons and rhinestones. Little bear on stick matches. *Photograph courtesy of the Sakamotos.*

The Sakamotos' audience is fellow arctophiles.

"All our bears are intended for the bear collector who likes unique and unusual handmade bears. We are trying to give the look, the feel and aura of an antique bear in mint condition, by using all the materials of yesterday. We want to give collectors the opportunity to experience owning a genuine antique reproduction. We have used all the materials — felt, genuine 1920 shoe buttons, mohair, excelsior, etc., and patterning of the old antique bears."

Garrett's favorite of his creations is such a bear. Janet describes him. "Garrett's favorite bear is one that we call *Oldie Bear*. He likes it best because it looks the most like an antique bear in mint condition. It is made of champagne mohair, has shoe button eyes, felt paws and feet, stitched claws, long arms, big feet, excelsior stuffing and an innocent face."

They may try to duplicate the essence of antique bears, but the bears are new, contemporary interpretations of old designs. And some are definitely a crosspollination of antique and modern bears that fall somewhere in between.

I can think of a case in point: a certain rabbit-toting portrait bear.

Garrett and Janet Sakamoto and friends. Garrett holds the *Grand Jester*, 17in (43.2cm) tall. 1983. *Photograph courtesy of the Sakamotos.*

SARA PHILLIPS

Sara Phillips with her bears. 1983. *Photograph © Lee Wolf, courtesy of Sara Phillips.*

Dressed Bear, approximately 1½in (3.8cm). Made of velour; clothes made from antique trims; straw bonnet. Bear marked with "SARA" tag sewn into back. 1983. *Photograph © Lee Wolf, courtesy of Sara Phillips.*

"I sort of strive for the effect that Beatrix Potter's dressed animals achieve — finely detailed and 'old world' looking in dress design.

Sara Phillips is describing her bears. Fully-jointed, painstakingly dressed, (their clothing employs antique silks and laces), the tallest of them stands 1¾in (4.5cm) high.

"I think it's fun to dress a bear in an outfit you'd expect to see on a fine doll — sort of a contrast to see a furry little animal wearing beautiful old silks and laces, instead of a delicate doll wearing them," she says.

Sara's bears run the gamut from bare bears, who sport only a bow to jester bears, a confederate soldier, and *Prince Charles* and family. Any one of them could hide nicely in a walnut shell. But she reserves the shell for her *Nutcracker Bear,* with wide-open jaw.

A miniaturist, the Maryland teacher first made bears in 1981, when she could not find acceptable teddies to fill a miniature setting, "The Teddy Bear Shop," that she was building. "I was disappointed in the lack of fine miniature jointed bears when looking for some to put in the shop. I felt that almost everything had been produced in perfect detail in miniature, why hadn't someone done the traditional old jointed teddy bear?"

After much experimentation, she came up with her own designs, adapted from techniques used on full-sized bears. From Margaret Hutchings' *Teddy Bears and How To Make Them,* she learned basic construction, and from the Bialoskys' *Teddy Bear Catalog,* she got a feel for the classic bear's personality.

These she translated to miniature scale, using velour for bodies, felt for paw pads and polyester fiberfill for stuffing. With bears of such a small size, a lot of improvising had to be done to approximate the orginals without details overwhelming the bears. With a background in miniature-making, these things are second nature by now to Sara. "Usually I design as I go along, or I know what I want to do and just do it from my head," she says.

The clothing takes the most time. She tries to make each bear one-of-a-kind. It takes approximately a week to make one. "I definitely feel the clothing can change the bears' personalities. A rather docile-looking bear can become very dignfied when attired, and vice versa. If anything, the clothing seems to add to their personalities somehow.

"I like my bears to be somewhat 'fancy,' with lots of details. I like using old laces and trims for dressing because they are better made and have more detailing than contemporary materials, and they're also softer — current trims seem to be stiffer."

Sara's eye for proportion and detail transforms tiny bits of fabric into lively, humorous, fashionable bruins. Some are "stock items," like the *Jester Bear,* her most popular ted, who comes in all colors. Other favorites are a *Bonnet Bear* dressed in hat and necklace, and *Zotty-Style Bears,* with open mouths and curved-down paws.

But the "limited edition" and "one-of-a-kind" bears are where Mrs. Phillips excels. She describes two. "I did a series of ten 'trunk bears' — bears that came in their own little trunks with accessories. The bears were 1in (2.5cm) high and dressed, and the trunks each had a drawer (for the accessories) and a mirror. I'm currently (1983) doing a series of 20 peddler bears; each bear is dressed (including hat, hooded cape and apron) and carries a little basket filled with wares including several bear-related items."

Perhaps her most famous was a winner at the 1983 Philadelphia Zoo Rally: *Prince Charles, Lady Diana* and *Prince William*. The parents were in wedding garb, the baby in christening gown. "I copied the costuming as closely as possible — although I took liberties and put the Prince of Wales' crown on Prince Charles, which he did not wear for the wedding."

Sara's big problem is time. Each bear takes too long to make — at least a week — time that is shared with her full-time job as a special education teacher for the mentally handicapped. She considers them art objects, not toys, because of the detail and care she puts into them. For this reason she aims them at collectors, and labels them with ribbon tags imprinted with "SARA," and sometimes the bear's number.

The long hours involved in each bear's creation start paying off when it nears completion. "I probably enjoy getting a bear into its last stages of development the most. Then it's really starting to take shape and sometimes I don't want to stop working on it, even if I have to, because I want to see the final product."

She is rarely disappointed. Her tiny, well-dressed bears achieve the look she seeks — "finely detailed and old-worldish," like bearish cousins of Beatrix Potter characters. And they do Peter Rabbit one better — they can fit into a thimble.

Confederate Bear (Civil War soldier), approximately 1¾in (4.5cm), standing next to reproduction of Civil War bullet. Velour; antique metallic braid trim; felt boots and hat; crossed swords and ostrich plumes on hat. 1983. *Photograph © Lee Wolf, courtesy of Sara Phillips.*

Peddler Bear, approximately 1¾in (4.5cm) standing. Ultra suede; dress of antique trims; apron of tatting; straw bonnet; velour cape with ribbon trim. Antique basket contains honey jar, fuzzy bear, bear head lollipop (made by Joyce Shivers), tiny Fimo peddler bear (made by Whim C. Bears), two tiny baskets hang from rim (one straw, one silver), tiny Mexican jug and brassbell. 20 bears in "Peddler Series." Marked with SARA tag on back, #1 on other side of tag. This is the prototype of the series. 1982. *Photograph © 1983 by Lee Wolf, courtesy of Sara Phillips.*

Bumble Bear, approximately 1½in (5.8cm) without antennae. Velour; wings of "opalescent" cellophane. 1983. Bear marked with SARA tag sewn into back. 1983. *Photograph © by Lee Wolf, courtesy of Sara Phillips.*

Jester Bear balancing in thimble, 1½in (3.8cm) high excluding hat. Velour and felt; Fimo jester stick. Bear marked with SARA tag sewn into back. 1983. *Photograph © 1983 by Lee Wolf, courtesy of Sara Phillips.*

Dressed Bear, approximately 1½in (3.8cm). Velour; dress of antique trims; straw bonnet. Bear marked with SARA tag sewn into back. 1983. *Photograph © 1983 by Lee Wolf, courtesy of Sara Phillips.*

Clown Bear doing single arm handstand, 1½in (3.8cm) high excluding hat. Made of velour. Marked with SARA tag sewn into back. 1982. *Photograph © 1983 by Lee Wolf, courtesy of Sara Phillips.*

Dressed Bear, 1in (2.5cm) standing height. Velour; dressed in antique trims; straw bonnet. Marked with SARA tag on back. Sample bear. 1982. *Photograph © 1983 by Lee Wolf, courtesy of Sara Phillips.*

Royal Bear Family — Prince Charles, Princess Diana and *Prince William.* Sizes: approximately 2in (5.1cm), 1½in (3.8cm) and 1in (2.5cm). Velour; costumes mainly of antique trims. One-of-a-kind set. Bears marked with SARA tag in backs. 1983. *Photograph © 1983 by Lee Wolf, courtesy of Sara Phillips.*

FAITH WICK

Faith Wick and her *Clown Bear.*
1983. *Photograph courtesy of Faith Wick.*

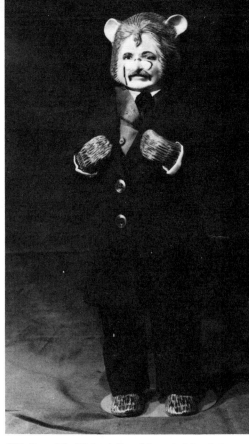

T.R. Bear, 16in (40.6cm). Porcelain portrait head of Theodore Roosevelt with bear "fur" hair and ears sculpted in porcelain; porcelain paws; balance wire armatured cloth body. Wears "Roosevelt-type" suit. 1983. *Photograph courtesy of Faith Wick.*

When Faith Wick introduced her original bear-dolls at the 1983 Teddy Tribune Convention, I was not really surprised. But I was pleased. Another fine doll artist had joined the ranks.

Faith's bears are bear-dolls; there is no mistaking it. One look at her *Theodore Roosevelt* bear will settle the question. His porcelain head combines a Roosevelt portrait face (glasses and all), "fur" sculpted hair and bear ears. All four paws are bearish. But the suit is Rooseveltian.

Her other bears boast the same construction: porcelain head and limbs and wire-armatured cloth bodies. They include *Teddy Bear Claus* (a Santa bear), a bear clown and a bear dressed in a bandleader's uniform.

The doll artist's bears are not teddies, but real bears with stern, slightly benevolent expressions, dressed rather incongruously. "I like costume," she says. "So the bears are designed for this as well as total personality."

The Minnesota native got her inspiration from native bears. "I've lived all my life in the Northwoods. Real bears are a part of my natural surroundings," she explains.

She started bear making with her humanoid bear and it was like eating potato chips — she could not stop. "I made *TR Bear,* then *Bear Claus* and the *Clown,*" she says. Bear making is addictive like that for many artists. Once you start, the ideas, the puns on words, the strange combinations of bear and costume pop out of ones mind and are impatient for realization — if the artist has a certain mind-set. Faith Wick seems to have it. When asked if bears were people to her, she replied, "OF COURSE."

The NIADA artist has been designing dolls for a long time — since before we met at a 1973 doll convention. She has gone a long way in the decade. She chiefly does commercial work — the bears will be reproduced by T.R. Wick Studio, Coleraine, Minnesota, for several firms, both domestic and foreign. Her work is ubiquitous and has won numerous awards, although now she does not compete. In 1976, she was selected Minnesota Artist of the Year and went to Washington, D.C. to meet President Ford. Her work has been in public exhibitions too many to mention, and her audience is a bit different from that of many doll artists; it is largely men.

Faith does not consider her bears or her dolls toys, but "sculpture for interior design," and she makes her bears 16in (40.6cm) high because it is "best for the shelf." She does not seem to feel that bear making is much different from doll making. "It's a nice addition to doll making. I like making a variety. I'm just beginning!"

At the rate the doll-bear artist works, (she has designed over 200 dolls), Faith Wick bears should be soon proliferating, finding their way to homes with both doll and bear collectors. I would not be surprised at all.

Teddy Bear Claus, 16in (40.6cm) tall. Porcelain bear head and lower limbs; balance wire armatured cloth body; Santa suit trimmed in fur; pointed hat trimmed in berries. Carries package. 1983. *Photograph courtesy of Faith Wick.*

Bear Drum Major, 16in (40.6cm) tall. Porcelain head and lower limbs; balance of body wire armatured cloth; drum major suit; tall black hat. 1983. *Photograph courtesy of Faith Wick.*

Teddy Bear Claus. Close-up of head. Note textured "fur" sculpted into the porcelain. *Photograph courtesy of Faith Wick.*

THERESA MAY

Variation of *Certified Public Bear*, 18in (45.7cm). Non-jointed; gray pinstripe knitted suedecloth; burgundy ears, vest and pads; gray boots; white collar; burgundy print tie with "pearl" tie tack. Vest pocket contains a tiny "ledger." Purchased white hat. *David and Susan Erickson Collection.* Signed wrist tag reads "Trunkful O'Teddies: Handcrafted Bears by Theresa May," with name of bear handwritten. Early bears of this type, beginning in 1978, had signed tag reading "The Beargeoisie: Bears for all occasions handcrafted by Theresa May." Theresa says: "I have made over 700 bears by this basic pattern, but dressed in a variety of ways. This was my first commercial bear type. Some of the bears are signed, but most are not. The clothing is mostly non-removable." *Photograph by Theresa May.*

Theresa May and some of "The Beargeoisie." *Photograph by Arrowhead Visuals. Courtesy of Theresa May.*

"Making things, to me, is like breathing. I couldn't NOT do it! I must be making something to be content, and bears fill that need beautifully."

Theresa May of Austin, Texas, is a multi-media bear artist, although she is not sure that the label applies to her. "I do not really consider the bears I make 'art.' They may be well-designed (a matter of opinion). I certainly strive for fine craftsmanship and care in detailing. I am always pleased when a collector buys one of my bears, but I am especially pleased if it is because the bear struck a chord, elicited a response," she says.

Theresa's bears have always elicited responses from onlookers, whether they be of plush or of paper. She is best known for character bears, having made them since 1978. Known as "The Beargeoisie," they are attempts to rep-bearsent actual people — famous and not — by means of costumed bear.

The bear tribe, which now numbers in the hundreds of immortalized individuals, was an offshoot of a Christmas project, Theresa explains, "I was short of cash Christmas 1978, and in lieu of buying presents for my husband's small niece and nephews, I made them bears from a commercial pattern I had bought when my own daughter was a baby. I took the bears to work for 'show and tell,' and they were a big hit. At my husband's suggestion, I had put a little vest with football star Earl Campbell's number on it on one of the bears. Earl had just won the Heisman Trophy, and that bear was for a six-year-old sportsminded boy. It wasn't long before we were calling him *Earl Campbear* and thinking of other 'bearsonalities.'

"My boss at the time was so taken with 'Earl' that my co-workers and I collaborated on a bear for his Christmas gift. We dressed him in a gray pinstripe jacket and gave him a phone and other appropriate bearaphernalia. In short, I got started making bears purely by chance."

Soon, Theresa was designing her own bear patterns to fit the personas of her character bears. But it is really the clothing that "makes" the May bear. It is also the part of bear making Theresa prefers. "Costume is one of my great loves, and I'll use any excuse for a chance to whip up something exotic," she says. "All my character bears have clothing, of course. Some of the more elaborate ones, such as *Little Bearry Blossom* (Japanese), have relatively accurate ethnic garments — even wigs! I've even done a *Scubear Diver* in a black wet suit, mask and fins. I believe that clothing for bears is very similar to clothing for people. Casual clothing (or no clothing!) permits casual behaviour — playing, sleeping, messy eating, etc. More formal clothing tends to foster better behavior — sitting quietly, asking permission, etc. However, some of my bears misbehave no matter how they are dressed."

The dressed bears are actually variations on a theme. Theresa usually does not design a new bear for each personality (that would mean by now she would have had to design over 700 new bears). "The basic bear pattern for these character bears is the same," she says. "—an unjointed 18in (45.7cm) classic bear. The bear fabric has usually been a knitted suede cloth, not plush, in everything from teddy bear browns to gray and tan pinstripe to blue paisley. The clothing is, for the most part, not removable and sewn into the actual construction seams of the bear. These bears are firmly stuffed, since they were designed for adults and professional people, and not for hugging."

She tells how she designs a bear: "My design procedures vary. If I am designing a stuffed bear, I might start with a pattern which already works and alter it some way — make it fatter, taller, change the nose, etc., or I might start completely from scratch, drawing the pieces bascially freehand on a brown paper sack and then sewing up a model to see if it works. My sewing and art background are a great help, in that I have a strong sense of proportion and scale, so usually only minor alterations or adaptations are needed. I rarely carefully graph anything out; I prefer the casual approach. Since many of my bears have been custom orders or customer requests, they are, in effect, one-of-a-kind. I have in the past made about 125 to 150 bears per year, not counting miniatures and paper bears. Once the design is worked out, I work rapidly. Most of the trial and error is done in my head. Hundreds....The only 'trick' I employ is to make sure that the bears I make please me. If they make me happy, then I can bet that someone else will like them, too."

Theresa's art background includes a B.A. in history of art-architecture/English from Texas Tech University in Lubbock, Texas, and post-baccalaureate work in the history of pre-Columbian art, studio art and music.

The character bears are her best-known products, and they have included "portrait" bears, such as a Greek Priest and one custom-made for Bette Midler (Bearre Midler), ordered by several devoted Midler fans when the singer performed in Austin, Texas, one spring. "Much of my business has been to customize a bear for some individual, using their coloring, clothing preferences, jewelry and other physical characteristics, as well as appropriate props in the design," she says. "The most amusing thing about my

character bears is remembering the number of times that I have made a bear purely from someone's verbal or written description of a person, only to find out that the bear I have made REALLY LOOKS LIKE THAT PERSON when I have finished it! Bears are so adaptable and flexible!

But, she would like to get away from the character bears. Truth be told, she prefers to work in two dimensions.

"I suppose I am still best known for my character bears, although I am striving mightily to discontinue those. I am introducing both jointed and unjointed plush bears, as well as a new series of water-color-type drawings of bears. I think I enjoy making the drawings best, since I can see more quickly exactly how they will look. I can also get ideas about costume, expression, etc., worked out better on paper than in fur. But I love all of the types when they are done."

In 1983, Theresa's poster designs won first prize for both 1983 and 1984 convention posters at the Teddy Tribune Convention held in Minnesota.

Theresa combines both loves, costume and drawing, in her bear paper dolls. "As a girl, I loved paper dolls and always had a huge box of both commercial and homemade ones in my room. I decided, in light of interest both in bears and in paper dolls, that I would design a series of bear paper dolls to be colored and cut out." They include some distinctively American character bears: *Teddy Jim,* a Texas Cowbear; *Bearabella,* a Southern Belle-type, *Bearonimo,* an Abearican Indian, *Queen Elizabear* and *Bearilyn Monroe.* She has designed a paper doll bear for this book: *Little Bearry Blossom,* after the plush bear described above.

Theresa is eclectic in her approach to art. "I work in many media," she says. "My main hobby is miniatures, in the pursuit of which I use paint, wood, paper, needlework and fabrics of all kinds. I also make clothing for humans from time

Teddy bear muffs made by Theresa May. Child-size in either honey gold or snow white plush; fully-lined; swivel head; lock-washer eyes; embroidered mouth; pompon nose; red neck ribbon; red plaid or polka dot bow. First made in 1982. Not a limited edition. Signed tag reads "Trunkful O' Teddies: Handcrafted Bears by Theresa May." *Photograph courtesy of Theresa May.*

Cowbear on Rocking Horse. Drawing by Theresa May. 5in by 7in (12.7cm by 17.3cm). Watercolor. © 1983. Matted in gold, signed and dated. *Photograph courtesy of Theresa May.*

Tiny Teddy by Theresa May. Made of Fimo clay; jointed; 1/2in (1.3cm) high.

Theresa May with her limited edition, *Bearlequin. Photograph by Juan Miranda, courtesy of Theresa May.*

to time. I find that I use the same skills and attitudes in making bears that I use in any creative project. My standards for construction are relatively high, but I will use whatever works to get the effect I am striving for. I am not a 'materials' snob, but I do believe in quality in both design and construction."

The designer has always aimed her bears at young-at-heart grownups. "I made my original bears not necessarily to 'play' with, but for fun, definitely. Since they were designed for adults, they were suitably 'adult' looking, but were meant to appeal to the child in all of us. Since those original bears, I have made many others for many purposes, both 'play' and 'non-play.' I don't think I would consider my bears sculpture, unless you categorize them as 'soft sculpture.' To me, sculpture implies a static nature, and I never envision my bears, either the ones I make or the ones I own, as 'static.'

She now marks her bears. The first ones only carried a wrist tag reading either "THE BEARGEOISIE, HAND-CRAFTED BEARS FOR ALL OCCASIONS," or "TRUNK-FUL O'TEDDIES, HANDCRAFTED BEARS BY THERESA MAY." Some bears are signed. All the limited editions are signed, dated and numbered on their feet. Future editions will have sewn-in labels.

Theresa is very fond of teddies and lives with a bunch. "Bears are people to me, although not every bear to the same degree," she says. "All my bears (that I own) have names and relationships within the group of bears. They have likes and dislikes and they have special places where they like to sit. Some can do tricks; some make me happy just by being quiet and sweet. But the one thing they all have in common is wanting MORE bears to live at my house! Sigh!"

The Texas bear maker finds that her bear mania is infectious. She works full-time as Direct Mail Manager for the University of Texas Press in Austin. As you may recall, she tried out her first bears on co-workers. They have never been the same.

She tells this story: "I was surprised at work one summer day by a teddy bear party complete with a human-sized costumed bear who read a proclamation in my honor, a teddy bear cake, punch, publishing-oriented teddy bear graffiti on the blackboard, and a coterie of attendant teddies brought from my co-workers' homes for the festivities. These wonderful people regularly tolerate my bringing bears and assorted bearaphernalia to work for 'show and tell,' but I never expected to be feted in such a unique way. It was the highlight of the summer."

Theresa May spends 40 hours a week at her publishing job, and probably as much time again at making bears. She has lots of future goals for them.

"I plan to design and make bears as long as there is a demand for them. I certainly have not exhausted the stock of ideas I would like to try, and if I weren't making bears, I'd be making something else. I am introducing new bears this fall, have several new ones on the drawing board for next year, and am working on an exclusive limited edition. I would also like to write bear stories and illustrate them. I'd like to do an entire series of authentically costumed ethnic bears, not necessarily for sale. I'd also like to get more sleep."

If Theresa May, by her own admission, "must be making something to be content," she must be happy indeed.

Little Bearry Blossom

Little Bearry Blossom. Paper doll bear done especially for this book by Theresa May. Size: 8½in by 11in (20.3cm by 27.9cm). Theresa has also done a plush bear of the same name. © 1983. *Courtesy of Theresa May.*

Bearilyn Monroe

GENTLEMEN PREFER BEARS

WITH BEARILYN MONROE

Bearilyn Monroe. Paper doll bear by Theresa May. © 1982. Size: 8½in by 11in (20.3cm by 27.9cm). *Courtesy of Theresa May.*

BEARONIMO
An Abearican Indian

Bearonimo, an Abearican Indian. Paper doll bear by Theresa May. © 1982 Size: 8½in by 11in (20.3cm by 27.9cm). *Courtesy of Theresa May.*

CATHERINE BORDI

Catherine Bordi and some of her bears. 1983. *Photograph courtesy of Catherine Bordi.*

Catherine Bordi *(The Chocolate Bear)* at work in her "bear factory." A finished 14in (35.6cm) *Pinecone Forest* style, powder gray bear is sitting on the sewing table. 1983. *Photograph by Peter Nuding, courtesy of Catherine Bordi.*

"M & M" was the first visitor bear, and he stayed the longest. He came packed with two cassette tapes and a "Chocolate Bear Bar," another of Catherine Bordi's confections.

"I'm something of an artist with food," the bear maker says. "Each of my bears has a recipe on its tag. My bears are called *Chocolate Bears,* partly because almost everybody likes chocolate, and partly because I wanted an excuse to make up a recipe. It makes them a little different."

Bordi bears do not need a recipe to stand out in a whole den full of bruins. Their high quality and excellence of craftsmanship and design put them paws above some of their competition. It has been this way from the beginning.

Influenced by the Steiff *Papa Bear,* and intrigued by the idea of reproducing antique bears, Catherine designed her first ted in the fall of 1980. It was little and filled with birdseed. The California bear maker aims for a bear with character, combining features found on early teddies and on real bears, but on few contemporary teds. "The modern bears look much less like real bears than some of the antique bears," she says. "If you look carefully at some of the old Steiff bears, they have features which real bears have and which modern bears do not have.

"For instance, they have a very flat head across the top and a long snout with shaved fur (almost any animal has much shorter fur on its snout than it does on the rest of its head, and the rest of its body). I like small eyes on a teddy bear beacuse a real bear has really small eyes in comparison

with the rest of its body. And great big eyes on a bear make it look cute, not in a way I like at all. What is most important to me is the blend of the best of the antique bears and the most appealing qualities of the real bear. I'm not after bears that look like Nelson Rockefeller, Dolly Parton or the Easter Bunny. It's not my style."

Bordi Bears are classy and stylish. The first ones were dubbed, logically, "Original Style." Made of domestic synthetic plush, they had unshaved longish snouts, were plump, fully-jointed and lacked the distinctive suede cloth label she started sewing into the back seam of every bear after number 100. Later bears sport shaved snouts (like her "antique snouty" style), for which she became well-known. Early gray bears became so successful, they formed the backbone of her production for a time, and surprised many a shopkeeper who thought unrealistically-hued gray bears unsaleable.

The California bear maker has never had trouble with sales. From the first basketful of bears she brought into a shop, the teds have sold themselves, and she had more than enough orders. It is a good thing she loves making bears.

"I make bears today because I'm addicted. I love making and designing bears and I love having numbers of teddy bears in my living room.

"I spend an inordinate number of hours making them. Anyone who knows me can tell you. I never seem to have time for anything else. I enjoy it so much that I do it to the exclusion of so many other things that I enjoy. I work on

Sunday when I could be doing something else. I'll have to learn to make fewer bears."

This would hardly please customers, who have to wait for bears as it is. Catherine is the sole producer of *Chocolate Bears* and does not intend to expand her work force. "I do all the work myself," she says. "I don't have ANYONE helping me. I don't even like to have someone else sweep the floor. I guess it wouldn't hurt if I did, but no one's offered. I like to work by myself. I'm efficient and I enjoy my own company. I don't like to keep an eye on someone else or supervise someone else. That way, I have total control over quality which is very important to me."

Quality is a key word in speaking of Bordi bears. Catherine uses only the finest materials, including the same

Catherine knows whereof she speaks. She had no childhood bear. Teddy bear love came as an adult. She talks about the experience.

"Having a teddy bear in a way is like being in love and never getting over it. When you're in love, you see only the wonderful things about the object of your affection. You don't see that whoever it is has all these nasty habits on the side. You just see all the wonderful things.

"And when you have a teddy bear, you feel the same way. You endow the teddy bear with all the wonderful personality traits that you love. And, since the teddy bear never becomes cranky, irritable or frustrated, you can remain in love with him forever. You never have to come down to earth or have to learn to accept the bad with the

Antique style bears, 20in (50.8cm), 17in (43.2cm) and 13½in (33cm), were introduced in 1982 and became extinct in late 1983. Rich long fur; multi-shaded coloration of toffee-colored beige and brown; cotton velveteen paw pads; trimmed inner ears and muzzles. *Photograph by Peter Nuding, courtesy of Theresa May.*

European fur that German bear manufacturers Steiff and Hermann use. Her tools, fiberfill and industrial-strength sewing machine are all highest quality, and she is picky down to the smallest details — things like making sure that all the fur is pulled from seam lines with a sturdy needle. "It's a good way to tell whether or not the bear maker takes pride in his or her work," she explains.

Even the neophyte can tell that Catherine takes pride in her work. She is especially pleased when her bears find their way to adults who have never known the joy of loving a teddy. My bears are for adult collectors and adults who fall in love with them. There have been a lot of adults who fell in love with my bears who never dreamt they could fall in love with a bear, but it was love at first sight," she says. "I'm always pleased when that happens. I like that better than with a collector falls in love with them because when it's someone who's never fallen in love with a bear, then I know it's really special. It's really pure. It's the real thing. This does not belittle the collector at all, but it's special."

good with a bear. A bear can be all good. I guess that's what makes them so special. They are a magical fantasy creature."

Fantasy creatures, perhaps, Bordi bears are designed from first-hand observation of real bruins. Catherine goes to the zoo, armed with a camera, and snaps a shot each time the bear moves, in the hope of capturing a salient quality she can reproduce in plush. She studies these shots and photographs of teddies she finds in books, trying to combine the best of each.

"I start out with my pattern and just draw it differently — a little longer here, a little shorter there — cut it out in some fur and sew it up to see what will happen, and just keep at it."

She makes fully-jointed bears in six sizes: 13½in (34.3cm), 17in (43.2cm) and 20in (50.8cm) in American fur, and, in the higher-quality European fur 11in (27.9cm), 14in (35.6cm) and 18in (45.7cm). Her favorite is a 1983 design, a 14in (35.6cm) honey-colored European bear. She describes him.

"I designed him after a very, very early Steiff bear which I had the honor of meeting. This bear was made before 1910. He was in beautiful condition, probably owned by adults his whole life or by a very careful child, because he has all of his fur, his eyes and everything. His stuffing had settled so that his head sagged down on his chest, making him look real tired. He had this real wise, wise look on his face. I designed my 14in (35.6cm) bear after him in several ways: I have the head sagging down, although it's not sagging. It's on quite sturdily. It has nice long arms. Right now, to me, he is my perfect bear. I just love him and I love making him."

Catherine sent her perfect bear for a Maine visit and he stayed a year and a half. He is the classy golden yellow teddy bear artist in the cover photograph — the bear who was the longest "artist in residence." Eric-Jon named him *M&M* the day he arrived for an obvious reason. He is a *Chocolate Bear.*

LEFT: *Pinecone Forest Style Chocolate Bear,* 14in (35.6cm). Golden honey fur; ultrasuede paw pads (as are all Pinecone Forest style bears); lightly pointed ears resembling a real bear. *Photograph by Peter Nuding, courtesy of Theresa May.*

BELOW: Antique style black bear, 17in (43.2cm). This bear also available in 13½in (31.8cm) and 20in (50.8cm). *Photograph by Peter Nuding, courtesy of Theresa May.*

Pinecone Forest Style Rich Cinnamon Bear, 11in (27.9cm). Chubbier than the larger sizes, he is more of a baby. His muzzle is shorter than in the larger sizes also; the ears are perfectly round, not having attained their slightly pointed mature shape. He can grow to be as large as 18in (45.7cm), however, he has big brothers to prove that! *Photograph by Peter Nuding, courtesy of Catherine Bordi.*

ROBERTA VISCUSI

Roberta Viscusi and friends. *Photograph by Marla Murphy, courtesy of Roberta Viscusi.*

A hospital career and a passion for bears have meshed for California craftswoman Roberta Viscusi. For over 24 years she has worked at Napa State Hospital where she is nursing supervisor and psychiatric technician. When she began designing bears, she looked to the needs of patients.

She has come up with a line of original plush bears to be companions for convalescing children — or adults. The bears' injuries are just like their owners'. She equips these teds with arm or leg casts, neck braces or head bandages.

A teddy whose hurts match yours, who feels just as badly as you do, cannot help but make a patient feel better. "The *Ouchy Bears* have a therapeutic purpose: to soothe and eliminate anxiety in injured folks (children especially)," Roberta says.

She makes them with "removable injuries," so the teddies can "get well" with the patients. The fur parts under the casts are protected by plastic. "The cast can be signed and dated by friends and left on the bears forever, or can be removed at the same time as your cast is removed," she explains. "This is a great idea to help eliminate a child's fear of having a cast removed. A child also forgets his discomfort because he's worried about teddy's. Of course, when he sees how brave teddy is it also helps."

Roberta has always liked teddies, but became obsessed with them in 1982. When her co-workers found out about her mania, they responded, "You've worked here too long."

She has won them over to the extent that they now give her bears. They can see that the nursing supervisor's teds are comforting patients in ways no human could. Stories of teddy's salutory effects with the physically and emotionally needy are legion; Roberta knows of his powers firsthand.

"I was given a bear by my uncle the night I arrived from California to live with my grandmother in Connecticut for a year. I remember being homesick and crying. Uncle Bill went out and came home with *Teddy*. The year was 1947. I was so pleased to have him to comfort me. We were very close friends. I shared all my secrets with him. He sopped up a lot of tears over the years, especially in my teens. We traveled back and forth across the USA every year and moved to England when I was 15. We visited Scotland and Wales, also. I almost married at the age of 18 but things did not work out and if it hadn't been for *Teddy,* I'd have been severely depressed, but again he comforted me.

"In 1959 it was time for us to return to the United States as my father's tour of duty was over. For four days we stayed in transit waiting for the fog to lift so our plane could take off. At least a half dozen times we were wakened in the middle of the night and boarded the plane only to have to unload and wait again.

"One night I had been sleeping on a cot next to a wall with *Teddy*. I was awakened and told to "hurry — the fog has lifted; we are leaving." It was three o'clock in the morning. We all ran for the plane and after it had leveled off in my

Ouchy Bear with cast and crutch by Ro"bear"ta. Bear is "signed" on cast. 1983. *Photograph by Marla Murphy, courtesy of Roberta Viscusi.*

sleepy state I reached for *Teddy* to settle down and complete my sleep when I discovered he wasn't on the plane.

"I panicked, cried, got physically ill and felt my whole world had come to an end. We landed in Newfoundland and were told we couldn't leave the plane due to a storm but Dad convinced the pilot to wait while he ran in and telephoned England to hear that they could not find *Teddy* and had not seen him.

"To this day I still feel his loss. I get a sick feeling in the pit of my stomach when I see a teddy who reminds me of him and in my mind's eye I can still see *Teddy* laying there between that cot and the wall where I know he must have fallen.

"I know how the English cherish the teddy bear and my only hope is that some caring person found him and he lives on in someone's collection. I wonder if he misses me as much as I miss him."

To make up for his loss, the Napa nurse has, in the last two years, filled her house with hundreds of teddies. Crowding got so bad, she purchased a double-sized mobile home for them. She calls it "Bearadise." It is here that she works on her bears.

Ro"bear"ta, as she calls herself, makes two types of teds: plush and clay. The clay ones, which she calls *E.T. Teddies,* made of Fimo clay, are 2in (5.1cm) and under. They are direct descendants of the first bears she made.

"The very first bears I EVER made were of mud when I was eight years old. There was a mama, papa and two babies. I built a shoe box house and wooden cars. Grandpa helped with the cars. *Teddy* and I spent many hours playing with the mud teddies which were sun baked and held together with grass cuttings."

Her techniques have become more sophisticated. The clay teds have distinctive heads, made by pressing her thumb down on the face. They are marked with a circled "R."

The fabric bears' birth stemmed from curiosity and cash shortage. "I really began making bears to see if I could do it. Then when everyone saw and wanted my teddies, I decided to sell them to earn money to buy for my collections."

After experimentation and encouragement from a collector-friend, Roberta came up with a repertoire of designs. Most are 18in (45.7cm) tall and fully-jointed. Few are identical. She prides herself on the fact that each bear is slightly different. This is achieved by combining pattern parts.

"I never cut any two bears exactly alike. I actually have 11 patterns that I've designed over a period of a year. Often I mix and match limbs, heads, tummies, sizes of eyes and shapes of ears so that all are different. Furs range from very short to 1in (2.5cm) long. Every color is used from time to time. I have even made a red and three green bears as special orders for St. Patrick's Day, etc. Noses are all different shapes and sizes, as are the snouts. There are pugged, turned up and long snouts, clipped and unclipped fur on snout. This all depends on demand. The local toy shop requests short snouts and little noses. Frowns are the most popular."

Roberta Viscusi with concerned, noseless bear. *Photograph by Marla Murphy, courtesy of Roberta Viscusi.*

Roberta's bears have become so popular she has needed to carve out chunks of time from her busy schedule to make them. "I work full-time in a hospital and the rest of the time I spend trying to make teddies — I'd guess three to five hours a day. I find when I get home from work is best, when everyone is asleep. I usually work on them from 11:30 p.m. to 2:00 or 3:00 a.m. This is really relaxing and I set the bears on the kitchen counter for the family to greet when they wake up in the morning."

She has to be careful working at these hours, though, "I never make bears when I am too tired — my husband had to take apart a little fellow who had his legs on backwards."

She marks her bears with a numbered tag center back, reading Ro"bear"ta, and a signed and numbered card. She records each ted by color, number, size, special characteristic and name of purchaser. Roberta's audience is collectors and children. But, more than anything, "I love to see my bears go to older people who are lonely," she says.

The Napa, California, nurse knows firsthand the curative powers of a therapeutic teddy.

E.T. Teddies, 2in (5.1cm), in Napa, California, vineyard. Made of Fimo clay. *Photograph by Roberta Viscusi, courtesy of Roberta Viscusi.*

OPPOSITE PAGE: *Ouchy Bear* with cast and sling by Ro"bear"ta. Bear is "signed" on cast. 1983. *Photograph by Maria Murphy, courtesy of Roberta Viscusi.*

Original fully-jointed bear by Roberta Viscusi. 1983. *Photograph by Roberta Viscusi.*

18in (45.7cm) bears by Ro"bear"ta. 1983. *Photograph by Marla Murphy, courtesy of Roberta Viscusi.*

JACQUELINE ROBINSON TAPLEY

Jackie Robinson Tapley, creator of Mountain Bears with *RR Bear* and a few of his friends. 1984. *Photograph courtesy of Jackie Tapley.*

Jacqueline Robinson, age two, and her original teddy, who inspired her Mountain Bear Manufacturing Company. *Photograph courtesy of Jackie Tapley.*

When Jacqueline Robinson Tapley was two, she fell in love with a white teddy bear. He was handsome, fully-jointed, with long white fur and brown eyes. The white bear was Jackie's constant companion, traveling with her, sleeping with her and watching over her as she grew up, got married and had children.

Jackie Tapley and her bear now share a log house on a Maine mountain, not far from her birthplace. The bear's fur is spotty. He has had eye transplants, but he has not retired. He has a new job — overseeing the production of the Mountain Bear Manufacturing Company.

The company is a byproduct of Maine's long winters. Up here snow comes early. By December, lakes are frozen. Cars and trucks careen over thick ice, competing with ski-planes, snowmobiles, ice fishermen and skaters for priority. The snow lasts sometimes till May.

Winter is a slow time for the swimming pool business in Bangor and Jackie Tapley builds pools. February is particularly problematic. Often-leaden skies and snow dunes keep folks housebound, inventing creative schemes to combat cabin fever. Thus, in February of 1982, Jackie made her first Mountain Bear.

Actually, she says, she decided to "raise" Mountain Bears, in the way her family raises Morgan horses and registered cocker spaniels. These bears, she decided, would have pedigrees and registration papers.

By summer, she had made five white bears and a lot of pools awaited attention. So she left the bears with her mother at Special Acres farm for safekeeping.

From the beginning, apparently, Jackie's bears have led a charmed life. They sat for publicity pictures on June 22, 1982, at Margit's Studio in Bangor. That day, Special Acres burned to the ground. "Had they been destroyed at this time," says Jackie, "the project would have been stopped."

Later that summer Jackie was Down East on Mount Desert Island building a pool for Mr. and Mrs. Caspar Weinberger. Mrs. Weinberger, a writer, admired the bears and their studio portraits and volunteered to write them a book. In a few days, Mrs. Weinberger presented Jackie with the manuscript, now published by Down East Books as *That's What Counts — A Tapley P. Bear Storybook,* by Jane D. Weinberger. The photographs taken the day of the fire illustrate it.

Jackie's bears are now made in a cottage industry in Hermon, Maine. Several women cut, sew and assemble them according to her design. Jeanne Savoy is in charge of quality control, and strict standards are enforced. The bears come in three sizes: 15in (38.1cm), 17in (43.2cm) and 22in (55.9cm). The largest can wear baby clothes. Some play music. All Mountain Bears are marked by brass identification numbers on their left legs.

A pedigree comes with each bear. When it is returned to Mountain Bears, the owner receives parchment registration papers with a gold seal on them, a one-year warranty and the promise of mail from the mountain for the teddy bear for years to come.

Besides the white bears, Mountain Bear Manufacturing produces character bears: *Tapley P. Bear, Double R Bear* (railroad bear), Ski Bear, Black Beauty Bear and *Sweet Chocolate Bear.* Then there is the *Blue Nose Bear* (for the Bluenose ferry that travels between Bar Harbor and Nova Scotia), with a blue nose and a blue ribbon in her ear.

Jackie finds parallels between her two professions: "Designing pools and creating a beautiful yard or indoor pool is much like building/raising a bear. There is construction and beauty all wrapped into either of these talents."

When asked what gives her the most satisfaction about bear making, the Maine designer replied: "Giving the bears to people I love and care about. Seeing them smile with happiness and hugging a bear. The hugs will spill over to the humans in their life. Everyone needs more hugs than they receive."

When it is time for bear hugs, most often Jackie turns to her original white teddy. Together, after all, they have bred a mountainful of bears.

Gypsy Bear, designed by Jackie Tapley. *Photograph by Margit Studio, courtesy of Jackie Tapley.*

Nanna and *Grampie,* designed by Jackie Tapley. *Photograph by Margit Studio, courtesy of Jackie Tapley.*

Career Bears At Work by Mountain Bear Manufacturing Co. 1983. Designed by Jackie Tapley. *Photograph by Margit Studio, courtesy of Jackie Tapley.*

ABOVE: *Lady Mountain Bears* by Jackie Tapley. 1984. *Photograph by Margit Studio, courtesy of Jackie Tapley.*

LEFT: *Pedigreed Bear* from the Mountain Bear Manufacturing Co. Collection of Career Bears. Designed by Jackie Tapley. *Photograph by Margit Studio, courtesy of Jackie Tapley.*

DEANNA DUVALL

In 1976, Deanna Duvall was captivated by the look on the face of an antique teddy bear. For lack of the original, she began to design her own.

When she moved to New Jersey, she met a bona fide bear collector with a "teddy bear room" filled with old teds. The lady had seen Peter Bull on television, read his book, *The Teddy Bear Book,* and had been inspired to acquire piles of bears. Deanna was struck by the inevitability of this idea. So she bought Mr. Bull's book. Getting bears was harder.

"I soon discovered in my pursuit of teddies that they were difficult to find, as a quiet group of bear collectors had been working over the territory long before I arrived (1976). The price involved in purchasing old bears was very often prohibitive for me, so I decided to design a bear with all the features I loved best about my friend's bears."

Deanna had been involved in cloth toy and doll designing in California, and had the requisite skills to design her own bears, always bearing in mind the expressions embroidered on her friend's teds. "Even today I am always refining my designs in pursuit of what I saw in those dear little bear faces," she says.

The first three years the bear maker sold her work to local doll collectors and friends. Eventually, as bears became more popular, business picked up. Now she has a national mail order bear business. But the bears are made the same way, except maybe, for the cloth from which they are cut.

"Overall, I do not deviate too much from old early bears. I have never been able to get mohair/wool but find that there are sources now.

"I have always used acrylic fur fiber as I like a 'real' look about the bears and because I feel more at home with fabric. I am enjoying experimenting more with natural fiber fabric rather than heavy pile. I like velvet for its texture and slimming quality — plaid wool is fun (a subtle plaid) and other wool blends. I have always been a careful seamstress but it is easy to get sloppy with fur fabrics because you can't see the seams. The wool blends require careful attention."

Because she is dedicated to the memory of those New Jersey bears, Deanna is careful to keep a nostalgic look about her designs. "Bear making for me," she says, "is the pursuit of that whimsical, naive 'bear face' that stole my heart as I played with my friends's bears in her parlor. The colors, the natural fibers of the toys constructed at the turn of the century and the craftsman's input are very appealing to me. For a teddy bear to 'look very much like a real bear' and yet to invite confidence, affection and imaginitive play is what I want my bears to achieve. Because I'm drawn to the 'old' toys, I'm currently working on a bear on all fours on a platform with wheels. I've wanted one for such a long time and have not been able to afford them."

She describes her methods: "I've now developed basic patterns that I alter to suit need or desire. If I'm doing a bear to fit a piece of clothing that is dear to a person, then the bear's body must be altered. Sometimes I want a LONGER snout — just BECAUSE — so, when laying the basic design on the fabric, I make the adjustment when I mark the pattern

Deanna Duvall and her bears. *Photograph by Stardust Studio, Dave Kupetz,* © 1983, courtesy of Deanna Duvall.

on back of fabric. The most difficult moments in bear making for me are eye and ear placement. When embroidering the nose, I begin to anticipate the bear personality that will finally emerge with the mouth.

"Many aspects of the bear making process are tedious. Cutting out, sewing several limbs at the same sitting, some of the stuffing — tiring, but so important, all of them."

Deanna's bears range from 12in (30.5cm) to 5ft (1.52m) in height, (the five footer was a special order) but the most popular seems to be the 18in (45.7cm) size; he is easiest to dress. The bear maker does not spend much time making bear clothing, although she does love a well-dressed bear.

"I liked the traditional outfits first designed for the old bears — clowns, sailor suits, sweaters and others. I found making the clothing more time-consuming than the bears, so I use children's clothing I can adapt. Clothing adds more whimsy and can define a mood or celebration of a particular event."

The Oregon bear maker could make a bear a day if she wanted to, but her output varies, depending upon family responsibilities. "I have two boys at home and my husband is president of a university. I am afraid that bear making gets relegated to a No. 3 spot in priorities if need be," she says. So she has designed a kit for her bears that has been very well received.

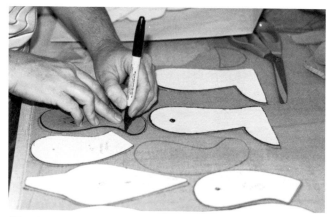

"Busy hands (belonging to Deanna Duvall) lay out and draw patterns onto a 3yd-long (3.8m) piece of knit plus fur. As many bears of the 18in (45.7cm) and 12in (30.5cm) variety as can be accommodated are fitted onto the piece, drawn around and then cut out. A laundry marking pen is used; each piece is marked by size of bear and joint place if required. Patterns are modified all the time, sometimes even during this step." — Deanna Duvall. *Photograph by Robert Duvall, courtesy of Deanna Duvall.*

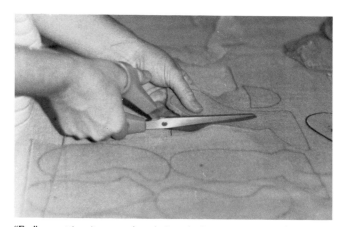

"Endless cutting, it seems, long before the bear even gets to the sewing machine. Many bears are drawn onto fabric before cutting starts. This is an important step that has to be done carefully in order to preserve the length of fiber of the plush." — Deanna Duvall. *Photograph by Robert Duvall, courtesy of Deanna Duvall.*

18in (45.7cm) tall bear strutting his stuff to show his ability to move arms, legs and head. The fabric is woven with a gray/beige color plush. Claws and nose are brown perle cotton thread and pads are beige wool felt. MY BEARS tag is in left leg seam. This size bear is the most popular for dressing and displaying. *Photograph by Stardust Studio, Dave Kupetz © 1983, courtesy of Deanna Duvall.*

This is *Wendy*. He belongs to Wendell and June Amos and shares their interest in boating. He is 18in (45.7cm) tall, beige knit plush, black wool thread nose and claws; fully-jointed. All Duvall bears are stuffed with polyester fiberfill and their pads are beige wool felt. He is wearing a baby's white terry cloth swim suit trimmed in red and green at each leg, navy at the yoke. "Yachting" is in red thread and the sailor hat is white with a blue pom on top. *Wendy* came directly from a boating trip by airplane to be photographed. *Photograph by Stardust Studio, Dave Kupetz © 1983, courtesy of Deanna Duvall.*

Duvall bears, marketed under the name "MY BEARS," are marked with a cotton tape that is usually in the back of the leg. They are usually unsigned and have never been numbered.

Since 1976, Mrs. Duvall has amassed a number of American teddy bears "because of the variety of expression and body build. I never knew you could combine such variations on long and short limbs and bodies as I've seen on the American bears," she says. And the recreation of these

bears still excites her. "I've been quite surprised at myself and my continued interest in the production of bears; I thought I would tire, but so far I've gotten great joy from each bear face and personality. I think that was what caught and held my fascination with the old bears — individual personalities."

The look on the face of that antique teddy that captured Deanna back in 1976 is, apparently, still a powerful inspiration.

29in (73.7cm) tall beige knit plush bear; fully-jointed; wool felt pads; black wool claws and nose. Tag in left leg seam. Wears a blue/white romper from the 1920s. Stuffed with polyester fiber. *Photograph by Stardust Studio, Dave Kupetz © 1983, courtesy of Deanna Duvall.*

This 18in (45.7cm) bear has assumed the name *Tabitha* for Halloween. Greize woven plush; brown perle cotton thread nose and claws; fully-jointed is easily dressed. This costume was borrowed from "Belle," Snoopy's girlfriend and has a black cotton under dress with black cotton witch's hat trimmed with a purple cotton band. The cape belongs to a 22in (55.9cm) dolly friend and is made of crushed nylon velvet lined in black tricot and has a hood. Pumpkin is papier-mâché with tissue paper; painted features. *Photograph by Robert Duvall, courtesy of Deanna Duvall.*

One-of-a-kind 5ft (1.5m) tall *Big Bert, the Scout Leader.* Jointed legs; arms and head sewn-on for some mobility but head is stationary. Leather feet, paws and nose; brown acrylic safety eyes. *Big Bert* is made of a long pile synthetic fur in gray tones. Made for Carole Osborn for a special teddy theme for the 1982 Central Florida Doll Club Christmas party. *Photograph courtesy of Deanna Duvall.*

Gladly Gordon, 34in (86.4cm) tall. Jointed arms and legs; stationary head; beige color knit plush; polyester stuffing; wool felt pads; black wool yarn for nose and claws. He is wearing an old sailor collar of navy blue wool trimmed in white braid and a red satin ribbon with brass sleigh bell. There are only three *Gladly Gordons. Photograph by Stardust Studio, Dave Kupetz* © *1983, courtesy of Deanna Duvall.*

KELLY REUTER

The Reuters: Karl, Kelly, K.C. (6) and Shelby (5.). 1984. *Photograph courtesy of Kelly Reuter.*

" 'Tis the Season to be Beary," could be the theme song of Kelly Reuter's business, "Teddy and Me."

Kelly designs and produces original rainbow-hued teddy bears for every holiday imaginable, and has since 1980.

"During the long, cold days of January 1980, I decided to design some bears that were different from any ready-made bears on the market," she says. "Although I love all bears, I personally felt the brown, jointed, antique-type teddy was entirely too common; you saw them everywhere and everyone sold them. When I went to buy a bear, I wanted something unique and different with lots of personality and appeal. I could never find what I wanted so I decided to design it, make it and sell it myself."

Kelly has always been fond of bears, and her favorite was of uncommon hue. "My first and very favorite bear was *Pink Teddy,* who was a gift from my beloved grandfather. *Pink Teddy* was approximately 10in (25.4cm) tall with a white body and head and pink arms, legs and ears. She was a constant companion and when it was necessary for her to be washed, I sat by the dryer the entire drying time, watching her go around and 'round."

When Kelly started to make her own bears, color was foremost in her consideration.

"I wanted a cuddly, sweet-looking teddy with a lot of personality in lots of different colors. The color idea is how the 'Bears of the Month' were born. I needed an interesting and appealing reason to make bears in lots of colors. Since I've always loved holidays, decorating, celebrations and all that goes with them, I decided to make a bear for each month. Each 'Bear of the Month' is an appropriate color, dressed accordingly."

The Amboy, Minnesota, resident had a lot of bear making under her belt before plunging into multi-colored bruins. "In 1977, when our first child was born, I decorated his nursery in shades of lime green with brown teddies all around. I made appliqued quilts, wall hangings, macrame teddies, etc., for the nursery. These things were probably some of the first bear items I designed myself. I also designed his first Halloween costume when he was a month old. It was

a brown fur teddy suit which made him look just like a live little teddy (with baby face poking out). I also made K.C. (and later Shelby, when she was born in 1979) many outfits with teddy appliques or in pockets."

Kelly came up with a bear that bore all the characteristics she wanted, but could not find.

"The basic bear for 'Bear of the Month' was the first one I designed. He has a short, round body with a full tummy, short, pudgy legs and arms, big round feet, a fairly large head with round muzzle (separate piece from head piece) and medium-size ears. All my bears (with the exception of the tiny angel-bear ornament) have pure black eyes. I feel these look the richest, most mischievous, have the most 'sparkle,' give the teddies personality. They also have black noses and black thread mouths in a little smile. Since then, all the bears and bear items I have designed are based basically on that same principle. I also make brown and bear-colored bears as well as the bright and pastel shades."

Kelly's distinctive simple teddy shape prevails in most of her designs. It has found its way into other materials: "The first bears I designed to sell were of synthetic plush and most still are today. Soon after I made the first plush bears, I designed some very tiny crocheted doll house teddies in fluffy yarn, and a larger ornament version in regular yarn. I also did some appliqued teddy-shaped pillows in gingham and a teddy-shaped quilt of quilted calico. I created a little bear named *Hoky* later which I did in crochet as a full-bodied finger puppet and in plastic-canvas needlepoint kits as four season ornaments and a trinket box. I have also done many types of edible teddies including teddy bread, cakes, cookies and candy. Recently I have begun making hand-painted folk art style teddies. I am also doing teddies in soft-sculpture, made from just one bootie sock." To date, Mrs. Reuter has designed over 100 bear items, and the ideas just keep

December Bears. Mr. and *Mrs. Santa Bear* from the "Bears of the Month" collectors series, 16in (40.6cm) tall. Non-jointed; white plush; red Christmas costumes. *Photograph courtesy of Kelly Reuter.*

Baby's First Teddy, 12in (30.5cm). Pink and blue teddies dressed in custom teddy sunsuits and bonnets. Each holds his own *Baby Bear. Photograph courtesy of Kelly Reuter.*

Shelby and *K.C.* bears. Special "going to a party" teddies ready for the Teddy Tribune Convention in Minnesota, August 1983. *Photograph courtesy of Kelly Reuter.*

coming. This is probably because inventing bears is, for her, the best part of bear making.

"I enjoy the designing aspect most, creating new bears and bear items. I have so many ideas I will probably never have time to make. It's so exciting to design a new teddy and see him come to life as I add his eyes, nose, mouth and stuffing. What joy to see the first edition of a new bear completed. What I enjoy least is having to mass produce and fill orders by a specific time. I enjoy working whenever I please and on whatever teddy I am in the mood for, rather than on things that "have" to be done. When I have the plans for a new bear formulated in my mind, I just sit down and make it without hesitation. I draw the pattern on a large bag, cut out the bear and sew it up immediately. Once I get the

idea for a new bear, I don't stop 'til the first one is finished."

Once the prototype is done, Kelly changes bear making procedures. Consequently, she has no idea how long it takes her to make one.

"I have never timed myself because I rarely sit down and make a bear start to finish at one time unless it is a new bear and I'm just trying out the design. When I'm producing bears in quantities, I try to do all the same pieces of each bear at one time and then all the next step, one right after the other.

She squeezes bearmaking into a busy schedule as wife and mother, but never makes bears unless she is in an upbeat frame of mind. Her recommendation to prospective bear makers is as follows: "Only make a bear when you have the time and are in the mood. That way all your bears will bring happiness because they were produced that way. Bear making should not be a chore; it should be something you really want to do."

Kelly really wants to make bears. Despite the vast repertoire she has invented, she feels she is best-known for her "Bears of the Month." These are the basic bear. The bear maker feels that clothing is very important in putting over her teds' messages. She has firm ideas about bear haberdashery.

"Many of my bears have clothing, all of my own design. I try not to cover up too much of the bear in most cases. I make a teddy in a cat costume for Halloween and one in a bunny costume for Easter, but rather than making the costumes to cover the whole body, as I would for my children's Halloween costumes, I make a cat and bunny jacket complete with hood, ears and tail. This conveys the idea without covering up the teddy.

"In many cases the clothing gives extra personality to a bear. I make pure white wedding teddies, but they don't take on the blushing bride and proud groom personality until I put on their gown and tux. Many teddies take on their own whimsical personality when you add overalls, a hat, a bow tie or even just a ribbon around the neck."

"Teddy and Me" bears are designed for collectors, but have saftey eyes and noses, so children can also play with them. Whoever gets them, these teddies are usually given as joyful gifts to celebrate a special occasion, festival or season.

That is the way Kelly Reuter likes it. For her, every season is the "Season to be Beary."

Wedding Teddies, 12in (30.5cm). Pure white teddies dressed in wedding clothes. *Photograph courtesy of Kelly Reuter.*

Betsy and Joey. Hand-carved wooden bears, *Betsy* wears a pink pinafore and bow. *Joey* wears blue overalls. Both are antiqued and have a satiny finish.

PAT AND MIMI WOOLLEY

"Woolley Bear" logo.
Courtesy of Pat Woolley.

WOOLLEY BEAR.

On the couch of her Manhattan Beach, California, home sit the bears that inspired Pat Woolley's career as a bear artist. Each has a story to tell. Some belonged to her mother, some to her grandmother and two were refugees from World War II. Pat loves them all, but they would not have affected her artistically had it not been for her daughter, Mimi.

"Mimi started us making bears," Pat states. "She started making miniatures (for her animal-house) when she was ten years old. A couple of years later we opened a booth at our local fair and sold doll house miniatures and Mimi's first miniature bears. Now Mimi is at college studying to become a veterinarian and her time is very limited but she manages to make a few mini-bears in what little time she has."

Mimi's bears are carefully, affectionately, hand-stitched of felt. She makes two types of Woolley Bears, a *Baby* bear 2in (5.1cm) tall with jointed limbs, and the seated *Mama* and *Papa* bears, with jointed arms. *Papa* is dressed in a jacket, *Mama* in a sun dress.

"Mimi was having so much fun with her bear work that I decided to do something that would complement hers, so I started doing a family portrait gallery of our bear family," Pat says. "I had such fun doing this, that I thought people might be interested in having a picture of their bears."

Pat's portraits of bears capture their personalities with a freedom and economy of line that still somehow smacks of old-world etching techiniques.

The artist has had extensive technical training. A graduate of the Académie Julien, in Paris, France, she also studied at the Art Center College of Design in Los Angeles, California, and has many years' experience teaching art at collegiate and secondary levels. She works in mixed media (textured acrylic with watercolor and pencil), oils, does various crafts (she is a specialist in European egg decorating), and does pen and ink portraiture. This is the medium she uses for the bears.

Pat's bear portraits transmit her deep affection for the teds she depicts. This stems from the key role a teddy bear had in her life.

"I was born in France in 1933," she relates. "I immigrated to the U.S.A. with my parents in 1940. The only toy I could bring with me was my beloved teddy bear, *Jackie*. This once pure white bear was given to me by my mother at about age two. He traveled with me extensively before 1939 to such exciting places as Hungary, Czechoslovaki and Poland (often with the German army in hot pursuit). *Jackie* has lived a pleasant life in Southern California for these past 43 years.

In 1946, my family and I returned to Europe and I was delighted to find some of the toys I had left six years earlier. Among them was a larger teddy named *Jimmy*. He had survived the war pretty well, despite getting very damp and having had a bad attack of moths, which took one ear and all the velvet off his paws. However, he also returned to California and now sports one fabric ear and fancy green and blue paws!"

Pat's portraits are usually done from photographs. She

Pat and Mimi Woolley and some of Mimi's bears. 1983. *Photograph courtesy of Pat Woolley.*

Two of Mimi Woolley's hand-sewn felt bears, 2in (5.1cm) high. *Photograph courtesy of Pat Woolley.*

does them for love as much as money. Perhaps, in the balance, the love wins out.

"Mimi and I have been 'into bears' for many years," she explains, "for the pure pleasure of them. We consider ourselves artists first and if we are rewarded for our work, fine; however, we do not like to see bears get too commercial."

As she works in her home, the family bears supervise from the couch. Sometimes one will leave the rest to pose. The rest sit quietly, content with their role as artistic inspiration.

Pat Woolley drawing portrait, "Mother's Teddy, 1909." Mother's teddy looks on. 1983. *Photograph courtesy of Pat Woolley.*

"Mothers' Teddy 1909—" '83

"Mother's Teddy, 1909." 1983 drawing by Pat Woolley. 5in by 7in (12.7cm by 17.8cm). *Courtesy of Pat Woolley.*

CHERYL LINDSAY
JOANNE PURPUS

Cheryl Lindsay holding *Baby Victoria* and Joanne Purpus holding *Roller Bear*. 1983. *Photograph by Frank Romero, courtesy of Cheryl Lindsay and Joanne Purpus.*

This is the story of a partnership that is no more. While I was researching this book, "Lindsay Purpus Bears" dissolved, Cheryl Lindsay and Joanne Purpus took personal bear making paths.

However, the products produced by the participants, singly and jointly, in their brief business association, are so important in the story of contemporary teddy bear artistry that I am presenting their story. When they were introduced, "Lindsay Purpus" bears became instant classics, setting a new standard for originality.

Lindsay Purpus Bears probably could only have happened in California. There, bear makers have an unequalled opportunity for cross-pollination and a ready marketplace.

A strong tradition of pride in handcrafts, a legacy of the 1960s and 1970s, flourishes in contemporary California. From this tradition, many bear makers have derived a calling. Most posess a background in the fiber arts. Such is the case with Joanne Purpus and Cheryl Lindsay.

Cheryl and Joanne were both born in Los Angeles, California, "though a few years apart," as they put it. Joanne's background is in the fine arts field. She worked in ceramics and sculpture, and finally turned to three dimensional soft-sculpture work.

Cheryl was her student for several years, learning to sew under Joanne's guidance. She earned a teaching credential in needlecraft and clothing construction at the college level, but dropped active involvement in the field to go into neonatal nursing.

She moved to Northern California to continue education at San Francisco State and U.C. Berkeley. The two women lost track of each other for about a decade.

In the meantime, Joanne continued to pursue her interest in fiber arts. As a child, she disliked dolls, spending her childhood with stuffed animals, bears a favorite. It was only natural that she should pounce on a course in bear making when one became available.

Mary Hardy was the teacher. Joanne says that Mary is "a delight to know," and considers her bear making instructor her inspiration. The class led to a renewal in the artist's interest in bears. The instructor's teds were fashioned from felt, using her own pattern, which had appeared in a magazine.

Joanne's "appetite was whetted for more complex bear forms" when she had mastered the felt bears, and she decided to design her own.

In December of 1981, the new, original teddies were given a pre-Christmas exhibit at the Palos Verdes Community Arts Association gallery. Called "The Art of the Teddy Bear," it featured 24 of her one-of-a-kind stuffed bears.

She used heavy wools, camel hair or velvet that cost up to $40 a yard, shoe buttons for eyes and flea-market snippets of lace and embroidery for trims on them.

"I wanted to use fabrics that homemade bears used to be made out of, like cut-up old winter coats that were too shabby to be worn," she said at the time, "but I couldn't find any, maybe because people in California don't wear heavy coats."

The exhibit was decorated with childhood photographs, garnered from friends, of children with teddies. Her bears sold out.

At the time (December 1981), the artist told a reporter that she "knew of just two other artists in Southern California producing handmade unduplicated bears."

An article about Joanne's bear making appeared in the *Los Angeles Times*. Cheryl's mother sent it to Joanne and they renewed their friendship.

At the time Cheryl called, Joanne was inundated with post-show bear orders and needed help.

"I was so happy to hear from Cheryl," Joanne told a reporter. "We had lost touch for a few years, but I remembered her as an exceptionally talented and likable young woman. When I admitted that I was flooded with requests for my bears and that I'd promised to design more, in limited editions, for eager collectors, she offered to help. I was jubilant because Cheryl is not only a superior craftswoman, she has rare creative ability." She could hardly feel otherwise. Joanne had taught her to sew.

In the intervening years, besides nursing, Cheryl had pursued a career as a custom clothing designer, becoming partners with Annabel Whitney Smith. Their garments, which wore the Cher-Anne label, were worn by such celebrities as Rick Nelson and his Stone Canyon band. This partnership had since dissolved. Now Cheryl had another opportunity for a fiber arts career. She and Joanne joined forces.

The women describe their spur-of-the-moment partnership as "an immediate success." They began filling gallery-generated orders, switching to original designs under the "Lindsay Purpus" label. An early customer was Earth Bound, a "collector bear" store in Long Beach, California. The women credit the encouragement they derived from the owners, Kim Shadley and Rene Charles, for the furtherance of their bear making.

The early Earth Bound limited editions were discovered by owners of other bear emporia, and orders began a never-ending pace. Soon, over 200 shops carried Lindsay Purpus bears.

From its inception, Lindsay Purpus sold wholesale. Shops ordered their bears, produced in limited editions, in staggering quantities. This instant popularity stems from the way the women designed them — always with an artistic, sculptural concept and a sensitivity to fine fabrics and careful construction. "A bear should be well made with quality materials. It should evoke a feeling of warmth and tenderness; it makes you feel good about owning it," stated the artists. This philosophy guided them as they developed their line.

Joanne, the bear lover, specialized in their design. Moving away from the felt, at first she used heavy coat woolens and some velvets. The velvets were discarded; wools became the main medium, with occasional forays into "a good quality plush." The teddies' design basically remained the same throughout the partnership. Fully-jointed, they came in two sizes: 14in (35.6cm) and 17in (43.2cm). Later, felt was once again introduced. A 3in (7.6cm) felt bear was added and the women began to experiment again with this medium.

Probably the most difficult design to perfect for Joanne was the standing bear design, which was incorporated into the Lindsay Purpus logo. Six months' work went into its development. "All of the ones that I had ever seen were the flat 'cookie cutter' types. It was so exciting to achieve success!!," Joanne stated.

The sizes selected for the teds are deliberate. These, the designers feel, are the best to show off the distinctive wardrobes, designed by the younger partner, for which their bears became known.

Cheryl loved dolls as a child, (she never remembers having a bear as a child — she feels that probably this has something to do with her fascination with them now), so designing the bears' wardrobes naturally fell under her aegis. The years of custom clothing work for people were well-used; "She went from designing clothes for big teddy bears, like Rick Nelson, to the little bears designed by Joanne," the women explain.

Joanne Purpus' first original bears. Jointed. 18in (45.7cm) tall. Made from heavy coat woolens, camel hair and velvets; paw pads of ultrasuede or leather; embroidered mouths and noses. Old shoe buttons from the 1930s used for eyes. Collars are old laces or embroidery pieces. "With these bears, I hoped to capture the feeling of the 1930s and the tenderness of the old, hand-made bears,"...Joanne Purpus. *Photograph by Roger O'Neill, courtesy of Joanne Purpus.*

Mariane Shadden Noe, Ann Shadden, Joanne Shadden Purpus, with bears. This childhood photograph of Joanne Purpus was on the cover of the program for her bear exhibit, "The Art of the Teddy Bear," at The Palos Verdes Community Arts Association in December 1981. *Photograph courtesy of Joanne Purpus.*

12in (30.5cm) semi-jointed bears (legs and arms only). Made from felt and adapted from a pattern by Mary Hardy. Old shoe buttons were used for eyes and large flat buttons were used for leg and arm "joints." These are the first bears Joanne Purpus made for sale, in 1981. *Photograph courtesy of Joanne Purpus.*

Original *Roller Bear;* 12in (30.5cm). English coat woolens; antique shoe button eyes; hand-embroidered face; the bear rides on a hardwood trolley and wheels (designed and constructed by Roger O'Neil). Designed for 1982 Los Angeles Museum of Natural History Invitational Craft Fair. Hand-signed and numbered under wooden trolley. Limited edition of 30 in assorted colors. The design is by Joanne Purpus and took six months of design time; this original three dimensional design is copyrighted and became the logo of Lindsay Purpus Bears, as it was their first joint project. It was available under the original company name, "Purpusful Bears." *Photograph by Roger O'Neill, courtesy of Cheryl Lindsay and Joanne Purpus.*

Some bears were designed, also, by Cheryl, including her early felt bears with button joints. She invented some woolen ones with wooden joints, and went on to revise the felt bear design in a project called *Purpusly Prairie,* combining a wool bear in prairie clothing with a small felt companion bear.

The exceptional quality and flair for fabrics in Cheryl's bear garments stunningly complemented the English wools and subtle surfaces of Joanne's bears. The fact that the bruins were done in strictly limited editions added to their appeal, and helped to minimize burnout when constructing garments. But the fact that such small amounts of any given fabric were required made retail fabric purchases necessary; this added to the cost of construction. It was worth the trouble, though. The outstanding clothing on Lindsay Purpus bears became their hallmark. The women describe their bears' garments.

"Cheryl designs the clothing worn by most of the Lindsay Purpus editions. Several of the bears are elegantly dressed in bridal satins, laces and ribbons, giving them a Victorian look. Others are dressed in calicos with eyelet accents and have a country flavor. The size of the bear and its costume definitely change the personality. *Heavenly Teddy* in white satin with quilted wings and sporting a silver halo is 'angelic.' *Clarance, the Country Clown,* is 'whimsical' in his calico clown suit and pointed hat. Both *Baby Victoria* in her christening dress and *Cousin Sara* in her crocheted baby outfit are 'innocent.' The clothing gives each new edition a completely different look and feeling."

Lindsay Purpus bears wore only the best. Their garb was adorned with satin ribbon roses, embroidery, laces and, sometimes, needlepoint.

Eventually, Cheryl acquired a helpmate for her bear haberdashery, as orders began to grow out-of-hand. The partners describe how this happened.

"As meeting up again happened with Joanne and Cheryl through the bears, Annabel Whitney Smith, Cheryl's former custom clothing business partner, came to a Teddy Bear Collectors Club sale only to find Cheryl there selling teddy bears. Annabel has now rejoined Cheryl to again form Cher-Anne and assist Lindsay Purpus with their productions."

Cheryl stated, at the time, "Being away and pursuing my education separated me from two of my favorite people and the very best craftspeople I've ever been acquainted with and teddy bears have now reunited me with my two best friends."

Bear designing, the friends discovered, was hardly child's play.

"We believe designing bears and clothing is basically hard work with lots of wasted fabrics and dark moments when we think we will never get from 'mind's eye' to finished

Clara, the Country Clown, 17in (43.2cm) with hat. Fully-jointed; English coat woolens; available in camel and gray; ultrasuede paw pads; antique shoe button eyes, hand-embroidered face. July 1982. Lindsay Purpus cloth label above upper right paw pad and a numbered certificate tied with a ribbon around one arm. Limited edition of 50 with matching *Clarance* set of 50. *First dressed bear designed by Cheryl Lindsay to be worn by the bear designed by Joanne Purpus.* Dressed in three-four color coordinated calico prints; large cotton and lace collar, lace around all four cuffs; pointed hat adorned with ribbons and matching lace. *Photograph by Frank Romero, courtesy of Cheryl Lindsay and Joanne Purpus.*

Clarance, the Country Clown, 17in (43.2cm) with hat. Fully-jointed; English coat woolens; available in camel and gray; ultrasuede paw pads; antique shoe button eyes; hand-embroidered face. July 1982. Lindsay Purpus cloth label above upper right paw pad and a numbered certificate tied with a ribbon around one arm. Limited edition of 50 matching *Clara* set of 50. First dressed bear designed by Cheryl Lindsay to be worn by the bear designed by Joanne Purpus. Dressed in three-four color coordinated calico prints; large cotton collar and cuffs. Pointed hat adorned with ribbons of matching colors. *Photograph by Frank Romero, courtesy of Cheryl Lindsay and Joanne Purpus.*

Rocker Bear, 10in (25.4cm) high. English coat woolens; antique shoe button eyes, hand-embroidered face; the bear rides on a hardwood rocker (designed and constructed by Roger O'Neil). Limited edition of 90. The original concept by Donald Lindsay using the copyrighted design for a three dimensional bear by Joanne Purpus. December 1982. Rocker is hand-painted by award winning tole painter Pat Saunders. She has copied the design in the Swiss embroidered ribbon which adorns *Rocker Bear's* neck on the rocker. Numbered on the rocker with a gold plaque. *Photograph by Frank Romero, courtesy of Cheryl Lindsay and Joanne Purpus.*

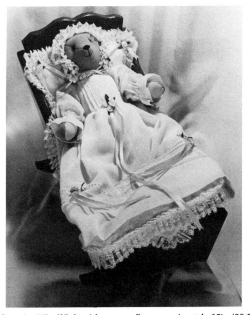

Victorian Jester, 17in (43.2cm); fully-jointed English coat woolens in camel or gray; ultrasuede paw pads; antique shoe button eyes; hand-embroidered face. November 1982. Lindsay Purpus label above right upper paw pad and comes with a numbered card tied with a ribbon around one arm. Limited edition of 50. Dressed in two colors of bridal satin; "Victorian" lace collar and trim; hat adorned with lace, satin ribbons and topped with either a bell or a plush ball. Clothing designed and constructed by Cheryl Lindsay and the bear by Joanne Purpus. Their first Victorian design. *Photograph by Frank Romero, courtesy Cheryl Lindsay and Joanne Purpus.*

Baby Victoria, 14in (35.6cm) bear; cradle approximately 12in (30.5cm) by 24in (61cm). Fully-jointed; camel wool with ultrasuede paw pads; shoe button eyes; hand-embroidered face. December 1982. Lindsay Purpus label above right paw pad; gold plaque at base of cradle and signed and numbered Certificate of Authenticity. Limited edition of 12. Original concept by Cheryl Lindsay; clothing constructed by Shirley Suchy, painting by award winning tole painter Pat Saunders and original bear design by Joanne Purpus. Dressed in full Victorian voile christening dress including pantaloons, two slips and bonnet adorned with lace, satin ribbons and roses. *Baby Victorian* rests upon a blanket and pillow adorned with matching lace, ribbons and roses. Her cradle is hardwood painted with a ribbon and rose design on an antique cranberry background. *Photograph by Frank Romero, courtesy of Cheryl Lindsay and Joanne Purpus.*

item," they wrote. "But we find it so rewarding when we 'do' manage to capture the magic. We are both basically designers and get more pleasure out of working through an idea from scratch to finished product. After a couple of 'completed' bears in a series, we often wish we could turn the production over to little elves. Designing is also the most frustrating part. Somehow there is so much yardage between a concept and reality, it is almost inconceivable, when the idea turns out, it is very rewarding!"

The women spent long hours making their custom limited edition bears, but their work habits differed. Joanne, who had some difficulty with her hands, found it hard to put in a full-time schedule. She put in about four hours a day. She stated: "It really helps to have a younger, healthy, and creative partner. It takes me a whole day to make a bear from cutting the fabric to the finished product, and since I only work a 'half' day, it takes two days to the finished undressed bear. A three bear week would be ideal but it doesn't happen. There is shopping for supplies, bear sales, correspondence, concepts for future projects — all part of the business and bear sewing in on top of the above."

Cheryl put in enormous work days, sometimes 16 to 18 hour ones, seven days a week, retiring from nursing to become a bear artist. She had to ask her family for help to fill orders, even with a six to twelve week delivery time for them.

"It's a blessing to have so many talented people in one family; my three sisters, my sister-in-law and my mother are all quality seamstresses who are very particular about

Lady Roxanne and her Rusty Roller, two-piece set approximately 18in (45.7cm). *Lady Roxanne* is 14in (35.6cm). Fully-jointed; contructed from hand-dyed apricot-colored English coat woolens with cream-colored ultra-suede paw pads; shoe button eyes; hand-embroidered face. Lindsay Purpus label above right paw pad and comes with a signed and numbered Certificate of Authenticity. Limited edition of eight, designed exclusively for Earthbound Collector Store in Southern, California May 1983. *Lady Roxanne* in cream moray taffeta with ecru lace collar and trim; sports two rust silk poppies on one ear and holds the tasseled reigns to *Rusty Roller,* a rust-colored 12in (30.5cm) roller bear constructed from English coat woolens with antique shoe button eyes and a hand-embroidered face. He rides on a custom-made hardwood trolley by Coleman Citchens. Around *Rusty Roller's* neck is an apricot-colored bow to match the bow around *Lady Roxanne's* neck. He also wears matching poppies at his neck. *Lady Roxanne* was designed and constructed by Cheryl Lindsay. *Rusty Roller* was designed and constructed by Joanne Purpus. *Photograph by Frank Romero, courtesy of Cheryl Lindsay and Joanne Purpus.*

Purpusly Prairie, 15in (38.1cm) with bonnet; felt bear approximately 3in (7.6cm). English camel coat woolens; ultrasuede paw pads; shoe button eyes; hand-embroidered face. May 1983. Lindsay Purpus label and comes with a signed and numbered Certificate of Authenticity. Limited edition of 50. Large wool bear was designed by Joanne Purpus; small felt bear was designed by Cheryl Lindsay. The clothing was designed by Cher-Anne, the clothing team of Cheryl Lindsay and Annabel Whitney Smith. The prairie clothing includes a pin-dot cotton dress and bonnet, eyelet apron, collar and cuffs. She also wears muslin and eyelet pantaloons. Her bonnet has ear openings and is adorned with satin ribbon roses. Her small bear is cream-colored felt with bead eyes and a hand-embroidered face. The dresses are available in six colors; slate, rose, peach, rust, forest and navy. (A few were dressed in specially requested colors to match people's home decor.) *Photograph by Frank Romero, courtesy of Cheryl Lindsay and Joanne Purpus.*

craftsmanship, and the strength to assemble jointed bears comes from my husband who also hand cuts each hardwood joint," she said at the time. "I've also had to hire professional seamstresses to assist with certain clothing projects. People don't realize what all is involved in running a teddy bear business besides the actual construction of the bears. First designing, then finding the right supplies for each project, cutting and sewing, keeping orders and supplies organized, keeping in contact with clients, shipping out orders and doing bookkeeping."

Cheryl's output was about 10 to 15 bears a week, using production-line techniques. She describes them.

"Sewing all camel bears at one time, threading elastic through casings, etc. This helps speed up things a great deal. Without this process, a single dressed bear could take 12 to 15 hours, start to finish, depending on the costuming involved."

Eventually, Lindsay Purpus bears added other crafts-people's talents to their production. The artists tell of one.

Pat Saunders, an award winning tole painter from Southern California, has incorporated her painting talent with Lindsay Purpus projects to create beautiful art pieces for the bear collector. "*Baby Victoria,* who is dressed in a christening outfit, rests in hand-painted cradle by Pat.

"She has also created a beautiful hand-painted box for *Poppin Bear,* a jack-in-the-box limited edition designed for Bear'n Grin It. Pat has hand-painted the rockers for *Rocker Bear* in the exact pattern of the embroidered Swedish ribbon that adorns the bear's neck.

"Sometimes bear making for Cheryl was what she described as a "real family project." Her favorite bear, *Cousin Sara,* named after her niece, Sara Jacobs, came about this way.

"She's my favorite because she's a real family project. This small camel wool bear wears a hand-crocheted outfit by my mother, Bonnie Salvail; the outfit includes a bonnet, bib and booties which are adorned with satin ribbon roses. The bear is Joanne's original design and is fully-jointed, has ultrasuede paw pads, shoe button eyes and a hand-embroidered face. *Cousin Sara* sits upon a traditional handmade quilt, created and constructed by Joanne. My nephew, Scott Sheleretis, assembled the Victorian buggy that *Cousin Sara* rides in; the buggy wheels are adorned with ribbons and on the back of the carriage sits a small bird's nest with a California quail inside. *Cousin Sara* was a limited edition of 25 and came with a signed and numbered certificate of authenticity designed by my sister, Ramona Salvail. My other two sisters, Linda Sheleretis and Charli Jacobs, assisted with this family project."

The business grew, and the name "Lindsay Purpus" became well-known to discriminating bear collectors. High priced items, intended as sculptural pieces, these teds seldom found their way to children's hands.

But the name caused some problems.

Often, collectors desired to discover intimate details of the elusive bear maker, "Lindsay Purpus." When he failed to attend shows, people would seize upon Joanne, after reading her name tag, and noticing the similar "last name," then congratulate her on "her" bears. Cheryl describes the experience as "traveling through the sale totally incognito."

"We also get curious reactions to the name Purpus with people believing we are unable to spell 'purpose' correctly. When we first opened a business checking account, the lady at the bank asked us three times to check the spelling for any errors before we realized she wasn't understanding that Purpus was a name, not a misspelling."

The joint bank account is no more. Lindsay Purpus Bears is a part of bear artist history, and the lucky purchasers of their joint efforts posess treasures, indeed. Created as sculptures, through a combination of artistic talents, these bears will never be duplicated.

In December 1983, the partnership dissolved, but the bears go on. Each designer has chosen to go her own way, to produce her personal vision of the perfect artistic teddy bear. Joanne will make *Roller Bear, Watch Bear* and a jointed bear. She intends to make all the bears herself, so will have a limited production. She goes by the name "Joanne Purpus Ltd. Limited Edition Bears and other Gentle Crafts." Cheryl, known now as "Elegant Fantasies by Cheryl Lindsay," is bursting with new, original ideas.

"Lindsay Purpus Bears" may be no more, but its tradition and legacy lives on.

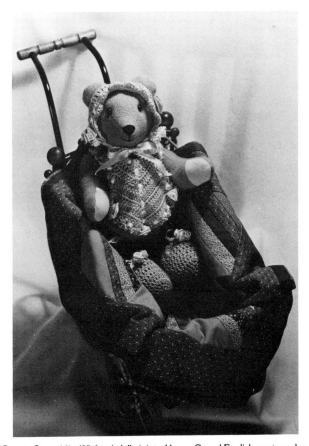

Cousin Sara, 14in (35.6cm); fully-jointed bear. Camel English coat woolen, ultrasuede paw pads; antique shoe button eyes, embroidered face is handmade. Limited edition of 25 comes with Certificate of Authenticity and Lindsay Purpus cloth label sewn above upper right paw pad. *Cousin Sara* wears a hand-crocheted outfit copied from an antique pattern. She sits upon a traditional quilt and rides in her own replica of a Victorian baby buggy. This edition is available in four colors; dusty rose, lavender, peach or slate blue. Clothing designed by Cheryl Lindsay with the original bear design by Joanne Purpus. May 1983. The traditional style buggy is adorned with matching satin ribbons in the buggy wheels and a bird's nest with a California quail inside. *Photograph by Frank Romero, courtesy of Cheryl Lindsay and Joanna Purpus.*

EARL KRENTZIN

Earl Krentzin and friends.

The Bear No. 250, playing with a Krentzin silver sculpture. 21in (53.3cm) tall with articulated arms and legs. Chocolate brown super plush with velour paws and pads; hand-embroidered nose, mouth, claws; leather button eyes; stuffed with polyester fiberfill; grosgrain ribbon around neck. Brass tag signed Krentzin and numbered No. 250 (sewn to bottom of foot). This description, except for color and number, applies to all Krentzin bears. *Photograph courtesy of Earl Krentzin.*

As I strolled past the gift shop in the Smithsonian Institution, I spied *The Bear*, "We meet at last," I thought, and smiled up at him. Outstanding among the dolls and toys on display, he was surveying the territory.

The Smithsonian is a proper den for *The Bear*. Although different from his creator's usual work, he too, is contemporary American sculpture.

For over three decades, Earl Krentzin, his designer, has been totally committed to silver sculpture. His academic credits include a BFA with distinction from Wayne State University, an MFA in metalsmithing from Cranbrook Academy of Art and postgraduate work in silversmithing on a Fulbright Grant at the Royal College of Art in London, England.

The whimsical works for which he is best known spring from his fascination with antique toys. Constructed from precious materials, they turn and spin and delight the viewer, bringing him, for a while, a bit closer to his childhood.

In his long career, he has created an enormous number of these playful art objects and once lent over 100 of them to an exhibit without even noticing they were gone. Art, to him should be enjoyable for both artist and viewer. "I have fun," he stated. "Sometimes people look down on what I do as not being serious enough. But humor always has been a part of art. And artists know how to preserve part of their childhood."

It was from this philosophy that *The Bear* emerged.

Mr. Krentzin, a collector of toys, had been searching fruitlessly for a suitable teddy bear. "Since childhood," he says, "I have liked bears and I do remember an orangey-colored mohair bear about 10in (25.4cm) tall with articulated arms and legs that I carried around for a long time." The bear remained elusive. Flea market ones were in bad shape; others, overpriced, so, with the encouragement of his wife, Lorraine, a fine artist, he decided in the summer of 1981 to create his own.

He describes the process.

"I looked for a pattern to make one (bear), but ended up designing it myself. I had this lining from an old coat and I made him out of it. It was so endearing that we decided to do a limited edition. The original bears were made out of muslin until the pattern was perfected. The prototype bear had leather paws and pads, pearl button eyes and was made completely by hand, no machine sewing. *The Bear* is still made out of super plush but has velour paws and pads and has leather button eyes. *The Bear* is now both machine sewn and hand-sewn. The main body pieces are sewn by machine. The ears are inset by hand. All features are hand-embroidered and the eyes are now leather buttons.

Mr. Krentzin only produces *The Bear* in one size, 21in (53.3cm), which he describes as "a traditional large sized bear. That size suits me and *The Bear*." However, for his own enjoyment, he has made *The Bear* in a 4in (10.2cm)

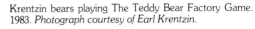
Krentzin bears playing The Teddy Bear Factory Game. 1983. *Photograph courtesy of Earl Krentzin.*

The Bear by Earl Krentzin. 21in (53.3cm) tall with articulated arms and legs. Super plush with velour paws and pads; hand-embroidered nose, mouth, claws; leather button eyes; stuffed with polyester fiberfill; grosgrain ribbon. *Photograph courtesy of Earl Krentzin.*

size, from a reduction of his bear pattern which was printed in *Americana* magazine in November 1982. Each one is different; his choice of fabric depends upon what is available.

His sources for materials are local: Kresge, Sears, Woolworth and Frank's Nursery (for the grosgrain ribbon that coordinates with the plush). The shape, as well as the fabric, vary, depending upon how the fiberfill stuffing conforms to the fur.

The only problem Mr. Krentzin experienced in his early bear making attempts came when a vital component of *The Bear* was locally unavailable. "There was difficulty in finding authentic shoe buttons to attach the arms and legs. After I used up my small supply, I discovered there was no source for these outdated buttons. I ran an ad in *Yankee* magazine's Swoppers' column which enabled me to swop collectible toys for 1000 shoe buttons."

Bear making is hardly a full-time activity for Mr. Krentzin. It is, rather, almost play. "I am a silver sculptor and the bear making is a relaxing activity when I am thinking up and developing new sculpture ideas," he says. "The entire process is a delight and a form of recreation from the demanding, precise, innovative creative work I do in silver and related materials."

With this in mind, he has worked his way approximately halfway through the planned limited edition of 250 bears at this writing. "My philosophy," he states, "is to enjoy the designing and making of *The Bear* and to stop before the enjoyment wears out."

The Bear will never be mass-produced. Mr. Krentzin explains. "It is truly a piece of sculpture because I have been a silver sculptor for over 30 years. *The Bear*, although based on the traditional teddy bear, is made and designed by a contemporary artist who has put much of my training and expertise into its creation. This bear must continue to be produced by hand, one-of-a-kind! It was conceived as a very special bear using the 'limited edition' art object concept. My bear is an extension of me and whether bought for adults or children, is identified with my primary art activity, silver sculpture."

Because of its art object status, *The Bear* has been featured in musuem shops such as those of The Dallas Museum of Fine Arts, The Fort Wayne Museum Shop, The Smithsonian Museum Shop and the Museum of Folk Art in New York, New York. Most of his bears, though, find homes through word-of-mouth.

Mr. Krentzin also makes his pattern available to the general public. "I feel that a collector who wants a limited edition bear is not the same person who wants to make their own bear. I am willing to meet the needs of both types of bear lovers."

Because of their price and the way they are sold, the artist feels that many buyers are probably aware of his silver work. Krentzin bears carry numbered brass tags signed "KRENTZIN," the same as other Krentzin sculptures. They come with an explanatory certificate signed by both artist and bear.

When number 250 is completed, the clan of Krentzin bears will be complete. All will have found homes but one. "One bear with a particularly long, dense, chocolate colored fabric is my favorite. He will be numbered No. 250 and will not be for sale."

Somehow, this bear has found a home in the Krentzin studio, where he enjoys playing with the silver sculptures. As he is also sculpture, he fits right in.

APRIL WHITCOMB

April Whitcomb with some of her tiny teddies. 1982. *Photograph courtesy of April Whitcomb.*

Four open-mouth bears by April Whitcomb, approximately 2in (5.1cm) tall. *Polar, Panda, Black* and *Buff.* Fully-jointed. 1982. *Photograph courtesy of April Whitcomb.*

"I want to make the best miniature teddy bears the world has ever see. Each one should be perfect." This is April Whitcomb's philosophy.

In the two years since she designed her first original teddy, the Massachussetts artist has come close to her goal. Her bruins are a delight — diminutive duplicates of old-time teds. Fully-jointed, they can sit, stand and "walk" on all fours. Some have tails that, when moved, cause their tiny heads to wag "no." Several sport open mouths with teeth and eager tongues, others closed snouts and "that loved look," as April puts it. And a honey-colored one is dressed as a perky bellhop.

There is something about these bears that makes grownups smile and melt inside. The salutory effect on folks delights April. "I think their purpose is to teach people to be children again and find joy in something so simple. Walk around an airport sometime with your teddy and suddenly people's faces soften up and you're no longer a stranger —it's a great ice breaker. The teddy bear will always be that. It's a link between people. It takes them back to childhood and their innocence."

She tells the story about the power of one of her bears: "At a party recently, a friend of mine showed a photograph of my bears to a full-grown state policeman and he just lost his mind. He started talking to them in a high voice as you'd talk to a child or a pet. It really was surprising, funny, but nice to see someone so unlikely just melt at a picture of them."

Some of April's bears. All are fully-jointed and are approximately 2in (5.1cm) tall. 1982. *Photograph courtesy of April Whitcomb.*

The bears are even better in person: "To see the bears in person and close-up see their faces you will feel (if you are a true bear lover, miniature collector, etc.) the effect I'm trying to create," she explains.

One wonders how anyone can put so much detail, can capture the essence of the originals in something 3in (7.6cm) high. What are they made of? "I like to leave some of my procedures and materials a mystery so as not to spoil the magic when someone studies one of my bears, but it is a mixture of sculpture. Six body parts are molded by hand from a plastic-like clay and then are baked in the oven. Next, when they are cooled, the mouths, paws and noses are painted and then the velvet fabric is applied. All the limbs and head are attached with nylon covered elastic thread and a bow is tied around his or her neck. Then a tag is attached, signed by me stating the number of the edition and the date. My mom makes the exquisite little calico hat boxes they travel in."

All her life, the Massachussetts artist, a member of the Good Bears of the World, has harbored a strong fondness for furry friends, especially small ones. "Teddy bears were more important to me than dolls because I am an animal lover — any kind." She has retained her bears. "I have so many bears now, big and small, that I don't have an exact count or any favorites. If any one of them were gone, I'd miss that particular one right away, but I love them all equally and would never dream of hurting their feeling by playing favorites."

It was only recently that April discovered that others shared her bear passion. In the daylight hours, she works as art director at Graphtex, a Massachussetts firm that prints textiles. One of her clients is Fran Lewis, of Bear-in-Mind, for whom April's firm does original artwork and prints T-shirts, totes, pillowcases and the like. A mutual interest in bears was the springboard for friendship. Through Fran Lewis, April met "hordes" of bear lovers and began to reason that perhaps they were seeking the same elusive perfect miniature bear as she.

"I had never found a miniature bear I thought was perfect. They were either too big and the plush too thick and crude or their faces weren't cute and appealing or they weren't fully-jointed — something was always wrong."

So, she began to invent. She knew just what she wanted to create and called upon her extensive art background (she works in many media) to help her. "Being an artist, and being very critical about my work and others', and having a mother who believes in me more than I do sometimes, pushed me into at least experimenting with constructing a bear in miniature myself. From the first, I seemed to be able to visualize exactly what I wanted them to look like. My first bear, which I still have and will never part with, was a huge success. Everything worked so well, it seemed as though I'd found my purpose in life."

Her first bear was the original April's Teddy with closed-mouth. Then came four open-mouthed bears: the buff-colored bear, the polar bear, the panda and the black bear. They have realistic padded paws, teeth and tongue, shiny nose and eyes. Two bears, copies of antique teddies with movable heads and tails followed. One is a honey-colored "Bialosky" type and the other is dark brown with buff nose and chest patch. An American antique reproduction who looks like Beggar T. Bear joined the den. The last was a reproduction of the antique bellhop bear, who is spiffy in red velvet cap and jacket, blue velvet pants and moves his honey-colored head when his tail is turned.

Sometimes April does special orders — not often. She made a 1in (2.5cm) tall bear — all white — for a lady in Florida with a roomful of white bears. A friend requested a bear wearing a black leather motorcycle jacket, for which she cut up a pair of leather gloves. "I must say he came out exceptionally well. The jacket did change his appearance. He looks like a little toughy — a Fonzie type." She only takes commissions from good friends and proven customers, however. They take up too much time.

Each regular bear requiries at least six hours to fabricate and they are done "from scratch" to completion, one at a time. "Every time one is created, he has a totally different expression from the last," she explains. "It's a little like being God and bringing children into the world for anxious parents."

Three of April Whitcomb's bears sit on her hand, two beige teddies surround a Bell-Hop bear (copy of rare antique with red jacket and hat, blue trousers, gold trim; tail moves head). Approximately 2in (5.1cm) tall. Fully-jointed. 1982. *Photograph courtesy of April Whitcomb.*

Panda, 3in (7.6cm) posed atop a gingham-covered box made by April Whitcomb's mother. Open mouth; jointed.

Dark Brown Bear 3in (7.6cm), by April Whitcomb. Closed-mouth; beige snout and chest patch; movable head controlled by tail.

She is adamant in her views that her bears could never be duplicated commercially. " I honestly believe that it can't be done without many sacrifices and cut corners, therefore yielding something totally different. I wouldn't do it —they're too special. I never let one leave home until he's perfect. I'm afraid someone else wouldn't know what perfect was."

Her standards are so exacting, her production is curtailed. Each of her bears will be done in limited signed editions of 50. Perhaps her total output so far is 60 bears, 25 to 30 a year. Some of them are newcomers; not content to stagnate, she is always trying out new designs.

Why does she make bears? "I do it because it's profitable, but mostly I do it because it brings such an expression of joy and wonder to his or her new "parent." Also, I get to meet and correspond with some wonderful people who share my interest."

She has displayed her bears at the Bear Necessities Rally in Boston, Massachussetts, and at a rally in Harmony, Rhode Island. Her love for bears has taken April and Fran Lewis all over the country, to attend bear rallies in Philadelphia, Pennsylvania, Minnesota and elsewhere.

Word-of-mouth has been her best advertisement. She is afraid of being swamped with orders if she were to take ads, and credits much of her success to the support of her parents. "They're behind me a thousand percent in everything I do, but they recognize there is something special about these creations. My mother makes the boxes they come in and, as one of my co-workers once said to me as he examined a box carefully, 'Hey, tell your mother to quit making the boxes better than the bears!' My mom will pick up fabrics from time to time for me to experiment with. They think of me all the time. Dad's a great salesman, too."

But it is the excellence and the magic in April's bears that sells them. "I try to put my heart into anything I do. My work shows that, but the bears, they show it best. They come to life and pass it on to others. They have an energy force in them and I'm not sure where it comes from originally, but it passes through me, to them, my little children."

Buff Bear, 3in (7.6cm) by April Whitcomb. Open mouth; jointed body.

Perhaps this force is love. The bears seem to thrive on it and to convey it to others. April is firm in her belief that bears are, and should be, ambassadors of love and innocence: "Teddies today are innocent (even in motorcycle jackets) if they are made with love and caring. And you can tell in one minute if a teddy is lovingly and honestly made. They may look different today than they did in the first decade of the 20th century, but they still represent the same things. They're still soft and cuddly, they love you no matter what, they're good listeners, even mischievous, happy or sad. And people everywhere of all ages still love them."

People of all ages seem to love April Whitcomb's bears. Many of them are of the opinion that she may already have reached her goal to make "the best miniature teddy bear the world has ever seen."

Woody Bear logo.

Woody Bear No. M165, 15in (38.1cm). Carved wooden masque and foot pads; balance of body brown plush; jointed at head and limbs; hard-stuffed; inset eyes. Signed on foot.

"Bears come from the woods. Wood comes from the woods. And we all know that Woody Bears come from the woods."

Bob Raikes is speaking about his work. An active sculptor, he has been working in wood since 1970. Since 1977, his main output has been original, hand-carved dolls. Wood Bears, an offshoot of his doll work, were born in 1982.

Raikes is self-taught, "I have had no formal art training," he says. "But, rather, I have been a student of the world and its people. I found its curriculum to be more extensive and its diplomas more to my liking. Life itself, a love for my fellow man and a belief in God are more than enough to inspire me to create."

Woody Bears are a combination of media. "Wood has always been the main focal point of all my work," Bob says. "However, I am always experimenting with the introduction of other materials and ideas in the search for the new, the more expressive. And, especially, in the case of bears, the more whimsical."

As with Raikes' dolls, Woody Bears are really a family business. Bob does the designing, carving and finishing details. Other family members have designated roles in their bears' construction. Bob describes the process.

"All my design work starts as a rough sketch, and evolves in a natural progression, as new inspiration presents itself. I do all my own design work. I try to keep the clothing to a minimum, concentrating, rather, on the sculptural characteristics that give each bear its own uniqueness.

"My sister-in-law, Cindy, cuts and sews the bodies. My brother, Mike, is in charge of all assembly work, as well as insertion of all the eyes, the spraying of the wood surfaces and the sewing-on of the ears and the tails. My wife does all the collars. Because of the nature of our bears, we want them stuffed hard. That is done by two high school boys that we employ."

The "nature of the bears" is a combination of hand-carved face, wooden foot pads and hard-stuffed, jointed

Ballerina Woody Bear. Fully-jointed; hand-carved; painted wooden masque face; carved and signed foot pads; balance of body hard-stuffed light brownish plush; pink tulle tutu and flower (at ear); inset eyes. Photographed at Mt. Shasta, California. *Photograph courtesy of Bob Raikes.*

furry bodies. They have a curious, alert expression, and are unlike almost anything on the market. They owe a lot to Bob's doll work, and it was through doll work that the sculptor got the idea for Woody Bears.

Woody Bear by Bob Raikes, approximately 15in (35.6cm) tall. Fully-jointed; carved wooden face and foot pads; balance of body hard-stuffed off-white fur fabric; inset eyes; blue bow. Photographed at Mt. Shasta, California. *Photograph courtesy of Bob Raikes.*

Woody Bear by Bob Raikes, approximately 15in (35.6cm) tall. Carved wooden face and foot pads; balance of body hard-stuffed black fur fabric; inset eyes; wears wire spectacles and red plaid tie. Photographed at Mt. Shasta, California. *Photograph courtesy of Bob Raikes.*

Woody Bear by Bob Raikes, approximately 15in (35.6cm) tall. Fully-jointed; carved wooden face and foot pads; balance of body hard-stuffed grizzled black fur fabric; inset eyes; striped bow. Photograph at Mr. Shasta, California. *Photograph courtesy of Bob Raikes.*

He stated in April 1984, "The doll art form has been my main interest and devotion for nearly six years. Doing nearly 30 doll shows a year, I was well aware of the excitement generated by teddy bears over the last few years. Doing a unique bear was an obvious challenge and extension to what I was already doing as a doll artist. Besides the obvious fun of creating something just for the fun of creating, I knew that I could make a bear that would have a large public appeal. And since I support myself and my family in this manner, it was a natural thing to do."

The dolls and bears are an integral part of the Raikes family. "Our children are always around these bears. And for them it is normal to have bears and dolls all over our dining room table, with the family eating at the counter in the kitchen. It's not uncommon to see my children sitting in front of a t.v. set with about 20 Woody Bears watching t.v. along with them."

But Bob does not think of his bears as people, despite their insinuation into family life. "Bears are bears, and people are people. Rather, I see them as extensions of our personalities. In that repsect I think that they are mirrors of humanism. In the same way a child wants a teddy bear for warmth and security, adults find in teddy bears reflections of the better natures of man, for adults, something very important to hold onto."

And adults seem to have strong reactions to Raikes bears. Bob denies that he designs them for adults. "They're made for those people who love Woody Bears," he says, simply. But he thinks of collectors, because the bears are numbered, signed, have tags sewn into their leg seams and come with certificates.

Once in a while Bob will bring a bunch of bears on an outing. He recalls one of the more memorable of these jaunts. "On one occasion, I spent half a day on the slopes of Mt. Shasta, with 20 Woody Bears for a photo session. After hiking a half a mile with them and my camera equipment through the snow, I spent several hours photographing them frollicking through the snow-covered woods with beautiful Mt. Shasta as a backdrop.

"After hours in the snow, I was wet and cold. The Woody Bears appeared to be having a great time. About that time, I realized that there was not film in my camera. I had to drive back to town to get film and do it all over again."

Dolls do not cause such problems, but the bears' personalities are so endearing, that the whole family enjoys making them. With everyone helping, they can produce about 400 bears a year. "A lot of late hours, for all," is Bob's comment. But it is his work that is the keystone of the production. Without him, no Woody Bears could come from the wood.

Bearbit, 10in (25.4cm), bear-in-a-rabbit-suit. Fully-jointed; white fuzzy plush fur; pink paw pads; white removable hood with rabbit ears; pink inside ears match paw pads; shoe button eyes; embroidered nose and mouth; pink ribbon at neck. 1984.

The Three Bears from the box (visitor bears) by Cappi Warnick. Left to right: *Bright Bear* (BB), 12in (30.5cm); *Bearbit,* 10in (25.4cm) and *Terry,* 6½in (16.5cm).

Bearbit arrived in a box about Easter-time. She smiled up at me, snug in her white and pink bunny suit. She had not come to celebrate the season. She came to pose. Two boy bear chaperones accompanied her.

Cappi Warnick refers to *Bearbit* as a "him." A note I found in the box read: "...I am also sending *Bearbit* in case you can use him. I am so pleased with him. His hood comes off."

Cappi ought to be pleased with *Bearbit.* She made him.

Cappi has made hundreds of original bears, in sizes from 1½in (3.8cm) to 24in (61cm) since she began in 1981. "I think I have a pretty good output on bears," she wrote in 1983, "although some of my customers don't seem to think so when they call and order six dozen bears (assorted sizes) and expect them in two weeks. I have made approximately 450 bears, all fully-jointed, in the last eight-and-a-half months."

Cappi's bears are snapped up by dealers and customers alike. I have noticed that dealers are both proud and secretive about her work. A nice lady who runs a bear store in Baltimore, Maryland, approached me in Philadelphia, Pennsylvania, at the Teddy Bear Rally. "I knew you were going to be here," she said. I stood, rooted, clutching my teddy, astounded that anybody would care. "I have with me," she continued, a wonderful bear by a bear maker who does work for my shop. I knew you were doing a book, and you've just gotta see it."

From her purse she extracted one of Cappi's bears. Made, as I recall, of some sort of bristly reddish-brown upholsteryish material, he was handsome. I wanted to grab him and sneak him home. Throughout the two-day bear rally, he peeked out of the shoulder bag. "I try to keep her a sort of secret," the bear merchant confided. "Her bears sell out as soon as I get them in. If too many people know about her, I'll never get any bears."

I wondered about this. Did she think maybe I would tell nobody?

This March (1984), at the Teddy Bear Outing in Washington, demand for Cappi's bears again exceeded supply.

What makes Cappi Warnick's bears so popular? A combination of old-fashioned styling, innocence, high standards of craftsmanship, and charm, is my guess. There is something nice about the way they feel in one's hand. Their slightly superior, bright expressions seem to say "bring me home."

Cappi got started making bears because too many teds said "bring me home" to her.

"About ten years ago (1973) I started collecting teddy bears," she says, "very quietly, of course. Back then people looked at you very strangely for having piles of teddy bears all over the house.

"I actually started making bears to help offset the cost of buying bears for my collection. My middle daughter, Durae, urged me to go to a miniature show in the area to see the tiny bears and that was the start of my bear making. I bought some Sculpy and Fimo and went home to try my hand.

"I made tiny 1/2in (1.3cm) to 1½in (3.8cm) jointed clay bears and sold them at various miniature shows. I don't make many clay bears anymore but I am making a set of bears, one for each month, sculpted with a costume suitable for that month, in a very limited quantity for 1983."

Cappi's fabric bears come in everything from wools to plushes, are all fully-jointed and come in a variety of sizes. "I enjoy making different sizes because I never get bored that way," she says. Boredom an stultification caused by repetition are common complaints among bear makers. "I believe that, in the future, all new bears I make will be limited to 50 or 100 of each. In that way I can keep creating and not get bogged down." She has started to do limited editions, intended for collectors, of not more than 25 bears per design. All are marked with tags sewn into a back seam. "The tags are handwritten with my name, the series number, the number of bear and year. I have a master book in which all bears are registered."

Working on bears ten to twelve hours a day, six days a week, has caused the designer to develop preferences among her creations.

Her favorite design is *Timothy.* "He was the first 18in (45.7cm) bear I made and to me he turned out perfect. He has the sweetest face and is spoiled rotten. He goes just about everywhere with me and loves when people say how cute he is."

This not uncommon practice, (that of toting one's ted), leads to problems sometimes, when arctophiles meet non-believers.

"Bears are definitely 'people' to me," the bear maker recounts. "At the Teddy Tribune Convention in Minneapolis this past August (1983), a friend and I (along with our bears) were shown to a table in the coffee shop at the hotel. A woman across from us asked about the abundance of bears she had been seeing around the hotel.

"I explained that we had come from all over the U.S., Canada and even England for this affair, with our bears. Well, she was astounded and proceeded to tell me about her dog and how, being an animate object, she could talk to it and take it places.

"I tried to explain to her that I could talk to *Timothy* and take him places (like restaurants, where I know they wouldn't let her dog in) and that there were quite a few guests in the hotel who would certainly agree with me as to the animation of their bears, but in the midst of it all, the lady rather quickly excused herself and left."

Cappi's bears are real to her granddaughter, too. "Every bear that I make has love in it because my three-year-old granddaughter, Erika Leigh, kisses and hugs every single

Big bear, 18in (45.7cm), is *Timothy. Timothy* is buff-colored fur with toffee velour paw pads. Small bear, 12in (30.5cm), is *Sam. Sam* is nutmeg fur with beige velour pads. They both have black glass eyes. Both are fully-jointed. Hand signed ribbon tags in back seam. *Photograph courtesy of Cappi Warnick.*

Jester Bear, 13in (33cm) tall, is called *J.T.* Tiny *Jester Bear,* 1½in (3.8cm) tall, is called *BoBo.* They are both turquoise and fuchsia pink. *J.T.* has black felt pads; band on hat. Beige coat wool heads. Both big and little jesters are made in assorted colors. *Photograph courtesy of Cappi Warnick.*

Bright Bear (B.B.), 12in (33.5cm) tall. Camel-colored coat wool; beige velour paw pads; fully-jointed; black glass eyes; plaid bow. Tag in back seam is hand printed. 1983. One of the "visitor bears" from the box.

Mother and Baby, Cappi Warnick's first limited edition of 25. Mother is 6in (15.2cm), has a white pinafore trimmed in lace, human hair eyelashes and felt eyelids over brown glass eyes. Baby, 1½in (3.8cm), has a white lace bonnet and lace-trimmed gown. Photograph courtesy of Cappi Warnick.

bear before it leaves my house. Sometimes I have to delay shipping an order of bears for a day, until Erika can come over and kiss them good-bye."

Mrs. Warnick designs instinctively. She has sewn for years, and even made her sister's wedding gown completely by hand. Ideas for bears occur while she is otherwise occupied.

"While I am sewing and stuffing bears, I am constantly thinking of new bears to make. After I have worked out most the bugs in my head (such as size, type of fabric, special touches like eyelashes, clothes, etc.), I then work out the pattern on paper and make one up. It then sits in front of me on the work table for a week or so while I am working on other bears. In this way, I can thoroughly check the new bear out to see if he needs to be modified in any way."

Cappi's family helps, at times, with the bear making, but only if they conform to her high standards. "My husband is a real sweetheart about the whole thing (bear making). He helps here and there with little things that need doing and cuts out the joints. He was putting them in the bears, but I had to fire him from that job because the bear joints were just too sloppy," she says. But "he brags an awful lot, to anyone who will listen, about my bear making."

The Warnicks' support of their resident bear maker is evident in the following story. "The best indication of how my family feels about my bears was my last brithday. One of my daughters went shopping to buy me a present with a new boyfriend whom we had not met yet. After watching my daughter spend 45 minutes going through several toy stores, the fellow asked my daughter what she was going to buy me. Maybe a skirt or pretty blouse?

"My daughter looked at him in shock and said, 'If I gave my mother something stupid like that, she would think I had lost my mind. I'm looking for something 'beary.' When the boy came over later in the week with my daughter for my birthday, he understood. My house is just about wall to wall bears."

I know the feeling. When Bearbit arrived, my house seemed just about wall to wall bears, too. Most of them were visitor bears. Charles threatened to donate them to the next wandering UPS man if I did not hurry up and photograph them so they could go home. Sylvia Lyons' bear, now going under the alias of Van-my-Man, had by this time moved in; he growled at the thought of stuffing those bears back into boxes.

I rather liked the feeling of swimming in bears, but the day came when they all had to go home. All but one. Cappi's in the box had concluded, "The little one with the big tag is yours to keep. Thank you beary much. Cappi." Wowsers.

I replaced Bearbit in the box, with Bright Bear, her chaperone, then kissed them good-bye.

I still think Bearbit is a girl.

Terry, the bear who stayed in Maine, 6½in (14cm). Fully-jointed; camel-colored coating fabric; lighter hue camel foot pads; black glass eyes; embroidered nose and mouth; ribbon at neck; holding Maine state flag.

Four of Cappi Warnick's bears out for some fun. *Timothy,* 18in (45.7cm) is pulling the sled. *Sam* and *Melissa* are riding. *Pennie* is pushing. *Photograph courtesy of Cappi Warnick.*

FRANK AND SUSY BIRD

Frank Bird and St. George Bear dragon steamer. Steam comes out of the dragon's mouth when in operation. *Photograph courtesy of Frank Bird.*

Bears brought Frank and Susy Bird together.

Frank's fondness for teddies was fostered by his mother who received a big, brown bear from a beau sometime before her marriage to Frank's father. *Benjamin Baxter,* as he has been recently christened, "was always a treasured member of the Bird home." says Susy. He and Frank grew up on Winnie-the-Pooh stories.

Susy grew up all over the world as an air force dependant and met her first teddy in Cairo, Egypt. He was medium-sized golden Steiff bear. Her brother had a panda and they would tie large scarves around their bears' necks which "transformed them into superbears who helped out under-dogs." She also owned a Berlin bear mug and a blue glass bear nightlight, long-lost but nostalgically longed for.

Bears played a part in Frank and Susy's courtship. They met at a naval hospital where Frank was recuperating from a near-fatal auto accident and Susy was a Red Cross worker.

Frank reintroduced Susy to bears. He would give her dramatic readings from *Winnie the Pooh* and *The House at Pooh Corner,* setting the pace for their ensuing relationship. Frank gave Susy a watercolor he did of *Pooh* traveling on a bee-surrounded balloon, and their first Christmas together, they exchanged bears, starting a custom of adding a new bear each Christmas.

Finally Frank decided Susy was a "bear" herself and trustworthy to marry. She was dubbed "Small Bear" or "Bosnian Bear." Frank has an extensive background in the arts. He studied painting in Spain and had a painting studio on Midway Island while in the Navy. Theater (he wrote, produced and directed a motion picture), printmaking sculpture and ceramics were his interests at the University of North Carolina at Charlotte. Ceramics won out as first choice there, where he won the Kokenes Award for outstanding achievement in the arts.

Frank's career as maker of bears on functional, everyday items began with a mug Susy asked him to make for a baby

Susy Bird and potpourri box. *Photograph courtesy of Frank Bird.*

gift. When a ceramics teacher saw the bear mug, he strongly encouraged Frank to make more. He says his combination of bears and pottery works because "Functional, everyday items are perfect vessels for bears since they are extroverts and like to be included in all parts of everyday life."

From the start when Bird pots with bears were displayed in a gallery near the University of North Carolina at Chapel Hill, they have been highly successful. Before leaving North Carolina for Texas, Frank made a desk name plaque with bears on it for Jim Hunt, North Carolina's governor.

In Texas, the Birds fitted their pottery studio and collection of bears into a century-old Victorian house and large barn. Susy joined Frank as potter/sculptor, doing the detail glazing on the bears; soon she started her own line of bathroom pieces from clay slabs.

Frank is known as "the bear man" by the customers who come to buy pottery and stay for a tour of the Bird bear collection. He claims it is hard for them to believe his name is Bird, not Bear.

Customers find out about him through word of mouth, at shows, through publicity, galleries, newspapers and public auctions, as well as mail order. Those who trek to the gallery receive a discount.

Frank handthrows every pot. He has high standards, striving for thin walls in the finished product. Each bear is handmade, one at a time, in 30 steps. The bears and pots are designed to stand on their own as fine works of art.

The Birds believe that the individual touch is what makes their work special and have avoided doing molds which

Jewel box. Stoneware. 1983. *Photograph courtesy of Frank Bird.*

ElBanco, bear bank guarded by *Desbearado.* Stoneware. 1983. *Photograph courtesy of Frank Bird.*

"would involve too much quality control to keep the product up to par." Frank's goal is "a harmonious blend of bear and pot."

Bears are generally 2½in (6.4cm) or smaller, depending on the size of the pot. Like the pot, they are made of stoneware and fired in a gas kiln to 2381° F. Unlike the pot, the bear is unglazed, but waxed so the rest of the pot may be glazed without affecting him. If the bear were glazed, detail would be lost and he would be slicker and "not as earthy." Frank says, "Bears, because they are bunchy and trianglar-shaped, particularly while sitting, make excellet handles for casseroles, cookie jars, etc."

Every three weeks, about 70 pots in each kiln get fired. Pieces with gold touches are refired in an electric kiln, where all the preliminary bisque firing is done. Then pots are signed and dated.

A special joy is making bear pots with surprises, and Frank makes over 40 different items, including "almost everything available for the kitchen and bathroom." His mirrors feature bears looking at themselves from the frame, brushing fur with tiny brushes. Sometimes they sport signature bluebirds on their heads.

Perhaps the most unusual pieces are the steamers. The sculptural scene on the lid incorporates a bit of steam from below. Frank describes his work: "*Napoleon Bearnaparte* and his cannon sit on top of a steamer, and, when in use,

steam shoots out the cannon. The St. George bear steamer has a dragon that will spew steam out of his mouth, and the prospector bear sits frying a fish over a campfire and steam will wisp out from under his black skillet. Plans are now being made to make a bear in a sportscar or a biplane so that steam will pour out the exhaust systems. Steamship with bear figurehead, too."

Smily bears climb, sit, squat and cavort all over Bird pottery. A Valentine mug shows a bear climbing the outside rim on his way to present a golden heart to a bear on the inside of the mug. Lamps feature character bears: a Knightlight (nightlight) has "a charging knightbear in full regalia on a horse outside a castle turret with a king bear looking on. The lighthouse lamp has a captain bear on a beach with a spy glass, sitting next to a palm tree. The mission lamp sports a rejoicing St. Francis bear and the Taj Mahal lamp has a turbanned bear playing a flute to a cobra."

When asked about the good and the bad sides of his art form, Frank replied: "*Every art form that is also a means of earning a living has its drawbacks such as the pressure of filling orders and getting ready for big shows. There are also the problems of the ceramic form itself, i.e., cracking, warping, over and under-firing, wet weather not conducive to drying of greenware on schedule. However, the rewards of bear making far outweigh the drawbacks. Peoples' reactions give the most satisfaction. The bear pottery brings so many smiles and makes for many lasting friendships* between artists and customers."

Of course, there is always somebody who does not like bears. Or, at least, someone who does not like pottery with bears on it. One woman said, "You make such beautiful pottery, but why do you put the little pigs on it?"

These types are rare. Frank feels that making bears is gratifying because, "In a world where nothing is certain, a bear can be 'your very pal'."

The Birds try to reach with their work, which, by this time is hundreds of bears, "those who delight in regaining a happy childhood or those interested in constructing one they never had." They feel that a bear can reach into the past and heal it and make the future more acceptable. Frank says, "You're only young twice — once when you are a child and any other time when you're with your bear."

Their response to today's wide acceptance of the teddy bear is: "The recent popularity of bears is very gratifying. However, there will always be those who permanently love bears and those who like them because they're "in." The current popularity has much to do with our interest in the past when one led a more relaxed life and had more roots and a sense of belonging as an individual. A bear is good, clean fun and an acceptable escape into fantasy. He can make you feel wonderful and giving. He supplies self-esteem in a world sadly lacking in that commodity. He thinks the best of you to begin with so, of course, you'll try to do

Knightlight. Stoneware. 1983. *Photograph courtesy of Frank Bird.*

Carrousel Bear made for Doris and Terry Michaud. Stoneware. 1983. *Photograph courtesy of Frank Bird.*

everything to meet his expectations. He's an unhurried friend who's delighted to give you all of his time. He can be your best friend without rights in return. We can have faith in ourselves because he has faith in us.

"Many teddies are as innocent as those of years ago. It depends, of course, on the maker and the owner. Some have made bears for money alone and have put no love in the process. However, an owner can redeem that. The audiences aimed at today include, of course, the more sophisticated, those who can afford to collect. However, one can also say that bears are truly getting the appreciation they should always have had."

There are three Birds now. Son Ian tries his hands, too, at bear making. The bears that brought the Birds together seem destined to become a family tradition.

DORIS AND TERRY MICHAUD
(The Carrousel Bears)

Doris and Terry Michaud and a few favorite antique bears from their collection. Terry holds *The Professor,* the bear that started them off. Doris holds *The Duke of Portobello,* found in the alcove of a shop on Portobello Road, London, England. He appeared in the 1983 Teddy Bear Calendar. *Photograph courtesy of Doris and Terry Michaud.*

For Doris and Terry Michaud, bear making is not "in the bag." According to Terry, there are two types of plush teds, "bag bears" and "collector bears."

Bag bears are inexpensive (usually under $10), machine-stuffed, mass-produced teddies with limited life expectancy. Hastily constructed, they are seldom jointed. Their eyes and snouts and sometimes their mouths may be plastic or felt.

Michaud bears, sold under the trade name "Carrousel," are specially designed for the adult collector market and have, intrinsic to their construction, characteristics deemed most desirable to the grown-up bear buyer. These include dense pile fur, glass eyes, humps on their backs, fully-jointed limbs and heads, hand-sewn noses and mouths (they smile!), a nice firmness and a nostalgic air. Terry terms the latter "the same innocence as his counterpart or 'forebear'."

Their creators are very knowledgeable in such things; they are collectors themselves. In fact, it was a futile quest for a contemporary bear with the salient qualities of antique ones that led them to design their own.

It all began with a wise old bear. For 15 years, Doris and Terry were involved in the antique doll and toy business. One day, in 1975, they acquired an old (1906) teddy bear whose intelligent eyes behind elderly eyeglasses prompted their daughter's favorable comparison of him to one of her *teachers. Dubbed The Professor,* he was awarded the job of guarding a sign reading "Wanted — Old Teddy Bears" at shows. Soon a barrage of bruins began bursting in on the couple. Today, the Michaud collection numbers over 400 and continues to grow in both size and recognition.

Always in search of a new recruit to the den, Terry visited the Bear Necessities shop in Boston, Massachussets, in 1979. He got into a discussion with owner, Tim Atkins, in

which they bemoaned the fact that nobody made contemporary teds with the characteristics of the oldies. Terry mulled over the idea and replied that he was going to make just such a bear. The bear merchant assured him that a bear market out there was growling for it.

The next two years were a time for exbearimentation, in which they solicited input from folk knowledgeable in the field. "We...had the privilege of meeting Peter Bull in late 1980, and he looked at one of our early prototypes, (now in his collection), and was very encouraging to us to continue," recalls Terry.

In 1981, the design was ready for the final test. "We sent the samples to Tim and his reaction was immediate: How much and how soon?" says Terry.

The first "Carrousel" bears went on sale that year. Reaction from customers was prompt and positive, and, in 24 months, over 60 shops from coast to coast picked up the line, a remarkable accomplishment, since news of the bears had spread almost entirely by word of mouth. Merchants see them in other shops and contact the Michauds. The name of the company and its address appears on a printed tag sewn into each bear's right paw.

To keep up with the demand, the couple's original construction methods have been upgraded a bit. Terry describes their progress: "We started with acrylic plush from fabric stores and our first teddies were stuffed with recycled bank records. That gave them the "crunchy" feel of a straw-stuffed teddy. As the demand for our bears grew, we soon outpaced the supply of shredded bank records and switched to polyester fiberfill. Our pattern has stayed basically the same, but our methods of producing them have changed. For example, I used to cut all of the joint discs by hand. We finally found a supplier, but the minimum order was for 20,000 pieces. That was a major step for us.

Uncle Sam. Limited edition for 1983. *Uncle Sam Teddy* commemorated the 125th birthday of Theodore Roosevelt. A limited edition of 1000, he stands 22in (55.9cm) tall. Red and white striped pants; a red bow tie and grey flannel coat and hat; navy blue star-spangled vest matches the band around the hat; fully-jointed white plush; a goatee at mouth level. The edition number is stamped on the brass fob on his vest. *Uncle Sam* comes specially gift boxed. *Photograph courtesy of Doris and Terry Michaud.*

We graduated from buying a few yards of plush at a retail fabric shop to buying from a fabric mill. This also requires rather large minimum orders."

However, there is little "automation" in their production. Terry describes one recent innovation: "We have a custom-built cutting table that will hold four rolls of material and allow us cutting space on top. We recently changed to a cutting system that allows us to cut multiple patterns instead of doing them all one at a time. There are a few other minor changes, but to go beyond that we feel would sacrifice quality and we are not willing to do that. Each and every bear has to meet with Doris' final approval. We have 11 women assisting in several stages of our work, but only a few do the finish work."

The bears are fabricated in a sort of cottage industry. Jobs are delegated. Terry and Doris are responsible for design, finishing and marketing. The women who help with the construction each have special skills and duties. One cuts patterns; another affixes joints and stuffs; still others do preliminary sewing or are "bear couturieres."

But the final work is "in the family." Two married daughters, Mary Baese and Pat Messinger, are an important part of the "finishing team." No bear is "born," however, without Doris' blessing. Occasionally, an ornery bruin may be completely, or repeatedly, remade to pass inspection. Doris' standards are high.

Baby Edward, 13in (33cm) tall. Plush fabric; jointed; crocheted bib. He is listening to Charlie McCarthy play the drum. *Photograph courtesy of Doris and Terry Michaud.*

The Carrousel line encompasses both traditional and character bears. Teddies are in four sizes: 13in (33cm) *Baby Edward,* an 18in (45.7cm) *Sir Edward II* (their basic bear), a 27in (68.6cm) *Sir Edward III* and a giant 37in (93.9cm) *Sir Edward IV.* They range in price from $52 to $300. The Michauds also make a series of eight costumed character bears in the basic 18in (45.7cm) size. Terry and Doris enjoy making these most because of the added dimension the clothing to the bears' personas.

The dressed bears include *Bearzo, the Clown; Burnt Umbear,* the artist, *Stutz Bearcat; Brother Theodore (*their most popular item*); Sun Bearnet Sue* and *Captain Smoky Obearn,* the fireman, who holds a baby bear in a bunting (Fireman, fireman, save my child). Two recent additions are *Nurse Bearnadette* and *Ted, the Good News Bear'r* (Terry's favorite, because he has always felt we should place more emphasis on the good news in the world. Specialty bears include a panda, *Boomerang, the Koala* (Doris' favorite because he brings pleasant thoughts from a faraway land), several sizes of teddy muffs and a teddy with beautiful long grey hair called *Theodore, the Greyed.*

A very special limited edition, produced in honor of the 125th Anniversary of the birth of Theodore Roosevelt, who is recognized as the father of the teddy bear, is called *Uncle Sam Teddy.* He was limited to an edition of only 1000 and his brass watch fob was stamped with his edition number. *Uncle Sam Teddy* is an all-American teddy bear. In Terry's words: "It is appropriate that *Uncle Sam Teddy* is American from top to bottom. The teddy bear's roots are American, from the cartoon that inspired him to the humble store of the Morris Michtoms in Brooklyn where he was created. We do not attempt to downplay the importance or the quality of teddy bears made in Germany or in any other country. We simply take pride in the fact that here is a teddy bear that is

Just Ted. A departure from Carrousel's *Sir Edward* series, this recreation of a 1924 teddy bear from the Michauds' collection is the first in a planned series of recreations. Original ted on the right. *Just Ted* on the left. 1984. *Photograph courtesy of Doris and Terry Michaud.*

Sir Edward II, passenger. *Baby Edward* at the wheel. *Sir Edward II* is 18in (45.7cm) tall. *Baby Edward* is 13in (33cm) tall. Both are made of plush fabric; jointed and have "Carrousel" tag in left foot pad. *Photograph courtesy of Doris and Terry Michaud.*

100% American and proud to stand up and be counted with the best of them."

The Michauds have also done special edition bears, such as the black plush *Jester Bear* designed in 1982 for Hobby Center Toys, who boasts a pink and turquoise ruff and matching bell-trimmed jester hat.

In two years' time, bear making has revolutionized the Michauds' lives. Doris is a full-time bruin-builder, and Terry, who has a half-time consulting business in a non-related field seems to also spend full-time with the bears. In the near future they both plan to devote their entire energies to the business. Besides production, they take their furry friends, both new and old, on tour.

The couple is very proud of their product's high standards of quality. They refuse to compromise in making bears, or to have their designs executed by others. Terry talks about his bears; "They have not been produced commercially by anyone other than us. Compromise? Only the artist himself can determine if the commercial work is successful. It is our opinion that mass production techniques (or production by someone not familiar with the product or artist) strongly dissolve the personality of the creator in the finished work."

When asked his philosophy, he replied, "We try to put a little of ourselves in each teddy that is produced by us. We feel each and every person who buys one becomes a very important part of our family."

With such a wholesome philosophy, and a product to match, success for the Carrousel Bears is surely "in the bag."

BARBARA SIXBY

Barbara Sixby started bear making in March 1983. Her first bear was not a huge success. It was intended as a gift for her boyfriend. "The bear didn't turn out so well," she says. "He was so ugly he (the boyfriend) never got him."

She has been a collector of bears, and had definite ideas about them. "I could never find any really character bears. I'm really picky about the types that I buy and I always had to have them with really cute faces and everything. So, when I started making them, this is what I had in mind. I just thought I'd try my hand at it and see what would be the finished product."

Barbara never had any fine arts training. At this writing, she is attending college in California, taking pre-med, with the idea of becoming an M.D., having graduated from high school at sixteen. But, she says, "My mom just let me do a lot of arts and crafts when I was little. I think that helped me making the bears."

After the abortive first bear, her boyfriend, Mark, encouraged her to try again. "He never really criticized what the bears looked like, even the first ones," Barbara remembers. So she went to work, taking pieces and ideas from various sources, finally coming up with her own concepts. She had to design original bears; other people's directions and patterns were too complicated: "When I started out, I designed all my patterns myself. I found it was too hard to follow someone else's. I tried once and couldn't finish the bear."

The bears improved, and Barbara's mother, who originally thought they were funny-looking, offered to help. Selling some bears, they figured, might help defray high tuition costs.

So Barbara became a part-time bear maker and full-time student. By May of 1983, She had her first showing and the bears "took off." Soon she had so many orders, she had to re-evaluate priorities.

"I never thought it would go from going to school full-time and doing bears part-time to doing bears full-time and going to school part-time," she said. But it has.

Barbara designs for the collector, since this is where the market is, and what she understands. Truth be told, she prefers old bears: "Really old antique bears, the ones that have a lot of worn spots. You can tell they've been loved. I like the old bears that look at you in a special way. The ones that seem to always be saying to you, 'I need a new home. I need more love'."

Her own bear making ideas stem from what she looks for in others' work.

"With the new bears that are out today from the bear artists, I look for mostly character. Being a bear collector, sure, quality is important. But I think that the character of the bear is utmost important. For me, when I see bears that resemble others, I usually don't buy them. Each bear has to be different. They have to be telling me something. They have to give me a reason to take them home."

Zücker bears, ("sugar bears," Barbara's name for her critters) are full of such reasons. They sport wonderful crooked smiles, impish, inquisitive expressions and are full of

Barbara Sixby. Size: 5ft 2in (1.57m). Material: 100% American. Date: December 17, 1965. Limited edition: one-of-a-kind. Manufactured by: Mr. and Mrs. Ronald H. Sixby. Where: Alameda, California. *Photograph courtesy of Barbara Sixby.*

pizzaz and style. They come in all sizes and shapes — from less than 1in (2.5cm) to over 5ft (1.52m) tall, with and without ostrich plumes, turbans and outlandish getups.

"I'm being labeled now with making character bears," she explains. "I think the funniest thing is most people say that my bears have an expression of disinterest. They're looking all around and are just concerned with what's going on all around them."

Costume sometimes plays a part in determining the bears' characters. This most often occurs in limited edition bears, which Barbara prefers, since they give her a chance to experiment. "I do like doing limited editions, and one-of-a-kind bears. With the limited editions, I get to spend more time with each bear, putting time into a costume, giving it more detail than most of the bears."

She describes the role clothing plays in her work. "The only time I really design clothes for my bears is when I'm doing a limited edition or one-of-a-kind. The clothes play an equal role in the total look of the bear. Sometimes you get lucky and one bear can have a lot of personalities so you can dress him lots of different ways.

"I think that in the aspect of the dressing the bears, it's a lot like people. Some people only look good and show their personality with one type of clothing that they wear. They don't change it because that's not their personality. But there are other people that wear very flamboyant outfits, or they may be very casual. Whatever it is, it's what their personality is. It's the same with bears. You can't make them what they're not."

Goldish-copper color bear, approximately 16in (40.6cm) Fully-jointed; enjoys berries.

Hubert. Designed November 1983. Material: fake fur. *Hubert* is a kit which includes everything needed to make him except for stuffing and thread. *Photograph courtesy of Barbara Sixby.*

Barbara takes great pains to make the clothing. "I'll get the whole thing done and I'll think, 'This just isn't right,' so I'll take it all apart, I just have to wait until I fall upon something that really makes the bear, that really brings out the character of that bear."

Character bears made Barbara's reputation, but she feels that, perhaps, she is even better-known for the innovations her brother has made in her bear business. He has mechanized them.

The mechanical bears that my brother and I do are just wonderful," she says. "They are so much fun because I really enjoy watching him design something new. He usually comes up with an idea and I have to make the bears for it."

Her enthusiasm shows, as she describes a favorite: "I have one — her name is *Charlotte* — and she's on a swing. She swings back and forth and her head goes from side to side. The bear, itself, in the swing is just over 3ft (.91m) tall." The mechanical bears, as well as the others, have won prizes.

Barbara's bears have become so popular that there is at least a six months' waiting period for orders. Shops order dozens at a time and she supplies over two dozen stores on both coasts. In the first year, she has made countless hundreds of bears and bear making has taken over her lifestyle, as well as that of her family. Fortunately, they are enthusiastic and supportive.

Her working methods have changed considerably, as well as sheer quantities of supplies.

"I've always used the fake fur with making the bears but when I started I'd go to the retail stores and buy a couple of yards. Now I go to the mills and buy bolts at a time.

"The procedure of making the bears has changed some, just because of the quantity of bears that I do. When I first made the bears, I would make the whole bear at one time. And now, in a day, I'll either sit down and concentrate on just sewing bodies or legs or arms or heads or making their faces or putting the bears together. Rarely do I make one bear at a time. Usually I make a couple dozen at a time!"

Her days are full of bears. "A normal day of bear making for me usually starts about 7:30 a.m. And, if I'm really occupied in what I'm doing, sometimes I don't even bother getting dressed and I'm running around in my robe all day.

"I wouldn't really be able to tell you if my bear making methods were unusual because I haven't really talked to other bear makers about how they go about making bears. The only thing that keeps me going is I have an extra room in our house and it's just for making the bears. I have all my supplies in it and I have my table set up with my machine and everything. And on the table, I have a blanket and my puppy sleeps there with me all day. And I have my little Sony Walkman. I start out in the morning with some really uppity music and by the end of the day, I'm down to Roger Whittaker.

Barbara's father cuts out joints. Her mother draws up patterns, cuts them out, stuffs bears and helps with finishing. Tim, her brother does the mechanicals. And, her boyfriend, Mark, helps in lots of ways — including encouragement.

"All I have to do," she says, "is ask and they're all there, ready to help. It's nice to have my family involved in what I'm doing because they are really great. Sometimes our dining table is just loaded up with bear supplies and bears when I've been working out in the living room all day and, so I won't have to clean anything up or move anything, we'll usually end up having dinner on t.v. trays."

Barbara's bears sell through word-of-mouth, are available at shops and at shows. She does a lot of shows, but never has anything but samples to show; her waiting list is very long. And sometimes she just burns out trying to fill orders, wishing collectors would realize that quality takes time, especially when it is, essentially, a one-girl-bear making operation.

"If I'm doing my 9in (22.9cm) bear, and I'm doing them all myself, in one day I can do a dozen or more. If I'm doing my large bears, I can do maybe three a day. But, then, again, that's working on them for more than eight hours."

She has been approached about commercial production of her bears but has not given it much thought, since, unless the setup were similar to that of Steiff, where much is hand-crafted, the quality of the finished product might be questionable. And she would not want her name on anything inferior.

Still, she takes time to design new bears because this is what she prefers and it comes easily.

"I think I'm really lucky in designing new bears because I'm able to sit down and draw it out freehand on a piece of paper, cut out the pattern and lay it out. And, just by eyeballing it, see if it'll come out proportionwise. Making a new bear, desiging it, is really a piece of cake. And I think I'm really lucky because I've talked to other artists who struggle with making a new bear."

When she gets down because of order backlog, inevitably Barbara will receive a card or a call from a delighted customer. "Really, I think the most enjoyable part of it is seeing the enjoyment that other people get out of them," she says. It is often at shows this happens. At one, Barbara had a little bear which she had designed in December 1983. "His name was *Willy,* and he was a limited edition of 100. He's all dressed in little overalls and a little hat and he flies a kite. A lady came up to me during the show. She said she's never bought bears and she didn't collect and that she really liked the bears. She was looking around at my table and spotted *Willy.* She just had to have him because, she said, it looked like her husband and his name was *Willy,* also. Anyway, she

Oswald, 36in (91.4cm) tall. Made of cinnamon plush; wearing a vest and long tie. Designed May 1983. *Photograph courtesy of Barbara Sixby.*

Bernice, approximately 18in (45.7cm) tall. Made of various colors in plush; wears fancy hat and collar. Designed in April of 1983.

Jenny-Lynn Waugh and Bernice's hat.

Willy. Cinnamon plush; wool overalls with a handkerchief sticking out of his front pocket; a non-matching wool railroad hat; flies a kite that shows patches. He really loves flying his kite. His edition is limited to 100. *Willy* is marked with a button pinned to his pocket, with his name, Zucker bears, the number of the bear and how many are in the edition, the date, and Barbara's signature. This *Willy* belongs to Barbara's Mom and is a prototype. Designed December 1983. *Photograph courtesy of Barbara Sixby.*

ended up placing an order for him. She was going to give her husband *Willy* for his birthday."

Barbara has definite ideas about men and teddy bears. After all, her attempt to make a bear for a special man got her where she is today — up to her ears in bears.

"To me, it's really wonderful to see a man hold and cuddle a teddy bear, just like a little kid."

She tells her most memorable experience of this ilk.

"I was judging a teddy bear contest in San Francisco. A man came in with his teddy bear and he happened to be a Hell's Angel. He had a medium-size teddy bear that was all dressed up in leathers identical to his — down to a little spiked collar and arm band and hat and he was even riding a little motor cycle.

"He entered his bear in the best dressed section. He ended up winning first prize, Best of Show, for it. He was telling us, the judges, after the contest, that he even straps him to his motorcycle and he rides down the street with him. to me this was really great because it shows that anyone's heart can be taken by a teddy bear."

Of all the bears she has made, Barbara's favorite was designed for a man.

"I think my favorite bear is the one I did for Ted Menten for his *International Bear Hugs.* When I finished him, he just won my heart. The expression on his face was so adorable I didn't even want to part with him. For the December issue, Ted called me and told me I could design a bear. I had to make two of them. One he kept, and one was raffled off. And, when I had to pack them up in a box and ship them off to New York, my whole family was sad to see them go."

But Barbara's most-loved bear is the one she's shared with another male, her brother.

"My Mom used it at night with both of us, so we wouldn't be scared of our bad dreams. She would always tell us that, if we had a bad dream, all we had to do was to hug onto our teddy bear and he would make all bad dreams go away. That one bear chased all our bad dreams away."

Barbara Sixby at this writing, all of 18, may be America's most prolific young bear maker. When asked how she does it, she says, "I guess my philosophy would be, 'the bare facts of bear making is bear with it!!"

The Prince. Cover Bear for December, 1983 issue of *International Bear Hugs.* One of two bears made especially for Ted Menten. One was raffled off to a newsletter reader. *Photograph by Ted Menten, courtesy of Ted Menten.*

BEVERLY PORT

"There is a child within every adult. I want to make a bear that calls to that child and awakens even those who sleep, a bear that satisfies the yearning in people's hearts for their "lost" bear, to make a bear that people will love and enjoy always, to make the perfect companion and confidante; as were teddy bears of childhood."

Beverly Port's call was heard, over a decade ago, up and down the West Coast of America. In the beginning, it was a lonely cry, the cry of the child inside herself, the child who was seeking, through her own artistic achievements, to somehow replace her own lost bear — to awaken in others the memories of the importance of "Teddy Bear Love."

"I probably liked teddy bears before I was born," she says. I know a teddy bear awaited my arrival along with my dad and mom. When I was six, my dad won a 30in (76.2cm) teddy bear for a nickel on a punch-board. I can remember the big brown paper-wrapped package tied with string and how excited I was about what it contained.

"The big brown and gold bear was my friend. We had many visits and tea parties at my little red table and chairs. When we moved to Washington, a big packing box was lost; it contained my special teddy bear and my mom's best china and silver — never to be found!

"Thus began the 'Teddy Bear Trauma' for me. I thought no other could take his place and ever wished he would miraculously appear.

"At any rate, I didn't want another teddy bear until many years later when I was collecting antique dolls. Perhaps the best part of making teddy bears is recapturing some of that happiness from childhood in every bear I create."

Bev Port is probably America's foremost teddy bear artist. She has been at it longer than most; her influence upon all the rest is incalculable. It is no accident that the greatest number of artists in this book live on America's West Coast. It is here, her home territory, where her message has been heard the strongest. She has been preaching the message of the original teddy bear to anyone who might listen, for years — long before bears became fashionable. She began making bears as art objects to answer personal artistic and emotional needs in the late 1960s, finally coming out of the teddy bear artist's closet in the 1970s.

"My first public exhibit was at Bainbridge Arts and Crafts in the early 1970s. I made both jointed and non-jointed bears. *Theodore B. Bear* was the first publicly exhibited jointed bear in 1974. I made bears and dolls for my sisters and my children before that."

Beverly is perhaps best known for her original dolls; it is hard to say, though. Her work in both complementary fields is outstanding. The bears and dolls developed simultaneously, out of the same artistic drive. An art major at Olympic College, the Washington State doll artist is adept at many media.

"I work with porcelain, wax and cloth in doll making. I use oil paints, acrylic paints and china paints. I also draw and paint pictures — plus work with color pencils, and make paper dolls."

Beverly Port with her father and 30in (76.2cm) teddy bear, 1939. "Old Teddy" was brown mohair with lighter brown muzzle. Bev's Dad, P.J. Matteson, in middle. Bev holds her Easter bunny. *Photograph courtesy of Beverly Port.*

All of the above are used in her bear making. Her first attempts to recapture her childhood bear went to family members. She made bears when she was a child herself.

"I began making teddy bears, dolls an other toys for Christmas presents for my family when I was little and learning to sew. I wanted to do 'my own thing' even at a young age, so I made my own patterns. I've never used a commercial pattern."

She began simply, progressing with each bear, finally gaining the confidence to offer her bears to the general public as her repertoire expanded.

"Cloth was the first medium I used for small hand-sewn teddy bears. I first made small one-piece felt bears; then jointed velour and velvet ones. I also modeled teddies for ornaments and figurines. I have progressed through the years — making larger sizes, using both acrylics and mohair materials.

"I've also combined fabric with porcelain faces with modeled mouths with tongues (some have teeth); and glass eyes inset into the eye sockets. I've made mechanical bears with heads that turn by moving their tail; others with tails that wind a music box, and other novelty bears including candy containers, perfume bears, bears-on-wheels, patchwork bears, character bears — they have become more detailed.

Love Bears © 1977 by Beverly Port. Golden brown porcelain bisque; black eyes, noses and mouths; jointed with wire at arms and legs; modeled like "old fashioned" teddies with long arms and humps on backs; red hearts on ties around necks with "LOVE" on hearts. Incised mark on back with artist's name, date and ©. *Photograph courtesy of Beverly Port.*

Baby — A Bear for all Seasons, © 1980 Beverly Port Originals, approximately 15in (38.1cm) tall. Fully-jointed pale gray acrylic plush; wool felt paw and foot pads; swivel neck; antique shoe button eyes; black embroidered nose, mouth and claws. Her blue print bib, ruffled hat and blanket are handmade. She also has a pillow with birth month "March" on it. Her blanket has teddy bears printed on it — a different scene for each month of the year. She has a music box in her body that plays "Rockabye Baby." A "Time Machine Teddy."

One mechanical bear is mounted on a music box and both arms and head are moved by the mechanism in the box."

But it was her gentle other-worldly classic teddy that first grabbed the public's attention. She began to integrate the salesrooms of doll shows with original bears in the mid 1970s. The public responded with enthusiasm.

"When I first exhibited my jointed teddy bears in the mid 1970s, they caused quite a stir at doll and toy shows, for the great surge of teddy bear makers was yet to come. People who had ordered my original dolls also 'special ordered' teddy bears from me. Some people thought new handmade bears would NOT be of general interest to the collecting public, yet I've seen the handmade bear become an important category in collecting right along with the two categories of 'antique' and 'new commercial manufactured.'

Doll collectors began to broaden their interests, especially those who were already "closet" bear fans. Many of them were traditionalists.

"People who ordered my original dolls asked me to make my version of the timeless classic — the early-style teddy bear so in the late 1970s the *Time Machine Teddies* were born and copyrighted and exhibited in 1980."

Before *Time Machine Teddy,* her best-known ted, many doll-bears — crossbreeds of doll making and bear making techniques greeted the doll-buying public. They were snapped up.

"I made the character bears, *Tedward, Tedwina* and the large patchwork bear, *Patches, the Bear with a Secret* in 1974 and 1975 and copyrighted them in 1976. I also made and copyrighted the *Lavendar Bear King and Pinkerton of Oz* in 1976. This group of jointed bears appeared in the UFDC Doll News, Winter Issue, 1976, along with *Bearby,* a portrait child in a teddy bear suit."

Jingles © 1980 by Beverly Port, 15in (38.1cm) from head to toe. Full-bodied muff; jointed arms; swivel head; old shoe button eyes. Body is the muff lined with red. Legs below muff. Ribbon of red, blue and green around neck with same color tiny bells — so named *Jingles.* Squeaker in body. Happy face — helpful teddy bears — glad to keep your hands warm. *Photograph courtesy of Beverly Port.*

About this time, Bev began to proselytize for the "Teddy Bear Cause." She wrote articles for anyone who would accept them, extolling the glories of beardom and she began giving talks and slide programs. Her first jointed ted, a diminutive fellow (and fellow writer) called *Theodore B. Bear,* joined her in her mission. He has the advantage over her other bears of a wealth of intrinsic knowledge. Made from a 1914 coat, he is "wise beyond his years," as Bev puts it. She is inordinately fond of this little guy.

"*Theodore B. Bear,* 5in (12.5cm) tall, would have to be my favorite bear creation because he has taken on a life of his own, separate from me — people write to him as well as to me. He wrote his own column in two magazines (*Doll Revue* and *Bambini)* from 1976 to 1982, narrates two UFDC (United Federation of Doll Collectors) slide programs, has written many freelance articles in the "Teddy Bear Cause," (almost wearing out his paw).

"He first wrote in 1975 for a UFDC slide program and Region 1 UFDC souvenir book. He wrote for *Doll Reader*™ in 1976 and his article is now included in the book entitled, *The Best of the Doll Reader.* As a handmade bear, he is proud to be included in Pat Schoonmaker's *Collector's History of the Teddy Bear.* He assists me with my column in *The Teddy Bear and friends*™ magazine.

Santa Bear © 1980 by Beverly Port, 16in (40.6cm) tall. Fully-jointed; tan plush; cranberry red Santa suit trimmed in white plush with three bells down the front of the suit; black shoe button eyes; black embroidered nose and mouth. He has music box in his body that plays, "Santa Claus is Coming to Town." Plump cuddly fellow. A "Time Machine Teddy." Beverly Port trademark neck medallion. *Photograph by Beverly Port.*

"He has traveled widely in search of the "Bear Facts" — twice to England for the big rallies there. *Nutshell News,* the April 1983 issue, also credits him with "spurring on" the teddy bear movement with his articles.

"Many times collectors have come to talk to me at shows and, on seeing *Theodore B. Bear* for the first time, all 5in (12.7cm) of him — they have exclaimed, 'Is that all the bigger he is? We thought he'd be about five FEET (1.52m) or more tall, all the writing he does!' Then they add, looking at ME — 'Well, of course, he REALLY IS.'"

Sometimes Bev brings larger bears on her travels. She finds that the general public not only bear collectors, is in tune with them, too. One more recent example of this sort occurred returning from a Teddy Bear Rally in California in April 1984. Bev brought along with her a humungous off-white bear she had just completed. The plane ride was their mutual maiden voyage in the clouds. "I had a hard time carrying both my bear-packed briefcase and my *Big Bear* onto the Alaska Airlines plane leaving San Jose, California. *Big Bear* is about 34in (86.4cm) tall and made of cream-color mohair. The flight attendants immediately took charge of him, saying he looked like a 'First Class' bear and carried him to the 'First Class' section (I was traveling 'coach'). After take-off, they presented him with his 'wings,' a balloon and two bottles of champagne. I was allowed to go up to the 'First Class' section and take his picture as he relaxed, visited with other passengers and turned to look out his window. His solemn air of dignity was not disturbed by all the attention."

In San Jose, Beverly led bear making workshops and gave talks on a number of aspects of bears, both antique and modern. The diminutive doll maker enjoys sharing her wealth of ursine knowledge with others, and it is largely because of her activities that enthusiasm for artist-produced bears has grown on the West Coast, in the last few years, to its current mania. Her love for them is infectious, and, by example, she demonstrates that producing original teddies can be, not a craft, but art. It depends on ones motives, methods and the audience he intends to please.

"My first intended audience is myself — I want to make what I enjoy — the best and most perfect teddy at the time I'm finishing him. However, all artists must grow or become static so as I finish one, I see how I can improve the next one; so they change and another idea evolves in my progress. Each one I strive to make the best. Many people like what I create and so my next audience is the collector wanting one to love."

There is a certain feeling about Bev's bears that puts them paws above the norm. It is not just that she has been making them so long she has learned to make them well. It's a combination of artistic flair, sensitivity to the essence of teddy bear mentality, and a predisposition to fantasy.

"I'm trying for a look of 'timelessness' — something artistic in expression, but capable of evoking an emotional response — the unforgettable bear. I am trying to capture the elusive bear I see in my dreams and bring him into my three-dimensional reality. 'Painting' with fabric; sculpting a classic that will be the heirloom of tomorrow — today."

Bev's bears are for children — most of all the child she once was — the child who appreciates a work of art.

"Many of my bears are 'play' bears. The stuffed fabric ones can be hugged and cuddled. Some are also sculpture. The cloth are soft sculpture. I make porcelain-faced and sculpted bears with glass eyes. Some have molded mouths and tongues of hard material such as porcelain, composition or polyform with soft stuffed heads, bodies, arms and legs. All are considered 'collectible.' "

Port Bears are so collectible because they appeal aesthetically and emotionally. Some of them seem animate.

"Bears are like little people — 'animal people' — and each one has a distinct and different personality. Happy, sulky, sad or any other emotion can be evinced by a subtle shaping of the head, turn of the mouth, set to the eye — an intangible 'something' that sets them apart — one from another — much as 'human people.'

"And many times the teddy bear definitely has a mind of his own and turns out looking like HE wants to. Strangely enough, there are sometimes the MOST MEMORABLE of bears and hard to let go to a new home.

"Perhaps the subconscious guides my hand and I sometimes feel as if I was only the instrument through which each new character must come into being. It's exciting to see a new bear 'come alive' — at a certain point I can't bear (no pun intended) to put it away — he NEEDS his eyes to see, then looks reproachfully at me until he has his nose and mouth finished. Of course, then he pushes until he has arms and legs to move about and voice or music box to summon his new owner. Each new character creates excitement as he/she is completed."

Some are especially appealing. Bev talks about one such bear, a sentimental favorite.

"Hunny Munny went to a UFDC Regional and when people stopped to talk to her, I explained about the honey-money pocket she wears. About how she says 'hunny munny, hunny munny, hunny munny' over and over until she drives the nearest human crazy and the human puts a penny in her pocket to keep her quiet.

"Later in the day a lady came up to the table, looked closely at Hunny Munny, leaned over and put her ear next to the bear's face. Then she looked up at me and disappointedly said, 'I don't hear her saying 'hunny munny.' My friend said she talked!!'

"Hunny Munny was my mom's favorite teddy bear and she crocheted her hat, scarf, mitts, booties and honey-money pocket. Mom lost her battle with leukemia in the spring of 1982. The bears still mourn, for a great friend she was. In the spring of 1984, Hunny Munny appeared on TV on Gary Collins' 'Hour Magazine' show from the first New York Teddy Bear store, called 'Teddys.' Her funny face looked out of mom's TV screen across from the place Mom always sat — and 'Hunny Munny' smiled."

Smiles are what teddy bears are about for Beverly Port. They are a means of transmitting love and good feelings in a too-troubled world.

"When people stop to look at my bears in shows or exhibits, they pat them, smile, pick them up to hug them and usually a 'teddy bear story' from their past is shared. Teddy bears seem to bring out the best in people and hit a responsive, nostalgic place in people's hearts — young and old alike."

Hunny Munny, © 1980 Beverly Port Originals. Fully-jointed; medium tan wool and mohair; swivel neck; antique shoe button eyes; black embroidered nose and mouth; dusky rose and green crocheted hat, scarf, mitts and boots with a honey money pocket hanging from a strap over her shoulder. She has a turn-handle music box inside her body that plays "Teddy Bear's Picnic." She mutters "hunny munny" over and over until someone puts a penny in her pocket for honey.

And this is why the doll artist continues to spread the gospel of teddy bears up and down the West Coast of the United States. From Washington State, her message has overtaken California, and bear makers are taking up the torch, most ignorant of who sparked the flame, or her reasons for so doing. Beverly Port may not have found her childhood teddy bear, but her over-a-decade-long quest has led to happiness and teddy bear love for countless thousands.

192

Bearby ©, portrait of a small girl dressed up in her teddy bear suit at Halloween. Pouty expression; swivel neck; jointed at shoulders and hips; porcelain face with glass eyes; fur fabric body. A musical doll, approximately 20in (50.8cm), her music box plays "Rock-a-by Bearby" (really "Baby"). She has a pink ribbon around her neck and holds a pink flower. Her name is derived from "Bear" and "Baby." *Bearby* won 1st place in "Portraits" division, Original Dolls, United Federation of Doll Collectors' Convention, San Francisco, California, 1976. *Photograph courtesy of Beverly Port.*

Mr. Pink, © 1980 Beverly Port Originals, approximately 20in (50.8cm) tall. Old pink mohair; antique shoe button eyes; collar and bow tie; completely jointed; swivel neck; old wool felt paw and foot pads. His tail turns a music box in his body and moves as music box plays. A "Time Machine Teddy." *Little Gruff,* © 1978 Beverly Port Originals, approximately 7½in (19.1cm) tall. Wool and mohair from an old coat; completely hand-sewn; accentuated hump on back; curved back with a little tail; extra long arms; paws curve downward; toes are extra pointed; shoe button eyes; black embroidered nose, mouth and claws; dark green crocheted hat and scarf.

Big Bear © 1980 Beverly Port Originals, approximately 34in (86.4cm) tall. Creamy-white long mohair; black button eyes; brown embroidered nose, mouth and claws. When his tail is turned, he moves his head back and forth. There is a growler in his body plus a music box that plays "Teddy Bear's Picnic." Fully-jointed; swivel head; suede paw and foot pads. *Baby -- A Bear For All Seasons,* © 1980, approximately 15in (38.1cm). Pale gray acrylic plush; wool felt paw and foot pads; fully-jointed; swivel neck; antique shoe button eyes; black embroidered nose, mouth and claws; red knit pants with the words, "Be My Bear," knitted onto it in white.

The Mechanical Nursemaid© 1983 with *Baby Brat*© 1978 Beverly Port Originals. The *Nursemaid* is dressed in white antique materials, as is the hat, bib and diaper of *Baby Brat*. Red flower trim and ribbon are imported from France. *Nursemaid* and *Baby* are made of medium brown antique material. *Nursemaid* has black button eyes and black embroidered nose and mouth. Fully-jointed *Baby* has open molded mouth with teeth and tongue. *Nursemaid* holds teddy bear rattle in one paw. Both her arms and head move up and down. She raises rattle to show *Baby* as she lifts *Baby* up with other arm. She looks down at *Baby* and then up with a look of anxiety as obviously *Baby* is still being a "brat." Music box is covered with antiqued red velvet and trimmed with gold braid and ribbon. Music box in base plays "Brahms Lullaby."

CAROL-LYNN RÖSSEL WAUGH

Carol-Lynn Rössel Waugh and *My Friend Bear*.

Carol-Lynn Rössel, Panda and Jack Rössel, Staten Island, New York, 1948.

Teddy bears are milestones in my life. Not that, until the last decade or so, I have had a bundle of them. In my childhood photograph album, nearly every shot contains at least one doll. But there is only one of me and a bear. The photograph is fuzzy and the bear does not really qualify; it is a panda. Probably it belonged to my cousin Jack; I have no memory of it.

The bears I do remember I still own. There is the 3in (7.6cm) fellow I got when I was born. His name is *First Bear*. His nose and mouth are loved off. His felt ears, even when I was small, started disintegrating, so I sewed them, and his foot, up with sturdy, thick green thread, which still dangles from the mends.

Next came *Second Bear*. He has a metal nose and a grumpy expression. When I was young, I borrowed my mother's lipstick and drew a nice, indelible, red smiling crescent over it. This bears was probably the start of my career, such as it is, as a bear designer. When I was six, I decided he needed clothes so I designed and sewed for him a high-fashion (?) suit of red polished cotton. It had a real button, a pocket, two snaps that still work and, inadvertantly, a drop seat.

The third bear was not named "Third Bear." I got more original as I matured. He entered my life when I entered college. I arrived at Harpur College, State University of New York at Binghamton, less than a week after I graduated from Tottenville High School on Staten Island, New York. It was July 1964. I was 17, lonely, miles from home, miserable. When things were at their nadir, a squashy chunk of brown bear arrived in the mail to keep me company. I called him *Care Package Bear*.

A special bear came my way on November 11, 1967. Charles gave him to me for a wedding present on the night we eloped. It was not a formal wedding; we told the witnesses on the way, while they were in the car and could not escape what their evening plans were. The bear's not formal, either, or really, even a bear. He is a koala. I named him *Wedding Present*.

The last important bear in my life you have already met if you have read the Introduction. *Oop* and I met in early November 1983, and we plan on a long relationship.

My kids have favorite bears. Jenny-Lynn's long-term pal is named *Butter Bear*. She used to be yellow (the bear, not the daughter). *Butter's* so unobtrusive she tends to get overlooked, until Jenny comes to her defense, like the time Eric-Jon decided she would make a fine wife for *My Friend Bear*.

Probably the most obtrusive of our bear den, which now numbers around 200 generic bears, *My Friend Bear* (MFB for short) is a real member of the family. I bought him for a quarter at a Winthrop, Maine, thrift shop about the time Eric-Jon was born in 1978. From the start, he was a favorite. I wrote a children's book about the two of them, cleverly called *My Friend Bear*. It was published in 1982 by Atlantic-Little, Brown.

Jenny-Lynn Waugh and *Butter Bear.* July 1977.

Jenny-Lynn Waugh and *Butter Bear.* May 1984.

Eric-Jon Rössel Waugh and *My Friend Bear.* April 1984.

So, an interest in teds comes naturally. So does an interest in art. Officially, I am an art historian. My area of study is American art and architecture, and I have a master's degree in it. However, I have not studied studio art, except for a couple of required courses. I never fit in well, somehow. I have this idea that art does not have to be "serious."

I remember one day, in drawing class, we were allowed to draw whatever we wished. Everyone else was busy with abstruse stuff. I drew a teddy bear with a honey pot. The instructor was appalled, exclaiming, "Deliver me from teddy bears and bunny rabbits!" As I recall, he specialized in large-scale paintings of dead crows. We were not on the same wave length. That bear drawing is the only specimen I saved from college.

If most of my art is homegrown, an aptitude for it runs in the family. My grandmother Rössel painted, but I never knew her. I use her paint box, though. It says, "Maria, 1896" on its inner lid, in oils.

In the early 1970s, I started making original dolls for Jenny-Lynn, attending my first doll convention in 1973, where I discovered porcelain. After picking peoples' brains for techniques and information, I experimented and came up with some atypical little dolls. I prefer little dolls — and bears.

Somewhere along the line, about 1975, I began to make porcelain teddies. It seemed the right thing to do. I had always liked bisque dolls with molded-on clothes. Animal dolls have been favorites since my brother, Greg, and I found some Steiff hedgehogs at the old Newark Airport gift shop in 1955. We created a whole fantasy world around them, and hedgehogs still evoke strong emotions in us.

The bears were a sort of compromise. They are about the size of Macki and Mucki (the hedgehogs, who have resided for the last two decades in my parents' freezer). Like them, some bears sport molded-on footgear and cloth clothes. Like the bisque dolls, they are porcelain — or they were, to start, and jointed like dolls. Some have molded-on clothes.

When I do them now, they are latex composition, which has the advantage of bouncing, not shattering, when dropped. Some have a combination of wire-armatured fabric bodies and latex heads. I really want my bears to be played with; I would like them to be play dolls, like the hedgehogs.

Most of my critters stand about 6in (15.2cm) tall. I make them like dolls, sculpting in clay, making plaster molds, pouring the latex in and decanting it. When it has cured and the seams are smoothed, I paint and seal the bears, string them and sometimes dress them although, I really prefer to sculpt clothes onto the bodies. It sure beats sewing a bunch of tiny identical garments. Actually, I like knitted clothes on them — and molded-on shoes, so they can stand.

I have never made a slew of any doll. I am not what you would call a producing doll artist, more a designer. I do things unitl they work, and then move on. A half-dozen of anything is big with me. Twenty is mind-boggling. So Waugh bears are rare.

I also paint, in watercolors. I am self-taught. Not that I particularly wanted to be, but when I signed up for watercolor class at Winthrop adult ed, and said I wanted to paint people, the teacher said she had never done it — maybe I could learn from painting trees and rocks. My trees and rocks were awful. But the kids came out fine. Soon, family bears began sneaking into the painting.

Most of my work is personal, sorta autobiographical — except my books. Well, maybe them, too, if you discount titles like *Murder on the Menu.* I do mystery anthologies with Martin Harry Greenberg and Isaac Asimov. Only one has anything to do with dolls. None, so far, have bears. But I have hopes.

I am mostly a writer, and, more than anything, an art historian. As such, I look upon this whole movement of doll and bear artistry a bit differently from most. Since I have been involved with it for a long time, its growth and development interest me both as participant and chronicler.

Dolls — and I really believe teddy bears are dolls despite the squawks from some circles — are, to me, a form of sculpture, one that has been nearly ignored. Their universal appeal spans generations, cultures, economics and artistic media. And, it appears to me, after almost a decade of studying the work of contemporary doll artists, that the formal art world is poised at the brink of acceptance of the doll as a full-fledged art form.

In this book I have tried to offer, as both artist and art historian, an accounting of the early development of the teddy bear artist movement. I have an idea that this book is only the beginning of the story.

"Old Ted." Watercolor 22in by 30in (55.9cm by 76.2cm). 1982.

"Storytime." Watercolor 15in by 22in (38.1cm by 55.9cm). 1983.

"The Architect." Watercolor 15in by 22in (38.1cm by 55.9cm). March 1983.

"Eric-Jon and Oop." Watercolor 11in by 15in (27.9cm by 38.1cm). February 1984.

"Bearing Secrets." Watercolor 8in by 10in (20.3cm by 25.4cm). One of Carol-Lynn's first paintings. The models are Eric-Jon and *Birthday Bear*. 1981.

"Ring-a-Rosy." Watercolor 11in by 15in (27.9cm by 38.1cm). 1983.

DIRECTORY OF ARTISTS

Some of the artists herein listed may be contacted at their home studios. When so doing, please enclose a self-addressed stamped envelope with your inquiry. Other artists' work can be found at the shops listed under their names.

These addresses were correct at the time this book went to press, but are subject to change.

MARIANNE ANDERSON
The Cat's Whiskers Paper Dolls
P. O. Box 39
Dundee, Oregon 97115
(paper doll list for S.A.S.E)

BALLARD BAINES BEAR
COMPANY
(Karin Mandell and Howard Calvin)
1826 114th Northeast
Bellevue, Washington 98007

LOIS BECK
10300 Southeast Champagne Lane
Portland, Oregon 97266

JUNE AND BOB BECKETT
Beckett Originals Studio
Route 1, Box 141-1A
Deer Lodge, Tennessee 37726

FRANK AND SUSY BIRD
Three Acre Woods Pottery
Route 2, Box 53 AB
Marion, Texas 78124

CATHERINE BORDI
Bears in the Wood
59 North Santa Cruz Avenue
Los Gatos, California 95030

CAROLE BOWLING
P. O. Box 272
West Roxbury, Massachusetts 02132

LOIS CARLISLE
208 Salida Del Sol
Santa Barbara, California 93109

JIM D. CLARK
4093 Browns Valley Road
Napa, California 94558

DEANNA DUVALL
My Bears
1405 Birch Street
Forest Grove, Oregon 97116

THE REVEREND CHESTER DANIEL
FREEMAN, JR.
Baskets and Bears
44 Congress Street, Apt. 302
Hartford, Connecticut 06114

HERTA FORSTER
c/o NIADA Information Chairman
Betty Motsinger
213 Maple Court
Addison, Illinois 60101

ELAINE FUJITA-GAMBLE
Fujita-Gamble Teddies
19609 19th Northeast
Seattle, Washington 98155

LORI GARDINER
2565 South Mayflower
Arcadia, California 91006

BONNIE HARRON
P. O. Box 13173
Sacramento, California 95813

MIRIAM HUGHES
106 Revere Drive
Harleysville, Pennsylvania 19438

HELEN HULL
37 Nixon Road
Framingham, Massachusetts 01701

BARBARA ISENBERG
Barbara Isenberg's designs are manu-
factured by the North American Bear
Co., Inc., and are available at bear
merchants nationwide.
North American Bear Co., Inc.
645 North Michigan Avenue
Room 810
Chicago, Illinois 60611

REBECCA IVERSON
Route 1
Amery, Wisconsin 54001

JANNA JOSEPH
Box 687
Dunedin, Florida 34296

DORIS KING
4353 Landolt Avenue
Sacramento, California 95821

EARL KRENTZIN
412 Hillcrest
Grosse Pointe Farms, Michigan 48236

SUSAN L. KRUSE
431 Wooden Drive
Placentia, California 92670

MARIA KWONG
Bearware
1525 South Crest Drive
Los Angeles, California 90035

JUDY LEWIS
1128 Riviera Drive
Santa Ana, California 92706

TOMMY AND PATSY LEWIS
Louisiana Bear Company
6030 Line Avenue
Shreveport, Louisiana 71109

CHERYL LINDSAY
Elegant Fantasies
1366 Eldean Lane
Oceanside, California 92054

MAXINE LOOK
Nostalgia Nook
115 Winthrop Street
Medford, Massachusetts 02155

SYLVIA LYONS
A "Bearable" Bears
20437 Viewpoint Road
Castro Valley, California 94546

PAT MARRISON
Beanie Pie
1700 Autumn Lane
Lansing, Michigan 48912

THERESA MAY
Trunkful O' Teddies
329 East Garrett Run
Austin, Texas 78753

SARAH MC CLELIAN
Sal's Pals
8622 East Oak Street
Scottsdale, Arizona 85257

MEREART BEARS
(Suzy Stewart and Joanna Meredith)
9851 Sagepike
Houston, Texas 77089

DORIS AND TERRY MICHAUD
Carrousel Bears
316 St. Nicholas
Midland, Michigan 48640

REAL MUSGRAVE
The Real Shop
3611 Marsh Lane Place
Dallas, Texas 75220
(catalog free with S.A.S.E.)

PENNY NOBLE
1142 Manhattan Avenue
Suite CP 245
Manhattan Beach, California 90266

MARGORY HOYA NOVAK
P. O. Box 1554
Novato, California 94948

MARY OLSEN
P. O. Box 264
Graham, Washington 98338

SARA PHILLIPS
30 Locust Street, Apt. 2
Manchester, Maryland 21102

BEVERLY PORT
Beverly Port Originals
P. O. Box 711
Retsil, Washington 98378

KIMBERLEE PORT
Box 632
Retsil, Washington 98378

JOANNE PURPUS
5700 Ravenspur Drive, #311
Rancho Palos Verdes, California 92074

BOB RAIKES
Woody Bears
P. O. Box 82
Mount Shasta, California 96067

TEROL REED
6563 South Saulsbury Court
Littleton, Colorado 80123

KELLY REUTER
Teddy & Me
Box 31
Amboy, Minnesota 56010

JANET AND GARRETT
SAKAMOTO
P. O. Box 3182
Torrance, California 90510

BARBARA SIXBY
426 Pine Nut Court
San Ramon, California 94583

JOYCE STAFFORD
Joyce Stafford seldom sells her bears
and only at U.F.D.C. conventions.
c/o NIADA Information Chairman
Betty Motsinger
213 Maple Court
Addison, Illinois 60101

JACQUELINE ROBINSON TAPLEY
Mountain Bear Manufacturing
P. O. Box 633
Bangor, Maine 04401

ROBERTA VISCUSI
Ro "bear" ta's Handmade Teddies
3009 Silverado Tri
Napa, California 94558

KAREN WALTER
Old Time Teddy Bears
304 Southeast 87th Avenue
Portland, Oregon 97216

CAPPI WARNICK
Bears by Cappi
940 Lance Avenue
Baltimore, Maryland 21221

CAROL-LYNN RÖSSEL WAUGH
5 Morrill Street
Winthrop, Maine 04364

WHIM C. BEAR
1100 Raymond Avenue
Napa, California 94559

APRIL WHITCOMB
3 Larkspur Way
Natick, Massachusetts 01760

FAITH WICK
c/o The Ehlers Co.
2675 Skypark Drive, Unit 303
Torrance, California 90505

SANDY WILLIAMS
Marmee's Doll House
2704 Belleview Avenue
Cheverly, Maryland 20785

PAT AND MIMI WOOLLEY
708 8th
Manhattan Beach, California 90266

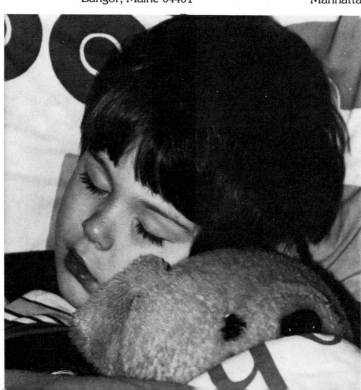